FLEXIBLE VISUAL SYSTEMS

The Design Manual for Contemporary Visual Identities

Dr. Martin Lorenz

slanted

WHY TO USE FLEXIBLE SYSTEMS

1. Working with systems is more efficient because the application can be automated.

2. Working with systems is more durable because the components can be optimized without having to overhaul the entire system.

3. Working with systems enables teamwork, as it is based on objectively comprehensible rules.

4. Thinking in systems makes empathy necessary for communication because design components have to be understood in context, as people will encounter them, which may be very different from how you encounter them.

5. Thinking in systems creates a sense for responsibility, as your work affects the system as well as everyone and everything involved.

6. Thinking in systems leads to the opportunity of criticism of systems because you realize that the system may be the problem, not its components.

7. Not working or thinking in systems corresponds neither to our today's communication networks nor to contemporary communication behavior.

GLOSSARY

Usually glossaries are located at the end of a book. In this book I make an exception because the terminology is intrinsically linked to my methodology and structure of this book. Understanding the concepts behind the terms in use gives you a head start on the content of this book.

Communication Design: Although this book is mostly about visual communication, we should not forget that communication design is not just using the visual sense. The touch, size, weight, and smell of this book for example plays a role in how you perceive its content.

Visual Identity: A visual language used by a company, organization, institution, but also product, campaign, person, or event to be recognized, remembered, and identified.

Contemporary Visual Identity: A flexible visual identity that communicates efficiently and effectively on today's communication channels. It is a visual language used to express messages rather than an image such as a logo that represents a singular message.

Visual System: A set of rules that define the visual language. Without rules, the articulations of the visual language might change from interpretation to interpretation of the designer who applies them.

Flexible Visual System: A flexible visual system is a visual language that can be used adequately in different contexts, for different audiences, and in different media without losing its recognizable identity.

A couple of terms I use often when describing the development of form-based systems:

Components: In this book I mostly work with geometric shapes, but they could be organic too. Components can be assembled into bigger, more complex forms, which increase their distinctiveness.

Assets: Components can be assembled to assets, like symbols, letters, lines, labels, frames, patterns, or any other illustration which will form part of the library of assets of the visual identity.

Application: The assets are applied to different formats. In this book I mainly focus on varying two-dimensional formats, but application systems may react as well to analogues and digital, two- and three-dimensional, moving and motionless, interactive or not interactive media, as well as any other data they are fed with.

Theoretical Part

GRAPHICS

Why to Use Flexible Systems 3
Glossary 4

INTRODUCTION

Stop Fixating on Logos 10
Identity Design Is Complex, Systems Can Be Easy 11
Corporate Identity ≠ Corporate Image(s) 12
A Little Head Start On Designing Flexible Systems 14
Spoiler Alert: In 3 Out of 4 Cases You Need a Flexible System ... 16
Get Into the Right Mindset 18

HISTORY

The Manual 22
The Stencil 24
The Building Blocks 26
The Program 28
The Tool 30

CONTEXT AND PROCESS

Forget about the Shortcut 34
When Does the Design Process Start? 36
Definition of the Communication Problem 38
The Process 40
What Is the Communicative Range of Your FVS? 42
Visual Language: Iconic References 44
Visual Language: Symbolic References 45
Precedent Models for Visual Systems 46
Model for Flexible Systems for Visual Identities 48
Form-Based FVS 50
Transformation-Based FVS 51
Mapping the Key Variables in a System Can Help You Focus 52

ARTICLES

What Is a Visual Identity? 8
How to Design a Flexible System? 9

Corporate Identity ≠ Corporate Image(s) 13
What Is a Visual System? 15
Does Every Visual Identity Needs a Visual System? 17
How to Think and Work in Systems? 19

Are Visual Systems a New Thing? 23

Where to Start and Where Not to Start? 35
What Type of Designer Will You Be? 37
How to Write a Design Brief? 39

How Flexible Does the System Need to Be? 43

How Do Flexible Systems for Visual Identities Work? 47

Too Many Options? Do You Need Help to Focus? 53

Practical Part

FVS: FORM-BASED

Construction of Components and Assets 56
Using the Assets 58
Regular Application on Different Formats 60
Irregular Application on Different Formats 62
Same Principle, Different Aesthetics 63
Identification through Composition, Color and/or Fonts 64
The Colors of This Book 66
Identification through Rules and Tools 68
The Advantages of a Grid 70
Create Grids with Geometric Shapes 72
Using Grids 74
Font Construction 76
Font Construction 78
Font Construction with Custom Components 79
Font Construction 80
Font Construction with Custom Components 81
Form-Based FVS 84
   Circle 87 | Right Triangle 105 | Acute Triangle 123
   Square 141 | Pentagon 159 | Hexagon (Right Triangle) 177
   Hexagon (Acute Triangle) 195

FVS: TRANSFORMATION-BASED

Transformation-Based FVS 232
   Circle: Gradation 236, Rotation 242, Repetition 248, Mirror 253
   Triangle: Gradation 260, Skew 266, Shift 272, Mirror 278
   Square: Gradation 284, Skew 290, Shift 296, Mirror 302

How to Develop Your Components and Assets 57
How to Use Your Assets? 59
How to Apply the Assets to Different Formats? 61

Working without Assets 65
What about Color? 67
Working without Grids 69
Which Advantages Does Using a Grid Have? 71
How to Create a Grid with Different Geometric Forms? 73
How to Use Grids? 75
What Kind of Grids Do I Need to Design Modular Letters? 77

Form-Based Flexible Visual Systems 85

Object-Based Flexible Visual Systems 215
Interaction-Based Flexible Visual Systems 221

Transformation-Based Flexible Visual Systems 233
3D-Transformation-Based Flexible Visual Systems 306
   Transformation: Objects 310
   Transformation: Reproduction and Recording 311

Epilog

How this book came to be 316
Acknowledgments 318

Bibliography 319
Imprint 320

INTRODUCTION

WHAT IS A VISUAL IDENTITY?

Corporations do not have a monopoly on visual identities despite the term "corporate identities" being commonly used to describe systematized visuals. Every association is defined by a common story, a (visual) identity, whether that story is created accidently or consciously. Organizations, institutions, events, as well as products, book covers, and media campaigns all need coherent visual identities too. Everything that has a series of communications to make needs a consistent visual language

From Logos to Systems

There was a time when logo design was almost synonymous to identity design and under certain circumstances it might still be, to a certain extent.

An example: A small family business makes shoes and sells them in their own shop. The shoes sell well as they are the only shoemakers in town. The family just needs to communicate that it is selling shoes. The only means of communication they need is a sign with a shoe in front of their shop so everyone knows where to buy shoes. Identification by the product, the shoe, is sufficient as a visual identity.

Now let's add a competitor to this example, Family B. Another family business that also makes and sells shoes opens a shop on the same street. Family business A no longer has a unique product. The shoe as an identification element is no longer sufficient.

A and B have two options to stay in business. They could offer different products. For example boots and sandals. In terms of the visual identity this would only mean that they need to change the symbol on the shop sign. A's shoe becomes a sandal, B's shoe becomes a boot.

The other option is not to change the product, but design everything that influences the buyer to buy at family A or B. Part of an identity is not only the product, but also by whom, how, and where it is sold. What does the shoe store look like? How does it smell, sound, and feel? How do the sellers treat their customers? What do the labels, the shoebox, and the shopping bag look like? How do they produce everything they need to make and sell the shoes? How do they treat all the people involved in this process?

Even the shape of the shoe, which goes beyond the pure functionality and type of the shoe, can become a distinguishing feature and thus an identification element.

In addition, A and B could communicate in public spaces and not just invest in distinction but as well increase visibility. Hang posters in the streets, place advertisements in newspapers and magazines, run spots on different media.

They could even hire well-liked public figures to wear their shoes. Potential customers would associate the values that their spokesperson transmits with the product, apart from just making it more visible.

All of these communication tools can be used to get the potential customer to buy at A or B. The communication process has suddenly become significantly more complex. The shoemakers have to realize that they communicate with different people, in different places, at different times and with different interests. They need a distinctive and visible visual identity, but that's not enough. They also need a flexible visual system in order to be able to communicate in a coherent, controlled, effective, and efficient manner in changing environments.

Social media has only made communication more complex. Not only have they created new communication channels, but also new forms of communication. While the recipients of traditional communication were passive, today they are very often part of the communication. Audiences like, share, and comment, thus influencing other recipients.

Now, if not before, a visual identity based on a symbol or logo is no longer able to adequately communicate. It does not adapt to the actors and surroundings of communication and cannot formulate adequate messages. It is too monosyllabic when eloquence is required. We need contemporary visual languages to be able to solve contemporary communication problems.

HOW TO DESIGN A FLEXIBLE SYSTEM?

Before you start browsing through this book I want to give you an overview which are the most important steps to follow when designing a flexible system for a visual identity. Each step refers to articles that offer insight and help, but can be skipped if you feel you do not need them.

1. Define the Communication Problem

Before you can decide how to communicate, you need to know who needs to communicate what, when, where, and to whom. These factors help you make informed choices during the design process and will influence your choice of shapes and colors.

2. Decide Where Your Solution Will Be Applied

Does your client need to focus on printed, animated, digital or analog media? Even if the visual identity should be applicable to all media, a focus on a specific media can make the visual identity special. If most applications are printed in short runs, you can use special printing and production techniques, while if the majority of the applications are on screen, you can focus on animation.

3. Select a Shape

Even geometric forms, as neutral as they might seem, convey messages to the person interpreting them. A circle might transmit playfulness and a hexagon might remind the receiver of a beehive. The form you choose to build your system with will influence the tone of your visual language.

4. Build Your Own Assets

After choosing a shape. What should you do with it? You could make symbols, patterns, lines, frames or even letters with them. Developing your own assets has the advantage that your visual identity will become more distinctive in comparison with competing visual identities.

5. Test Your Assets on Different Formats

Focus on the applications that you have to design, but always test your visual system on narrow, wide, large, small, loud, quiet, moving, and still applications too.

6. Present Your System on Mock-ups

Your client should understand how the visual system reacts to different formats and content. A large billboard on a busy street naturally has to be louder than an invoice or a receipt. Mounting your design on mock-ups helps to imagine how the visual identity will work in context. Present as well a design manual in which you document your process and the rules you have set up. The design manual is not only for the designer who will be working with the visual system you have designed, it is also a good tool for you to check whether the rules have been designed and applied consistently.

There are countless possible visual identities in these six steps. After you have mastered the tried and tested shape-based visual systems, part 2 introduces transformative systems. A transformative system is like a filter that distorts an image, font, or graphic in a recognizable way. The transformation becomes the identifiable element of visual identity and not necessarily the transformed.

STOP FIXATING ON LOGOS

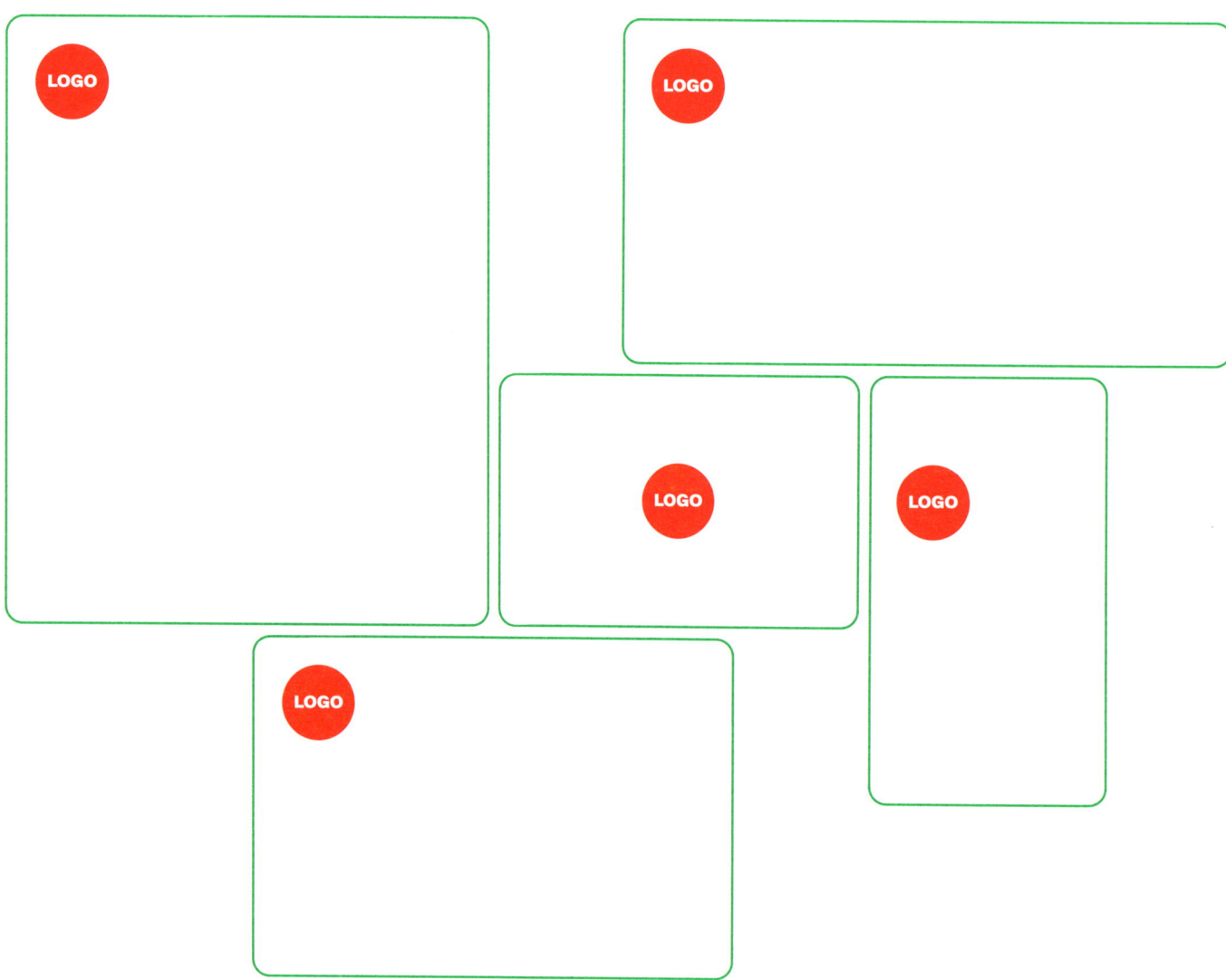

While a logo-based visual identity communicated the same message over and over again, a system-based visual identity is a language capable of articulating different messages in different ways to different audiences in different circumstances. Although the logo-based visual identity is anachronistic, it won't go away overnight. Our memories are branded with logos, like cattle is branded with hot metal. I do not use the term "branding," not just because of its cruel origin, but because of the ineffectiveness of this approach when building visual languages. Even though we grew up with logos, it does not mean that new visual identities still have to be based on them. Logos are very limited when it comes to adapting to different messages, contexts, and formats. A flexible system does not have this problem. We need to start to see and design identities in their full complexity.

IDENTITY DESIGN IS COMPLEX, SYSTEMS CAN BE EASY

One of the main functions of the visual identity is to make the association (corporation, institution, organization, event, or product) identifiable. As we humans perceive the outside world through our senses we can use any sense to make an identity recognizable. From the visual sense to smell, taste, sound, and touch. Choose the one that makes most sense for your brand. Communication nowadays is mostly based on images and text, but by shifting towards digital media, sound and movement becomes more important. Which means an identity can be completely based on recognizable movement and sound. Forms are still needed to express movement, but forms without some concept of movement rarely exist anymore. Even if the change from static to flexible visual identities and its further expansion to multi-sensorial and -dimensional solutions is inevitable, educational strategies are still very much focused on the design of specific deliverables without seeing them as part of a larger system. My approach stands in opposition to this way of teaching. It is my goal to teach approaches and perspectives and not a specific craft or aesthetic.

CORPORATE IDENTITY ≠ CORPORATE IMAGE(S)

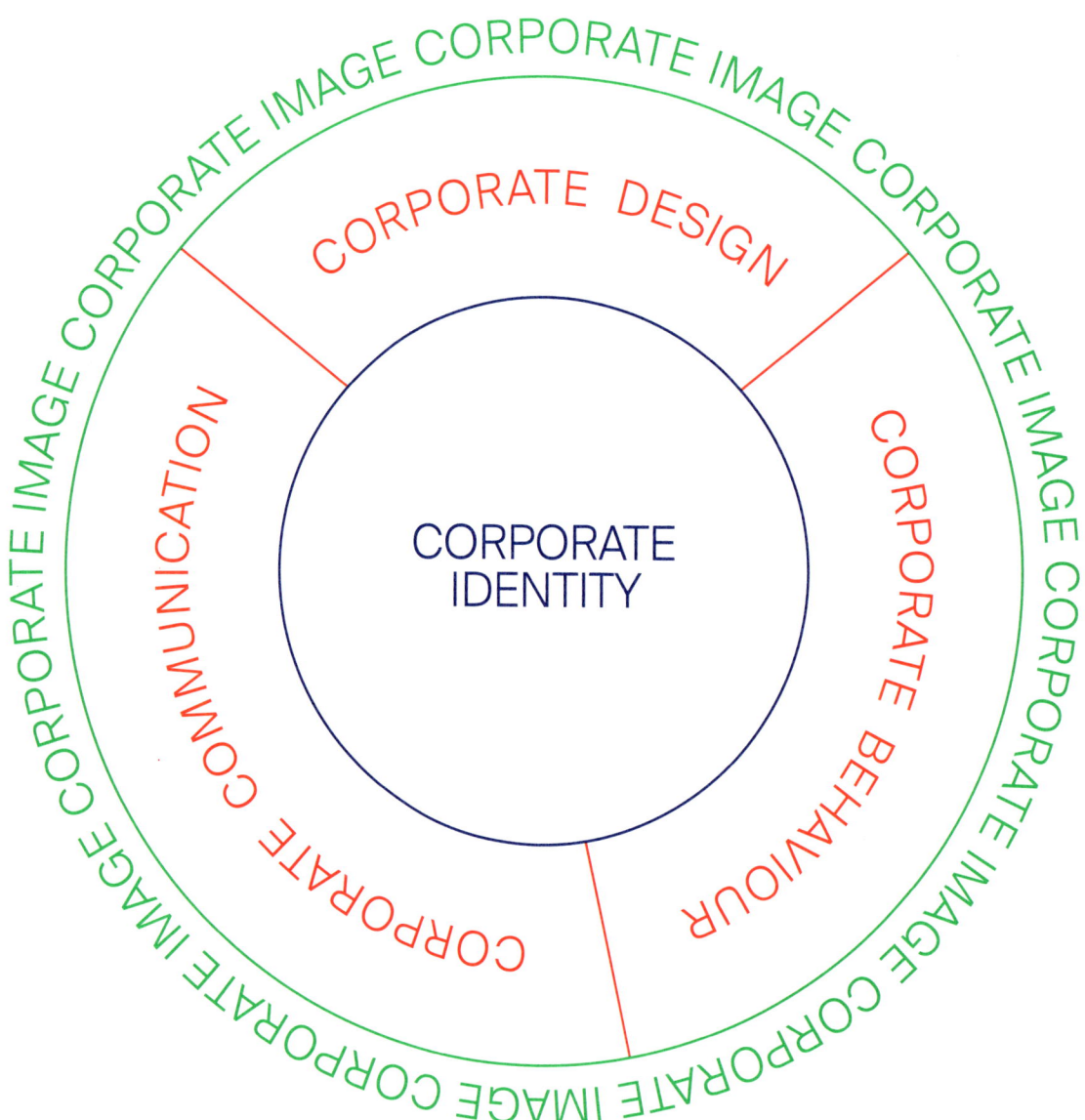

This is one of the very few pages in this book where I use the term "Corporate." I do so because it is the commonly used term, not because I like the term. I prefer using the term "Visual Identity," because identity design is not reserved for corporations, but can be used by institutions, organizations, events, persons, and products.

CORPORATE IDENTITY ≠ CORPORATE IMAGE(S)

Before we fully concentrate on the visual part of identity design, let us take a step back and take a look at the entire field of identity design.

**Corporate Identity ≠
Corporate Image(s)**

First of all, we have to distinguish between identity and image. Achieving the desired image is our goal as communication designers. The image is the viewer's interpretation of the identity we have designed. We study the recipient and the context in which we want the communication to take place to be able to guess how successful it is going to be. It would be presumptuous to claim that success is programmable. We humans and the world we live in are too complex to be able to guarantee communication. It is therefore much more efficient to understand visual identities as a process that needs to be observed and adapted from the inside and outside. To make this possible, we need flexible systems and not rigid structures. Rigid structures break easily, flexible systems adapt.

**Corporate Identity =
Corporate Design
+ Corporate Behavior
+ Corporate Communication**

What does a corporate identity consist of? A corporate identity is made up of corporate design, corporate behavior and corporate communication. The corporate design describes the visual appearance of a company. For small companies this might just be the business card, stationery, and website. In large companies, the corporate design can also be extended to retail design, uniforms, and products. Often not only the visual appearance plays a role, but all the senses that can be used for communication. Some stores use designed smells to attract clients from the street or car designers design the sound and vibration a car does. The corporate behavior defines how the company acts, internally and externally. Bad treatment of employees, customers, or the environment can result in a bad corporate image, even if the corporate design looks fantastic. Corporate communication can also have a negative or positive effect on the corporate image. You might love the visual identity of a company, but if an employee at a store on a hotline treats you badly you won't think well of the company anymore, you might even perceive the visual identity differently.

Not just that you expect a company to look, behave, and communicate well, you expect it to be coherent. In the best case, corporate design, corporate behavior, and corporate communication speak the same language. If the identity makes the promise to be a fun company, but the person picking up the phone is grumpy, the inconsistency would be interpreted as inauthenticity.

In this book I do not use the term corporate identity, but visual identity, as the system design is not only relevant for corporations, but for everyone who has to communicate a large number of different messages in a visually consistent manner. Be it a series of posters for a theater, a campaign for an institution or a series of book covers.

Why do I focus in this book on the visual sense, visual identities and not identities communicating through the other senses? I can not present any study which scientifically proves that the visual sense is the most important sense of identity design. It might be my perspective as a visual communication designer, coming from a two dimensional discipline, slowly opening up to three-dimensional design, who considers the visual sense as the most important sense for communication. However, you are holding a book in your hand, which is proof for my belief in the power of sound, touch, and smell of objects.

A LITTLE HEAD START ON DESIGNING FLEXIBLE SYSTEMS

One of the most effective visual systems is the simple modification of the edges of rectangles. The different types of rectangles can be used to place text or images inside of them, they can become interactive buttons or even shape devices such as smartphones, tablets, laptops, or computers.

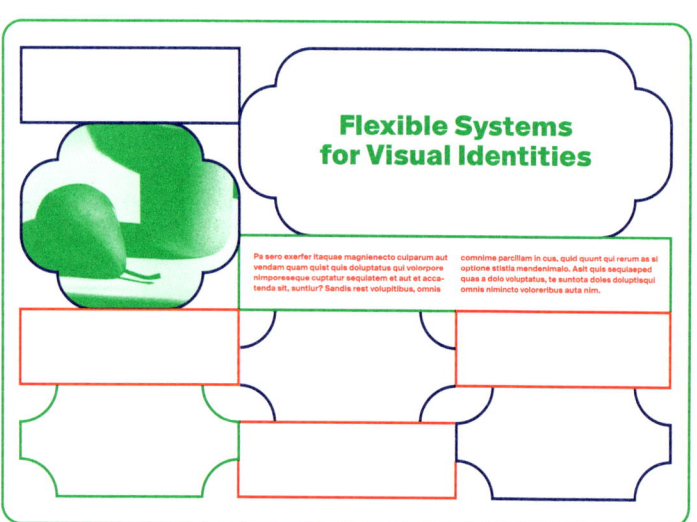

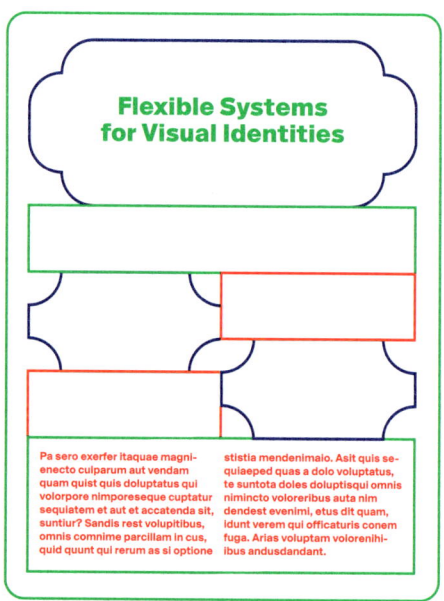

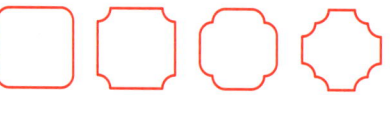

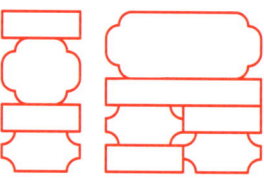

Components

The components of the visual system should be versatile. They should be combinable with themselves and other components. Therefore, self-contained forms with a strong character are not suitable. In this book, I use geometric forms which I subdivide in such a way that they can be combined in many ways. This increases the number of possible variations. An organic form could be an interesting shape to work with too, as long as it can be combined in many different ways. If not, you will end up with few ways to assemble them.

Assets

The assembled forms, as for example symbols, letters, lines, frames, or patterns are the assets that we use to design the applications. Since we created them from the same shapes, they are visually consistent with one another. They form a harmonious system. The assets must be so flexible that they can convey any message and emotion in any medium and format. Assets are not only defined by their shape, but also the properties of the shape, i. e. what can be done with this shape, like for example filling them with a texture, image, or color.

Applications

Adding a set of rules on how to apply the assets to a format, you have built a flexible system. The rules should define how the assets are positioned, adjusted to size, format, and content. The system is now under control and can be used by anyone, not just you, or even be automated, which speeds up the application process considerably.

WHAT IS A VISUAL SYSTEM?

How we design visual identities has changed a lot in the last ten years. Today, visual communication mostly takes place on screens and screens have different properties than paper. A screen enables images to be animated, made interactive and automatically adapted to the format, device, content, and user.

This book suggests a way of thinking and working that is inspired by the realities of communicating in a digital era and the work of pre-digital visionaries such as Karl Gerstner, especially when developing and applying visual identities. While in the past logo development was often the focus or at the beginning of the process, this book recommends a different approach. It assumes that only contextual communication has a chance of success and that the design of visual identities based on a logo is too rigid for our time.

If you look at the history of written language, it feels as if the history of visual language is repeating itself and we are again at the point where the representation of a concrete content by a concrete sign is insufficient and our visual communication has to evolve from sign to writing systems to do justice to the complexity of our communication. Except that this time it is not the complexity of the content, but the individualized formulation of the content that is the engine.

If we want to design context-related communication, we do not have to understand the visual identity as a rigidly formulated message (logo), but as a flexibly adapting language (system). It must be able to adapt to the time, place, medium, and person with whom it wishes to communicate. You will learn with this book how to design a flexible system that is capable of doing that.

To give you a little head start I have an example of one of the most common ways to construct a visual identity on the left page. The example also illustrates the methodology I find the most efficient. Choose or make a shape, use it to develop assets and then apply them. The assets as well as the application requires design rules which define the properties and the behavior of the shapes.

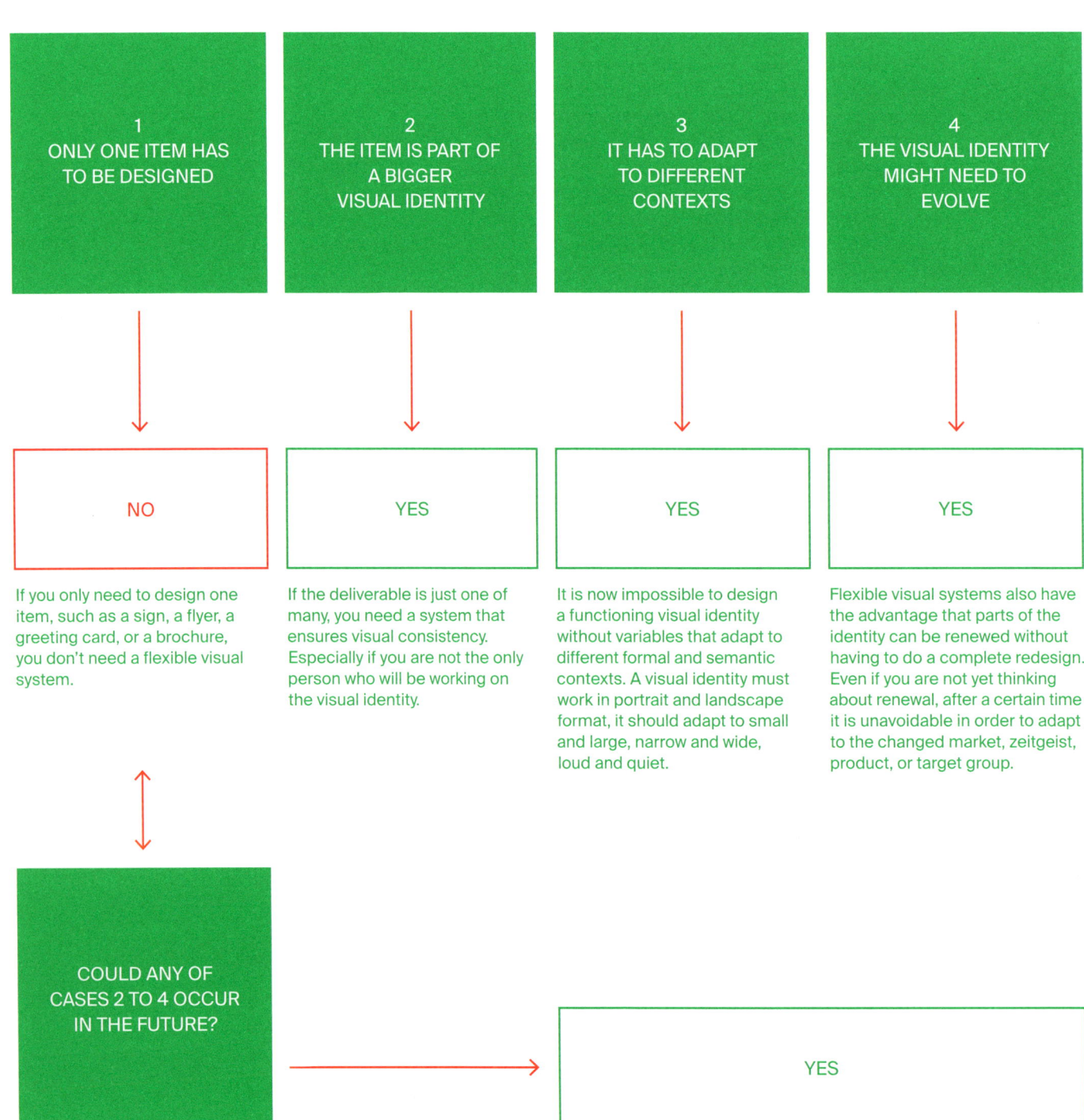

DOES EVERY VISUAL IDENTITY NEEDS A VISUAL SYSTEM?

Do you need a flexible visual system for your design? Yes! You and I know that. If not, you wouldn't have picked up this book, and I wouldn't have spent the last two decades researching, teaching, and designing flexible visual systems.

But even if we are aware that visual communication can no longer function without flexible visual systems, the question of necessity arises again and again. If you are with your client and have to explain why the initial phase of the project takes longer and becomes more expensive, if you have to explain to your students that logos are not visual identities and if you have to force yourself to invest time in systemizing what you have designed intuitively, I have a couple of arguments that should help you:

What to Tell to Your Client

As soon as more than just one application has to be designed, now or in the future, a flexible visual system saves time and money. It is true that the initial effort is higher because the system has to be developed first. However, the application process becomes faster (and cheaper) because all the design rules needed to design future deliverables are predefined by the system. With the right planning, even complex projects can be managed by small teams in a cost-and time-efficient manner. Even for large teams, systems are an indispensable tool for generating consensus and preventing internal and external communication chaos. Systems will save you a lot of headache, time, and money in the long run, and the best thing, they make you free to work with anyone you like.

What to Tell to Your Students

Often students come to class with an outdated definition of what a visual identity is. It is important to give them a theoretical and practical overview. Many feeds, blogs, magazines, and books do not help, on the contrary. They support the misconception that the logo is the centerpiece of a visual identity. It is absurd that the design press introduces a new visual identity with its new logo, when the final customer probably will see only the user interface of the website or app and barely notice the logo. This creates a false impression of how a visual identity works. The students should free themselves from their previous knowledge and think about visual identities without bias. They should look around themselves and analyze how to communicate what with them, when, and why. This sharpens the analytical eye, keeps the lessons up-to-date and provides an inventory of the requirements for the visual system. The versatility of communication makes the need for flexible systems evident.

What to Tell Yourself

Designing a system does not mean giving up intuitive working methods. Intuition is informed by knowledge, experience, taste, sense of time and context, and empathy with clients and target group. It is in many cases faster and better than rational working methods. However, a system will help you to know how you have to design the deliverables a year after you have designed the visual identity. This is especially important if you want a consistent appearance for your customer. In a year you, your taste and the way you design will have changed. Clear, objectively comprehensible rules will keep you on the right track.

GET INTO THE RIGHT MINDSET

1. Let the system do the work
2. The process is the result
3. Everything can be programmed
4. Program with everything
5. Do it wrong

HOW TO THINK AND WORK IN SYSTEMS?

1. Let the System Do the Work

We are used to working on concrete formats, like business cards, letterheads, brochures, or posters. Intuitively you would think of a concrete design in a concrete format. With system design, the approach changes. The concrete applications become examples of how the system is applied. In fact, when you design the specific applications, you think about the general rules and how they adapt to the different formats. You will notice that once these rules work, it is easy to work on other formats, while in the absence of a system, each design for a new format has to be invented from scratch, and therefore takes longer.

2. The Process Is the Result

Each approach leads to a different result. As you know by now, the system serves not only to control design, but defines the approach to design. The approach, whether you develop a form-based or transformative system, influences the outcome. So before you develop a system, be aware that the choice of system is a design decision.

3. Everything Can Be Programmed

Any design can be turned into a system. As soon as comprehensible rules are present in a design or subsequently interpreted, a system is present. The design of systems is about making subjective decisions into objective rules in order to be able to share them with other people or automate them with machines. This is exactly where the power of systems lies. When automating, you can accomplish much more than you would have been able to do on your own. Remember though: even when the process is computer aided and at times very complex, communication as described in this book remains between humans, which means that the start and endpoint of the process should also be intuitively understood by humans.

4. Program with everything

Programs develop their full potential when you program them. Let the programs do the work for you. Use variables. Automate as much as they can. Your task should be to develop concepts and systems, not to perform mindless repetitive tasks.

5. Do It Wrong

Although programs are great in executing systems, they are not great in helping you to develop new ideas. They were developed with preconceived ideas about what the design process and outcome should be like. That is very limiting as the process itself is influencing the result. Just look at the circular grids of Josef Müller-Brockmann and compare them to today's grid based design. Müller-Brockmann was far more innovative than we are nowadays because he used a pen, a compass, and a ruler which allowed him to think much more freely than we are able to think using today's layout programs. Although it's very tempting to go back to the pen, it's nonsensical to ignore the advantages processed design gives us. Instead we should start to hack our tools. Experiment with using the wrong programs and don't operate them the way they are supposed to be operated. Programs should always be the tools of the designer, not the other way around.

HISTORY

THE MANUAL

Construction of the Gothic minuscule by Albrecht Dürer from 1525.

The squares rotated 45 degrees are slightly larger than the straight stems to mimic the calligraphy downstroke.

The deviation from the grid in letters like the "S" is interesting. The first "S" is from Dürer, the following "S"'s are my proposals ...

... to find a system-compliant solution. This result is more consistent with the rest of the letters, but as well far away from Dürer's model, the calligraphic "Textura."

ARE VISUAL SYSTEMS A NEW THING?

Don't get the impression that there were no visual systems before the digitization of communication. Human sign systems have existed since the beginning of communication, as documented in cave painting. The systematization of written language simplifies the number of symbols to be learned and defines their meaning and function.

Genevieve von Petzinger examined cave paintings that are up to 40,000 years old, cataloged and compared them and came to the surprising result that the same 32 symbols appeared all across caves in Europe. This suggests that there was a sign system in Europe as early as the Ice Age that was used for communication between humans.

The Yì Jīng, dating from 3000 BCE, is one of the oldest sign systems that can still be read today. The signs of Yì Jīng consist of six horizontal lines arranged one above the other. Each line can be interrupted by a gap or remain whole. The permutation of these creates 64 different characters. A meaning was assigned to each character whose function is to foresee the future.

We find much more complex systems in movable type grids from the Renaissance, such as the book layouts by Aldus Pius Manutius (1449–1515). Peter Burnhill examined Aldus Manutius' typographical norms and was able to discover complex grids that indicated a close collaboration with Francesco Griffo, his punch cutter. The norms of Aldus Manutius are similar to contemporary grid systems in many respects, for example the modular dimensioning of positive and negative space.

While researching for my doctoral thesis, I discovered hundreds of visual systems in the history of typography. By categorizing the visual (typographic) systems according to their function and mechanisms, I hoped to find parallels to systems in contemporary flexible visual systems and learn from them. This only succeeded up to a certain point, since the function, i. e. the task of the system, has a direct influence on its mechanisms. The function of many systems has become obsolete over the years due to more efficient technical innovations (e.g. the stencil).

For reasons of space and time I decided not to use images, but I strongly recommend googling the red names.

The Manual

The design manual, even if it was not called that at the time, existed since someone had to apply the design of someone else who was not present during the application process and the design was too complex to be narrated by a messenger.

It is common for design manuals to use construction lines that are easy to reproduce. Geometric forms, which are easy to understand and reproduce, are often used to explain a construction.

The 500-year-old design manual by Albrecht Dürer did exactly this. He reconstructed Roman capital letters and Gothic minuscules in his book *Underweysung der Messung, mit dem Zirckel und Richtscheyt, in Linien, Ebenen und gantzen corporen* (Instruction in measurement with compass and ruler, in lines, planes, and whole bodies) in 1525. Dürer writes in the dedication to his patron and friend Willibald Pirckheimer that the book is not only intended for painters, but also goldsmiths, sculptors, stonemasons, and carpenters. In short, everyone who knows how to use a compass and a ruler.

One of the best-known design manuals in typography are the construction drawings of the Romain du Roi. The Romain du Roi was developed for the royal printing house of King Louis XIV by a commission in 1692. The so called Bignon Commission was directed by the French minister Colbert, headed by Abbé Bignon, who selected the royal typographer Jacques Jaugeon, the scholar Gilles Filleau des Billettes, and Father Sébastien Truchet, who's name you might know from the Truchet tiles.

The manual is based on a square format, which in turn has been divided into 64 squares. Each of these small squares was then subdivided into 36 smaller squares to create a grid system with 2,304 square modules. The grid helped to determine the position of the geometric shapes with which the letters were constructed as well as the forms of the letters themselves. The very detailed square grid is often referred to as the first bitmap visualization and the definition of the letter forms with geometric forms as the first vectorial

THE STENCIL

"Pour tracer géométriquement les lettres, les chiffres & les ornements." (For tracing geometric letters, numbers & ornaments.) Plaque Découpée Universelle (Universal Die-cut Plate), 65 × 113 mm, approx. 1879, J. A. David. The size shown here corresponds to the size of the original.

SYSTEM

The resulting letters. Note that even the sides of the stencil can be used to draw wider letters like for example the "M."

definition of a font. Since the function of the design manual was to make all fonts used in all documents printed by the royal printers of King Louis XIV look the same, we can speak of a flexible system for a visual identity. The formal coherence ensures recognition, the writing system ensures flexible use. I am disregarding the fact that the manufacturing method of the types made formal coherence in small font sizes impossible. Not only was it impossible for the punch cutter to implement a grid system with 2,304 square modules on a point size of 10 points, a font must also be drawn differently at different sizes to stay equally legible. You can tell from the printed publications that the punch cutter optically corrected the design manual.

It is in the nature of the manual that it is easy to understand and use. This often also means a simplification of the design. Constructed fonts, which have letter forms that are built out of modular components, such as the sans serif font samples from the 19th and 20th centuries for sign painters, show a strong simplification of the letters. This makes it easier to reproduce the fonts, but also means a loss of quality in the definition of the letters by disregarding optical corrections.

The font DIN 1451 was published in 1931 by the German Institute for Standardization (DIN). In 1936, DIN 1451 became the official font for German signposts, traffic, and street signs, as well as the lettering of the air raid shelters. DIN 1451 is the result of geometric construction. It has little typographical finesse. In 1995 Albert-Jan Pool designed a refined version of DIN 1451, the FF DIN, which was published by FontShop. In contrast to DIN 1451, the FF DIN has optical corrections and smoother curves, but preserves the aesthetics of a constructed font.

The use of constructed, sans serif fonts for informative lettering in public spaces in Germany goes back to the letterings of the Prussian Railway. Long before the DIN the Prussian Railway used design manuals to explain how the letters had to be painted, which set a trend. Information signs were no longer viewed as works of art, but as purely functional sources of information. Any additional ornament was considered a step toward illegibility.

Constructed typeface designs are also widely used in contemporary flexible visual identities. The modularity allows the designer to achieve formal coherence between all letters and makes it easy to add new symbols and pictograms. One example of this approach is the development of the grid-based typeface "Simple" by the Swiss design studio Norm, into "Simple Köln-Bonn" a version of the font that was enriched with a multitude of grid-based pictograms used in the flexible visual identity of the Cologne-Bonn Airport designed by the Ateliers Intégral Ruedi Baur Paris, Zurich.

The Stencil

Design manuals are intended to enable accurate reproduction of the intended design but almost every manual leaves room for misinterpretation, be it through an unrealistic template (as with the Romain du Roi), an incomprehensible template, or a stubborn designer who does not want to adhere to the rules.

Misinterpretations are impossible with templates. A stencil allows the unskilled and inexperienced to apply professional lettering quickly and easily. There is no need for a compass or a ruler. The only thing the designer needs is a stencil. Unfortunately not just one, but one for every size. While the Design Manual's description is based on scalable proportions, the size of the stencil template is fixed to one size. There are therefore stencils in many different sizes. To prevent the stencils from becoming unwieldy, there have been some interesting inventions in the history of stencil fonts.

Joseph A. David patented in 1876 a stencil system for sign painters, the Plaque Découpée Universelle. With this relatively small but universal stencil one was able to draw all lower and upper case letters as well as the numbers, the punctuation and all accents. Although you first had to learn to find your way around the complex grid of the Plaque Découpée Universelle, you had the advantage of only needing a relatively small template.

In the first decade of the 20th century, Georg Bahr, a vocational school teacher from Charlottenburg, Berlin, developed a new labeling tool. It was the shape and size of a ruler and came with a matching pen. Parts of letters were carved in the ruler and the user had to move the ruler to be able to draw complete letters. It took a while to write a whole word, but the stencil was handy and inexpensive. Bahr patented the stencil ruler in 1909. A year later, however, he sold it to his friends Paul Filler and Oscar Fiebig. Filler and Fiebig founded a company that produced and sold the

THE BUILDING BLOCKS

"Schönheitsformen Nr. 31 bis 45, Friedrich Fröbels Spielgaben" (Forms of beauty, Nr. 31 until 45, Friedrich Fröbels Toys), developed from 1834. Building symmetrical patterns is called "forms of beauty" or "art forms" in Froebel's pedagogy. The principle of developing compositions from a fixed number of predefined elements according to an inherent logic corresponds to a closed visual system that, by reducing the number and thus easily recognizable form, is suitable for the development of a visual identity. In contrast to Ostwald, on the following page, a grid is not necessary. It is the elements that determine the positions. Other elements result in other positions.

Bahr's Normograph. A little later they designed and produced the Standardgraph, a stencil template that had the entire alphabet with complete letters. Standardgraph became so successful that Filler and Fiebig renamed the company in 1967 to Standardgraph Filler & Fiebig GmbH. To this day, the company produces a wide range of stencils, mainly for technical drawings.

The idea of a stencil is still alive in many flexible systems. Shapes are used as containers for images or animations as in the famous identity of MTV by Manhattan Design from 1981. The shape serves as an identifiable element and the content is flexibly adapting to the specific message that should be communicated.

The Building Blocks

Even the most flexible stencil system wants to reduce the amount of possible forms to simplify the design process. Reducing the number of design options also speeds up the design process, simplifies the aesthetics, and makes the individual elements easier to recognize and thereby increases identifiability of the visual identity. Even if the elements are rearranged, the system remains stable. For all of these reasons modular systems are particularly popular when designing visual identities. However, modular systems were and are popular in children's toys too.

Artists like Josef Albers and architects like Frank Lloyd Wright are said to have been inspired by Friedrich Froebel's construction kits as children.[1] Froebel (1782–1852), the inventor of the kindergarden, developed ten games called "Fröbels Spielgaben" (Fröbel Toys) consisting of sets of geometric wooden objects. To each of the games a number was assigned that provided information about the appropriate age of the child and thus the level of difficulty of the game. Each level had a different educational goal. From rational thinking to mathematics to language. Although the connection has been never proven, it is likely that the games encouraged systematic thinking in future typographers, designers, artists, and architects. Especially when having a look at design, art, and architecture of the early twentieth century. Soennecken is a German office supplies manufacturer that, in 1913, developed a kit to teach primary school children to write. The construction kit contained seven components from which the children had to construct upper case letters. A grid helped to position the elements correctly. The letters looked very similar to the typeface Futura, designed by Paul Renner in 1927. Drawing the conclusion that Paul Renner was inspired by Soennecken is a bit far-fetched, but the fact that Soennecken commercialized a tool to teach grid-based letters shows that the ideas of the New Typography[2] were rooted in society long before the Bauhaus made them popular. It has to be mentioned that the usual tool to teach letters has been the feather. Using an additional tool to teach letters also means a differentiation between script based and constructed letters, which made it necessary to teach both models to children.

The "Kombinationsschrift" (Combination Font) by Josef Albers is not for children, but also a construction kit. In the magazine *Bauhaus, Zeitschrift der Gestaltung, No. 1* (Bauhaus, Design Magazine, No. 1) published in January 1931, Albers presents the "Kombinationsschrift 3." The biggest advantage of this writing system, according to Albers, is the savings that can be made with it. The font can be constructed from only three shapes, compared to an earlier version which needed 10 elements. The three elements were a square, a quarter circle, and a full circle. With only three elements, Albers was able to construct 27 different characters, as well diacritics and punctuation. Albers argues that reducing the elements in the type case to just three movable type forms (casts) helped the printer save storage space. In addition, the simple shape improved their longevity, especially if the shapes were made with less resistant material such as wood, glass, cardboard, paper, or neon tubes. Another advantage of the combination font was the

---

[1] Claims the author of the book *Inventing Kindergarten*, Nils Brosterman.

[2] In fact, even before Jan Tschichold, a German designer, wrote in 1925, only 23 years old, a book called *Die neue Typographie* (The New Typography), which would trigger a revolution in the design world. He supported innovative ideas by his peers, which at the time had been strongly influenced by ideas coming from the art world, such as the Futurists, Dadaists, and Constructivists, as well as ideas from the industry, such as Walter Porstman and the German Institute for Norms. Tschichold's intention with The New Typography was to move away from individualistic art and towards collective norms in favor of a more efficient and effective communication.

THE PROGRAM

"By drawing well-ordered lines between the network points while maintaining the associated laws of symmetry, one obtains an enormous abundance of the most beautiful surface patterns, only a small part of which had been discovered by previous jewelry art; scientific processing opens up the whole treasure for us." wrote Wilhelm Ostwald in *Frohes Schaffen. Das Jahrbuch der deutschen Jugend der Ostmark 5* (Merry Working. The yearbook of the German youth of the Ostmark), 1927

The drawings above show symmetrical line constellations in a grid of 16 network points. The repetition on three more squares demonstrates the possibility of expanding the line constellation to a larger pattern. In this book I call these small patterns, "components" to distinguish them conceptually from the "larger patterns," which are one of the possible design assets. For Ostwald, regular alignments, such as symmetric patterns represent beauty, harmony, and a source of new forms.

predictability of the line length, which was important when working with movable type. The last mentioned advantage is not really relevant for us nowadays, but another aspect of the font is very interesting in times of variable fonts. Josef Albers demonstrates in the article about the Kombinationsschrift published in 1931 the flexibility of the system. The construction kit is able to construct not only 27 glyphs with only three elements, but also up to four different variations of some glyphs and 12 different weights.

Building blocks are omnipresent in contemporary design. Design systems in user interface design are nothing else than responsive construction kits.

The Program

The term "program" was widely introduced to the design world by the Swiss graphic designer, artist, and author Karl Gerstner. Gerstner renounced already in the 1950s the logo based visual identity and opted for a flexible visual system, which he called "programs." From today's perspective one might think Gerstner would refer to computer programs, although they would come decades later, but Gerstner's definition of a program was neither limited to a specific tool, nor the time. This is what makes Gerstners perspective so interesting. In his two most influential books on programs, *Designing Programs* and *The Forms of Colors*, Gerstner created an multidisciplinary overview of the history of and form and color systems. He presented systems from mathematics, physics, sculpture, painting, writing, architecture, and photography and thus showed how rich the history of visual systems is, but also how little of them has arrived in our today's discipline.

Particularly impressing is the analysis and further exploration of a visual system of a Moroccan tile manufacturer. During one of Gerstner's stays in Morocco, he bought from Kamal Alí, a construction worker, a sketch that Gerstner used to create a variety of graphics.

While the previously mentioned types of systems are based on concrete forms the "program" defines a process to be followed. So instead of designing shapes, Gerstner designs systems that generate shapes or, as Gerstner would say, "instead of solutions for tasks, programs for solutions." Gerstner, interviewed by Ulrike Felsing, says "One day I realized that it doesn't make sense to design signets and then place them somewhere. The design itself must take the place of the logo." The visual identities Karl Gerstner designed for Boîte à Musique, Blech Electronic Center and Holzäpfel illustrate this statement. They are easy to recognize without the need of a logo. Dispensing of the logo even seems to make them more flexible and consistent.

Gerstner's definition of programs is not limited to graphic design, but expands to literature, architecture, urban planning, typography, photography, art, and music. The example on the left, designed by Wilhelm Ostwald, was presented by Gerstner in his book *Designing Programs*. Another interesting example made by Gerstner in the same book is a series of photos from a car. The cars themselves don't change, but the perspective from which they were photographed. The versatility of the imagery or flexibility of the system arises from the changing perspective. The controlled change of perspective as well as the not changing object with constant lighting ensure visual coherence and thus the recognition of the visual language.

Not changing the object itself, but rather the perspective from which it is viewed, is a rare approach in visual systems for flexible identities, but it still can be found. For example in the visual identity for the Netherlands Architecture Institute by Bruce Mau from 1993 and OVG Real Estate by Studio Dumbar from 2011. Another interesting example comes from Moving Brands for Swisscom in 2007. A three-dimensional object rotates around its own vertical axis and thus generates a large number of two-dimensional images, depending on the position of the object. According to Moving Brands, the object has been programmed in such a way that its shape can react to noise, movement, Internet traffic, or consumer behavior. However, the generated images still breathe the air of logo-based identities. Flexible logos were a common characteristic of the visual identity designed in the 2000's, a transitional phase in between logo- and system-based visual identities.

THE TOOL

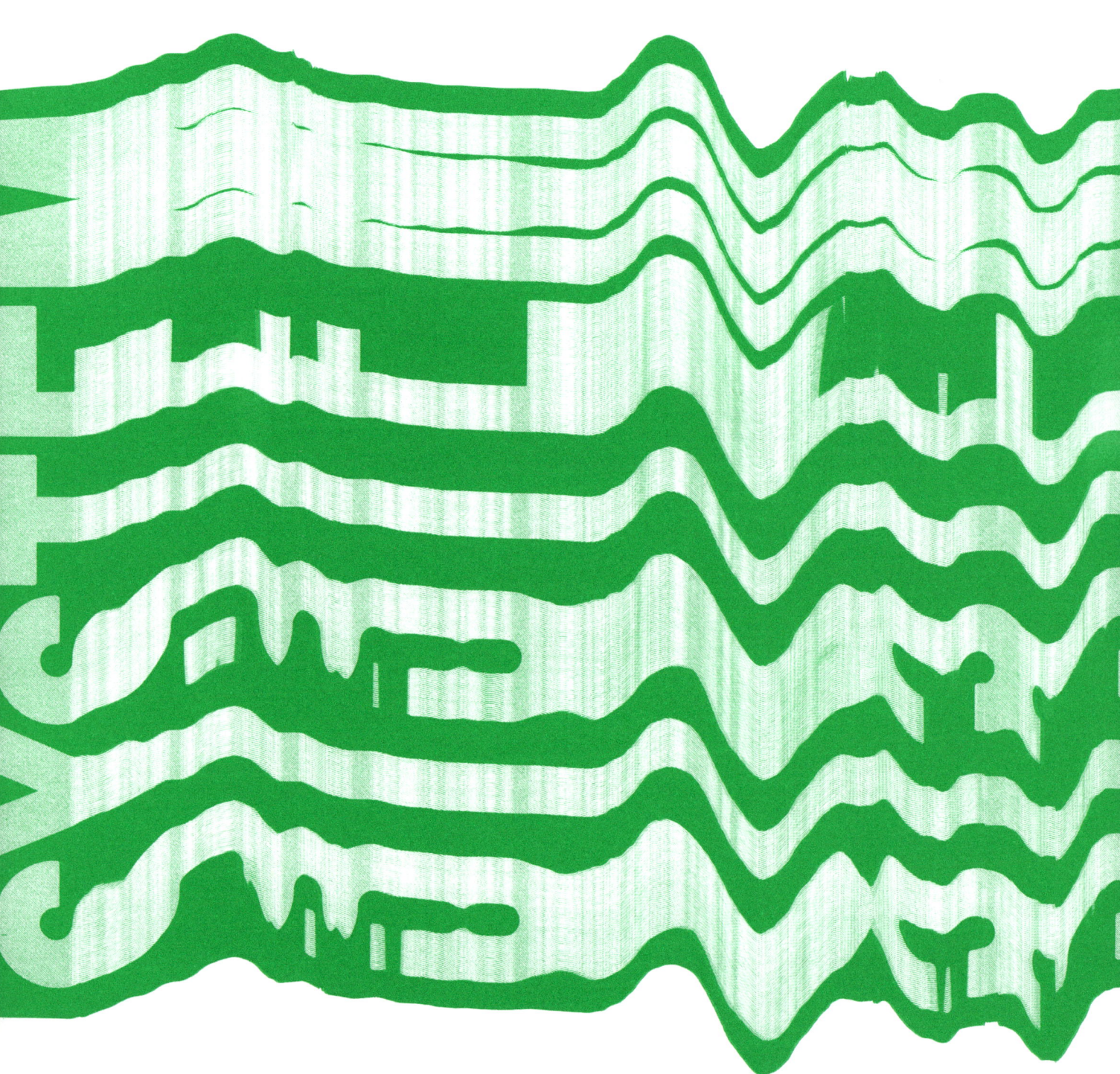

Anything can be used as a tool. In the example above I used a scanner to distort a lettering I made for this book. Even if I would have used an illustration or a photograph, the distortion itself would have made all scanned material look similar. This is an example for how a design process can become the identifiable element of a visual identity and not a specific element.

The Tool

The fifth historic category could have been the first. Tools were used since the beginning of systemic visual communication. They function as enhancement of visual expression, but as well as a harmonizer. Tools can give form consistency, which makes them a very flexible system for visual identities. While a program's objective is to be executed, ergo strive for automation, a tool, analog or digital, is the system to be used.

The influence of the tool on the form becomes particularly clear in the history of writing and starts with the pen itself, where the shape of the nib determines the distribution of contrasts in a letter.

The broad nib, held at an angle, creates the widest width in the shoulders and thus the darkest part of the letter. The vertical stems are slightly more narrow. In contrast to the shoulder, the upswings are the thinnest point. They are therefore best suited for connecting parts of the letter. The resistance of the nib on paper makes the upswings quite sharp, while the shoulders can be rounder.

Even with digitally designed text fonts, the contrast distribution of the broad nib is retained, as it has proven to be the most harmonious and easiest to read.[3]

However in every time and culture we can see a correlation between technology and form. The letters carved in stone look different from the letters written with pen and ink on parchment. Designing new tools means therefore designing new forms. Everything can be turned into a tool. A scanner for example can be used to distort letters or images, as I did on the left page.

[3] On behalf of the German Institute for Standardization (DIN), Albert-Jan Pool wrote a study on legibility in which he compared fonts based on the contrast distribution of broad and pointed nibs. Neither serifs nor weight played a decisive role. The most important difference was the contrast distribution.

CONTEXT AND PROCESS

FORGET ABOUT THE SHORTCUT

BRIEF → DEBRIEF

Visual systems can be used, among other things, to create visual identities, user interfaces, editorial design, data visualization, and environmental graphics. The commissioned deliverables provide some information about the functionality of the system, but you want to start somewhere else to provide your client with a design that can grow.

Forget about this shortcut.

Before you can start designing a visual system, you need to first know what you have to communicate, where, and to whom. In many cases you even need to take into consideration who is going to apply your system. A proper debrief will help you figure out how flexible your visual system needs to be. It cannot be expected of a client to know what the designer needs, so after a brief from the client should always follow a debrief by the designer.

DELIVERABLES

SYSTEM

Once you know all the requirements, you are ready to design the system and it's important to start with the system, not the application of the system. If you would start with the design of the deliverables, your design decisions would draw conclusions from specific cases and probably not be useful for other cases. Only a flexible application of the system taking into account all applications can deliver consistent solutions.

CONCRETE

ABSTRACT

WHERE TO START AND WHERE NOT TO START?

There are a couple of misconceptions about the design process when developing a visual identity. I give you two examples: Client A approaches you in need of a website for their company. The company does not have a visual identity. Maybe it has a logo the client made himself, because they heard that you need one if you found a company. But there is no visual system, nothing that tells you how to apply the visual identity to the website. You would need to add rules to the identity while designing the website. Starting to build an identity by adding rules as soon as a new deliverable is needed without having the overview of all deliverables that might be needed in the future, and no consistent system behind all of them, can only end in chaos. Not only will a lot of energy be wasted, the end customer will notice the chaos and make the company or organization untrustworthy.

Second example: Client B knows that before designing the deliverables they need a visual identity, but thinks that the logo is the most important piece of it. According to that belief, the logo needs to be designed first. The rest comes later. Colors and fonts are added, maybe as well a couple of decorative elements. This approach might be common, but it creates a lot of unrepairable problems. The most obvious problem is consistency. The visual identity becomes inconsistent if all elements do not originate from the same system.

It is not just clients that have these misconceptions, a lot of designers and even design teachers have them too. To a certain extent I get why: it is much easier to design a concrete form (logo) than a system that creates a situation-dependent (and thus constantly changing) form.

But our way of thinking and working is slowly changing. One of the reasons is undoubtedly digitization of communication. Hardly any visual identity can avoid being applied to different digital communication channels. We get used to setting up flexible design rules that work equally well on different formats and devices. What does our design look like when the browser window is made smaller or larger, the website is viewed on a desktop computer, tablet, or smartphone, when the device is held horizontally or vertically and which user navigates through our website and how? In this flexible environment, the logo as a static, unchangeable form becomes a pure profile picture that disappears with the first scroll or swipe. Text, typography, graphics, symbols, images, and colors take up much more space and thus play a more important role. On one hand, they make the visual identity visible, i. e. identifiable. On the other hand, they are more effective and efficient communication tools. You are able to formulate different messages on different levels. Take a look at Apple's visual identity. You don't have to look at the back of an iPhone to know it's Apple. The consistent use of rounded corners throughout products and user interfaces shows that you are holding an Apple product in your hands.

Summing up: The design brief needs to inform you about the larger context of your project. What should be communicated? To whom, how, and where? Who are the stakeholders (including those that will apply the system)? With this understanding, you can then design a system that is able to generate all deliverables while maintaining consistency.

WHEN DOES THE DESIGN PROCESS START?

Design starts before the designer begins. It starts when the design team is chosen. It's best when the designers working on solutions to a communication problem share perspectives with the target groups as well as the skills needed to design or the media that will be used to communicate. If, for example, you want to design an educational movie, it would be helpful to have educators and movie makers be part of the design team, maybe even a prospective student who would be the eventual audience for your work.

WHAT TYPE OF DESIGNER WILL YOU BE?

We tend to think that the design process starts when we switch on the computer but it actually starts, or should start, much earlier. The client choosing the designer and the designer choosing its team is already a design choice.

The Invisible Designer

When I was studying communication design in the 90s in Germany the common belief was that a designer had to be invisible like a good typeface is invisible in the way that it makes you only see the text, not the design of the letters. While that may be a noble goal in some settings, the invisibility of the designer is never full and complete.

Yes, designers are trained to be empathetic and to follow the needs of the people for which they are designing. It is an essential skill to understand the person one wants to communicate with, in order to know how to communicate. Yes, designers are also trained to be versatile in expression.

Designers should be like versatile actors, slipping with every new project into a different role. But this only works so far as we are able to imagine the role we are playing. There are experiences we have not had, because of the way we look or where and how we grew up. We can try to rationally comprehend how a certain message might be perceived by a certain person at a certain place and time, but it is going to be mostly guess work. We do not really feel it. Even the best actor cannot play every role.

The Visible Designer

If invisibility is impossible, why not embrace visibility? Instead of hiding one's personality, it could be used to transmit a message. I am not even talking here about star designers who give their name to add value to a product they are selling. I am talking about designers developing a distinguishable style and using it in every project. Undoubtedly this approach has advantages for the designer and the client. It is easier for the designer to become successful, because it is easier to be recognized, which is a marketing trick not to be underestimated in the saturated design market. The work by the designer becomes the visual identity. Clients appreciate the consistency in style because they know what they will get. There is no surprise, but also no risk and therefore no innovation.

The Systemic Designer

There is a third type of designer. Designers who understand that they can't make themselves invisible, but neither should strive for visibility. Instead, they understand themselves as part of a bigger system of actors. Persons with different perspectives, skills, and styles, essential to the success of this particular communication. These designers have to be in constant dialogue with the other actors, as well as never losing sight of the system that conditions the design process as well as where it is heading. Each of the actors are always stewards as well as sailors, and each of their perspectives are equally important.

A system as non-hierarchical has its advantages and disadvantages. A holistic approach helps the designer see a problem from different angles and therefore deliver a more effective solution, while an atomistic approach would probably oversee a side of the problem that might make the solution ineffective. The disadvantage is that non-hierarchical decision making processes can be very slow. To speed up the process it is of utter importance to have a clear problem definition and conversational and complementary team members. Both, not having a criteria for what could be a solution, as well as actors overlapping actions and entering into competition instead of collaboration, can bring the process to a halt.

DEFINITION OF THE COMMUNICATION PROBLEM

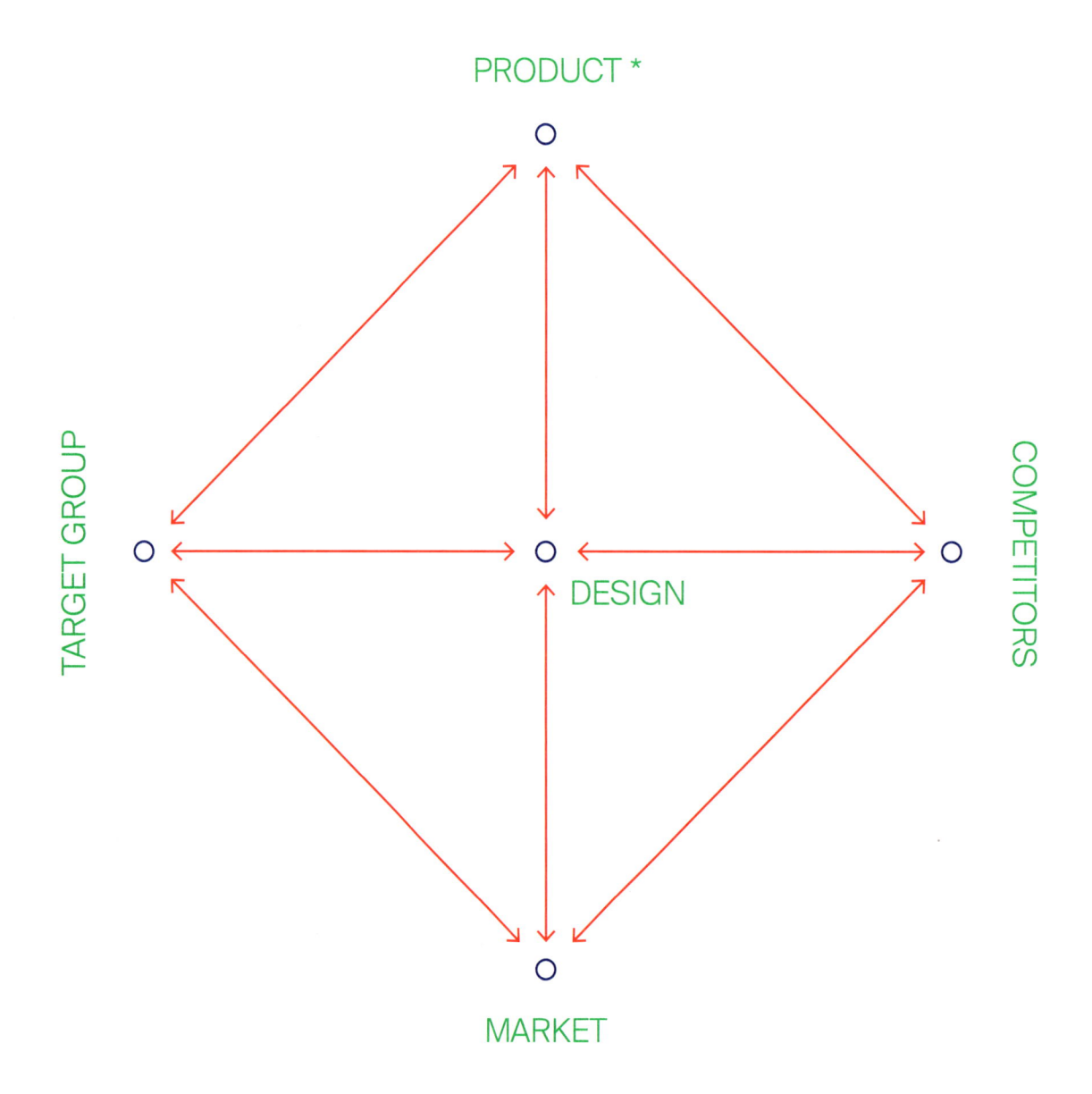

PRODUCT *

TARGET GROUP

DESIGN

COMPETITORS

MARKET

* I use "product" as an umbrella term for any content that needs to be communicated. A product could be a novel, a theatre play, a restaurant, an exhibition, but also a campaign by the city hall to get citizens to vote.

HOW TO WRITE A DESIGN BRIEF?

You cannot design something functional if you do not know what the function of your design will be. Unfortunately this function can be quite complex. If you are designing a visual identity, the primary function is to design a recognizable visual language, but which language makes the identity recognizable? It has to stick out from its environment and competitors, and it has to connect aesthetics and content with the target group. At the beginning of each design process there has to be brief. What does it need to contain?

A Problem Solvable Through Communication

Defining the communication problem is the starting point for every communication designer who wants to provide an effective solution. The designer needs to learn about the product or content, the target audience, the competitors offering a similar product or content, and the environment in which the competitor and client will operate.

It is important to identify the aspects of the problem that are truly communication problems. In most cases you would not even have received the commission if your clients had not detected their problem as a communication problem. However, it can happen that you are asked to solve a problem you cannot solve. Remember the article about corporate design, corporate behavior, and corporate communication? Your focus should be on the problems that can be solved with the right design, not how your client behaves or verbally communicates, even the best design cannot fix a problem coming from the product or content. Differentiating between your role and your client's role will save them and you from trying the impossible.

Understanding the problem definition as a system, i.e. the interaction of a number of influencing components, enables you and your client to determine the source of the problem more precisely. Maybe the target group is not the right one for the product. Perhaps the product would have a better chance in a different market, which would also change the definition of its competitors. The product may need to be changed because a competitor is offering exactly the same thing. Maybe there is no market for the product. Maybe a new market needs to be created.

The problem definition creates criteria that enables us to decide whether the developed design is a solution or not.[1] An incomplete problem definition can lead to the wrong design, having to start from the beginning again and leading to a longer and more expensive project, not to mention unhappy clients and designers.

Coming up With a Workable Problem Definition

Don't expect your clients to give you all the information you need. Your clients should be familiar with their product, target group, market, and competitors. But you can't expect them to know what you need to develop a visual identity. Only you know how you work and only the designer knows which problems can be solved with communication. Often a well crafted communication can solve many more problems than one would think.

There are four main areas to learn about. Discuss these points with your clients, even if your clients have already developed an analysis and strategy in their business plan.

1. Get To Know Your Clients and Their Products
What makes the product special or is there nothing special about it and the design has to be the differentiator? At first this question might make the product sound unnecessary. Why would you even bother developing a product that is similar to what exists?

---

[1] How do you know if a solution does not work? In the process, one of the participants usually gets the feeling that "something does not fit." This intuition must be pursued. Is the feeling just about personal taste, then it can be ignored. If it is based on the analysis of the communication problem, then the design needs to be adjusted.

THE PROCESS

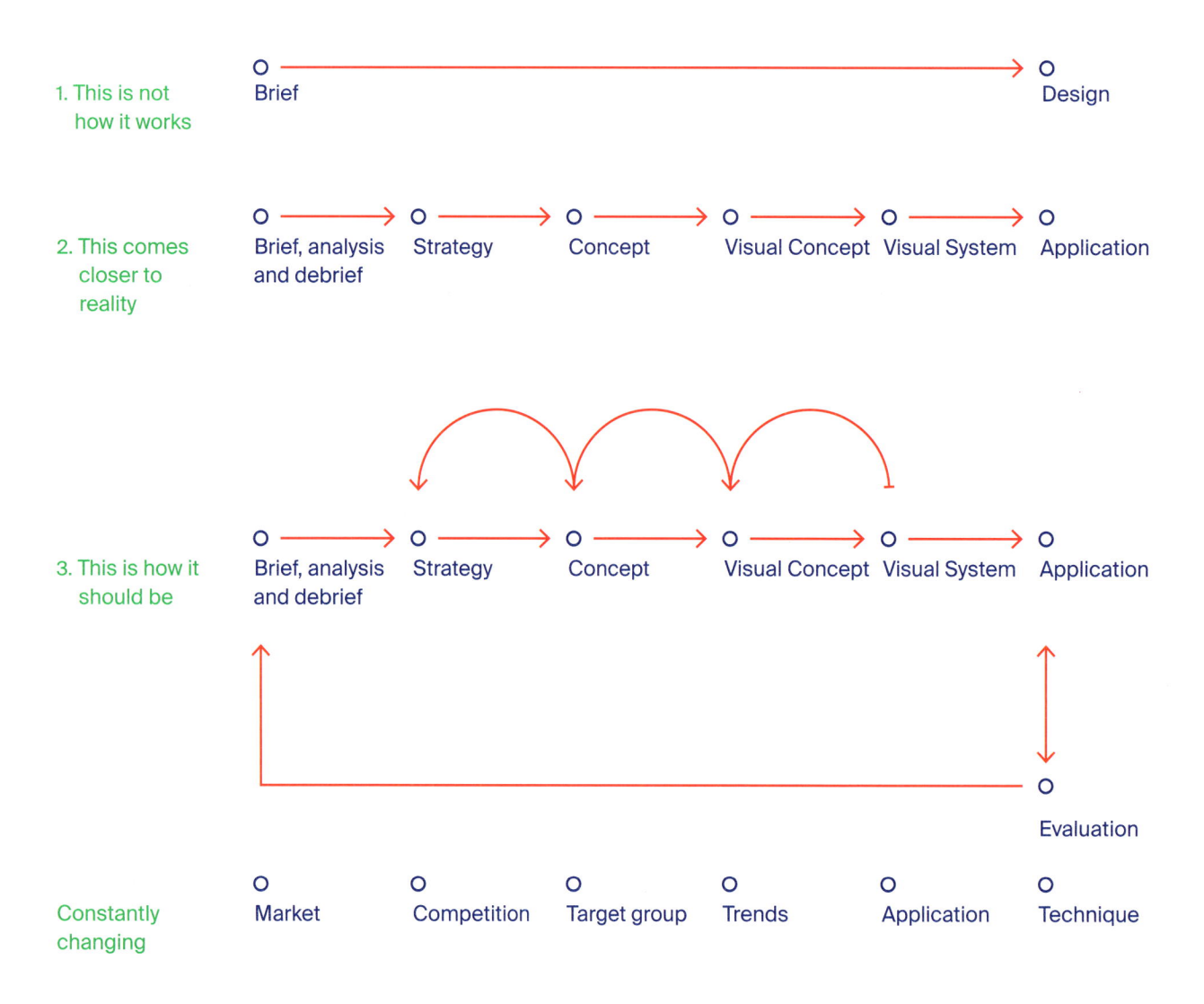

1. This is not how it works

○———————————————————→○
Brief   Design

2. This comes closer to reality

○——→○——→○——→○——→○——→○
Brief, analysis   Strategy   Concept   Visual Concept   Visual System   Application
and debrief

3. This is how it should be

○——→○——→○——→○——→○——→○
Brief, analysis   Strategy   Concept   Visual Concept   Visual System   Application
and debrief

○
Evaluation

Constantly changing

○   ○   ○   ○   ○   ○
Market   Competition   Target group   Trends   Application   Technique

On this page you see three illustrations of a design process. The first describes how some imagine the design process to be like, the second how it is and the third how it should be. The third process is a loop, instead of a linear process. The designers become not just the creators of the visual identity but as well their companions, evaluating if the previously defined still works.

The process includes nine phases: Brief, Analysis, Debrief, Strategy, Concept, Visual Concept, Visual System, Application, and Evaluation. It is important that each step is discussed and approved by your client, because if one step is a misstep you just have to back one phase and do not need to start over. Smaller steps make problems occurring during the process easier to detect and solve. However, I present the concept and visual concept together, because visual interpretation requires imagination, which is a tricky subject. It is highly subjective, based on one's own experience. Even for yourself that imagined is not equal to the visualized. It is always better to show than to imagine.

Watch out for changes in the market, competition, target group, trends, application, and technology. The world is changing quickly and something that once worked might not work anymore because of external factors. Another reason why visual identities should be flexible.

You underestimate the possibilities of design. Design can make a product easier to use. Just as content cannot exist without form. Communication and product form a unit. Communication design is always part of the product development, not just of its distribution. An example. My brother does comics about philosophers. The content is not new or unique. There are other publications with the same content. The way he communicates the content makes the product new and special. Other examples can be found in product and industrial design that even expands to the visual identity and its communication.

2. Get To Know the Current and Future Target Groups
Your clients should know their current audience. But they might think that their product could work even better on a different market with a different audience. That would mean that you not just need to learn about the current but as well the future target group. A new visual identity is also always a strategic tool in order to achieve a situation for your client in which they are not currently, but would like to be in the future.

3. Get To Know the Current and Future Competitors
When seeking placement in a new market with a new target group, new competitors also arise. Study the communication strategies of the competitors. The visual identity developed should be different from the visual identity of their competitors. How much they should differ depends on your communication strategy. Adapting to the visual code of the market without plagiarism can also be beneficial if you want to be quickly understood by your target audience.

4. Get To Know the Past and Present of The Existing Visual Identity and Communication
If your client and their product are new, you can skip this point. But if this is not the case and your client wants to keep their old customers, it is important not to abruptly break with the old visual identity. They could scare off the ones who have gotten used to the old communication. In this case you have to assess whether a gradual change is better than an abrupt one. A changeover to a new or renewed visual identity remains your job, otherwise your client would not have contacted you.

The Next Steps

When you have gathered enough information on the four points, the communication strategy arises almost automatically. It should be the logical consequence of what you have learned. After the strategy comes the concept and the visual concept, which is the idea for the visual communication. While defining the communication problem and analyzing all of its conditioning factors has been a very rational process, the exploration of different visual concepts can be very intuitive and experimental. You already created well funded criteria to decide later on which of your experiments work and which does not. Free experimentation is essential for innovation. If design would be a completely logical process, there would be no surprise, no innovation.

Having a visual concept is great, but not enough. In order to create a tool that can be used by yourself and others, over many years, you need to design a visual system that is easy to understand and apply.

In most cases you are also asked to apply the visual system to a set of specific deliverables, but even if you weren't asked, you should test your system on a wide range of different applications to make sure it works.

Even when your commission is completed, your work is not really done. A feedback loop should tell you how your target groups perceived the communication, which might mean you have to adjust the communication design.

How Does the Briefing for a Logo Design Differ From a Briefing for a Flexible Visual Identity?

While a logo design is the visual representation of a message, a flexible visual identity is a language that can formulate different messages. The concept that is formulated for a flexible visual identity describes the essence of the entity, the tone of the voice. Is it mostly calm and relaxed, energetic and loud, arrogant and distant?

In order to get to the description of the tone, it helps to let your client collect keywords. Start with ten keywords and reduce them yourself to the three most important words together with your client or work group. Words that describe the uniqueness of your clients' product. Avoid terms that your competitors would have chosen. Ordinary terms generate ordinary design. It is important that designers are involved in this process, as they quickly notice whether the chosen terms can be visualized or not.

The definition of the tone describes the essence of the entity. A modulation of that tone is obviously not out of the question. The overall language may be calm and composed, but when they speak in front of a large group they become loud and more determined. A flexible system for a visual identity also needs this leeway. It has to be subtle on an invoice, but expressive in a campaign.

WHAT IS THE COMMUNICATIVE RANGE OF YOUR FLEXIBLE VISUAL SYSTEM?

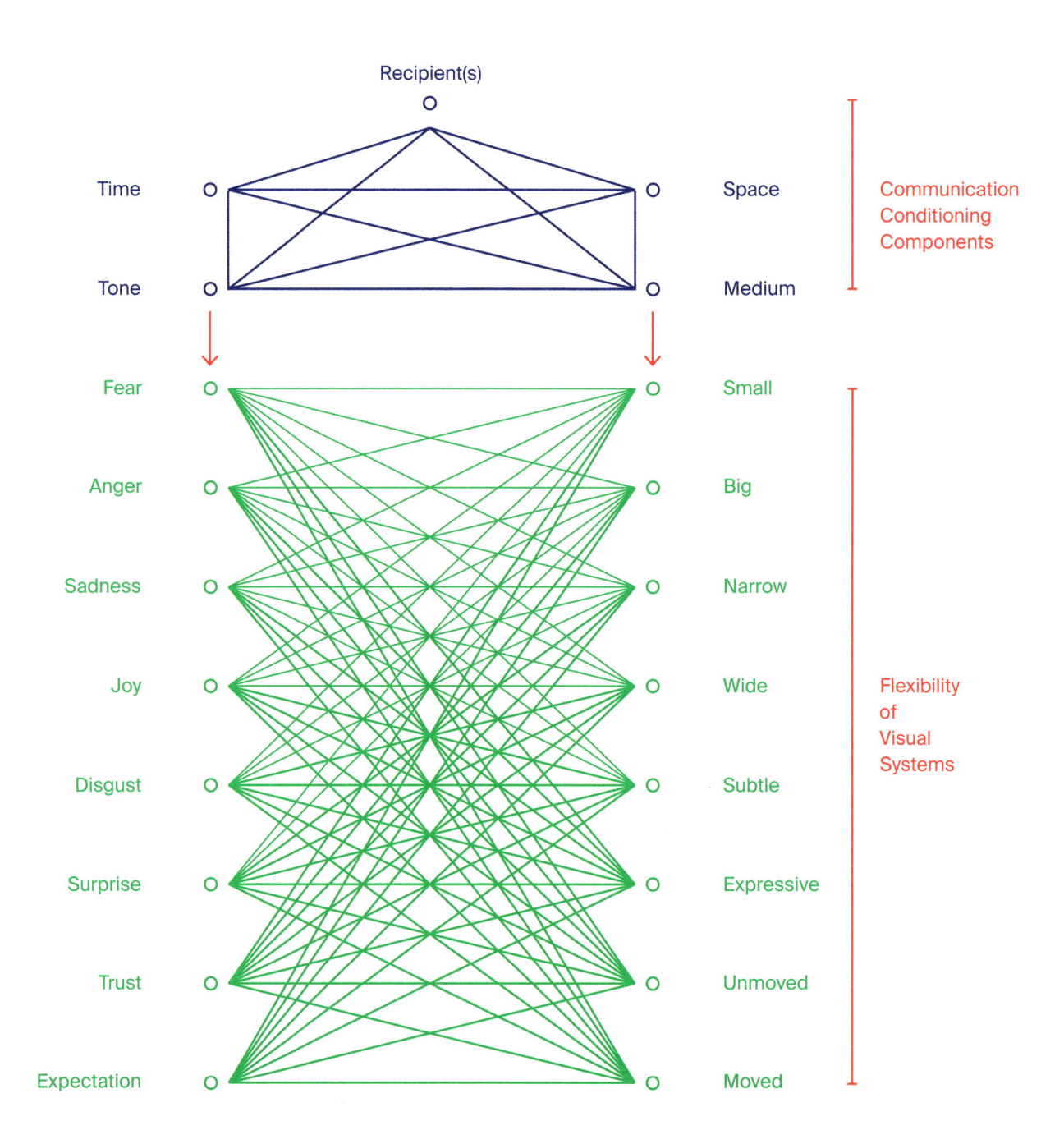

Recipient(s)

Time — Space
Tone — Medium

Communication Conditioning Components

Fear — Small
Anger — Big
Sadness — Narrow
Joy — Wide
Disgust — Subtle
Surprise — Expressive
Trust — Unmoved
Expectation — Moved

Flexibility of Visual Systems

Classification of emotions borrowed from Robert Plutchik (1927–2006), US American Psychologist.

HOW FLEXIBLE DOES THE SYSTEM NEED TO BE?

You now know what to communicate to whom and how. However, we did not enter much in the different articulations of the visual language. The temporal and spatial context may mean that you have to change the content and tone. Your visual system should therefore be prepared for these changes. The diagram on the left gives you an idea of the range of emotions or tones that various applications of your system may want to express

    Not all factors are always equally important and some can be completely ignored. Ignoring a specific articulation of the system can even be a chance to stick out. If your visual identity is mainly communicated through digital media, your visual concept can become unique by choosing movement or interaction. If your visual identity communicates mainly with printed media, you can use color systems, such as neon colors, or paper textures which cannot be displayed on screens.

    Before you can design a visual system, you need to know how, where, for whom, and perhaps even by whom, the visual system will be used. Your briefing will help you figure out how flexible your visual system needs to be. A project does not always need the full range of possible applications, but you should not build the foundation of your visual system too small either, if the building that arises from it may in the future be larger than initially planned.

    The specialty of a flexible visual system is its adaptability to changing contexts. They are languages that can be adapted semantically and formally. Like a spoken language, your visual system can be loud at times and quiet at others, small or large, narrow or wide. You can even change the emotional tonality depending on the context. To develop such a flexible visual system, you must work on the system and its applications simultaneously.

    If you do not do this, you run the risk of developing a dysfunctional system. A system that has not thought of landscape formats, for example, may not work in landscape formats. Therefore, always test for different formats, functions, and sizes.

VISUAL LANGUAGE: ICONIC REFERENCES

	Circle	Triangle	Square
Iconogram			
Pictogram			
Cartogram			
Diagram			
Ideogram			

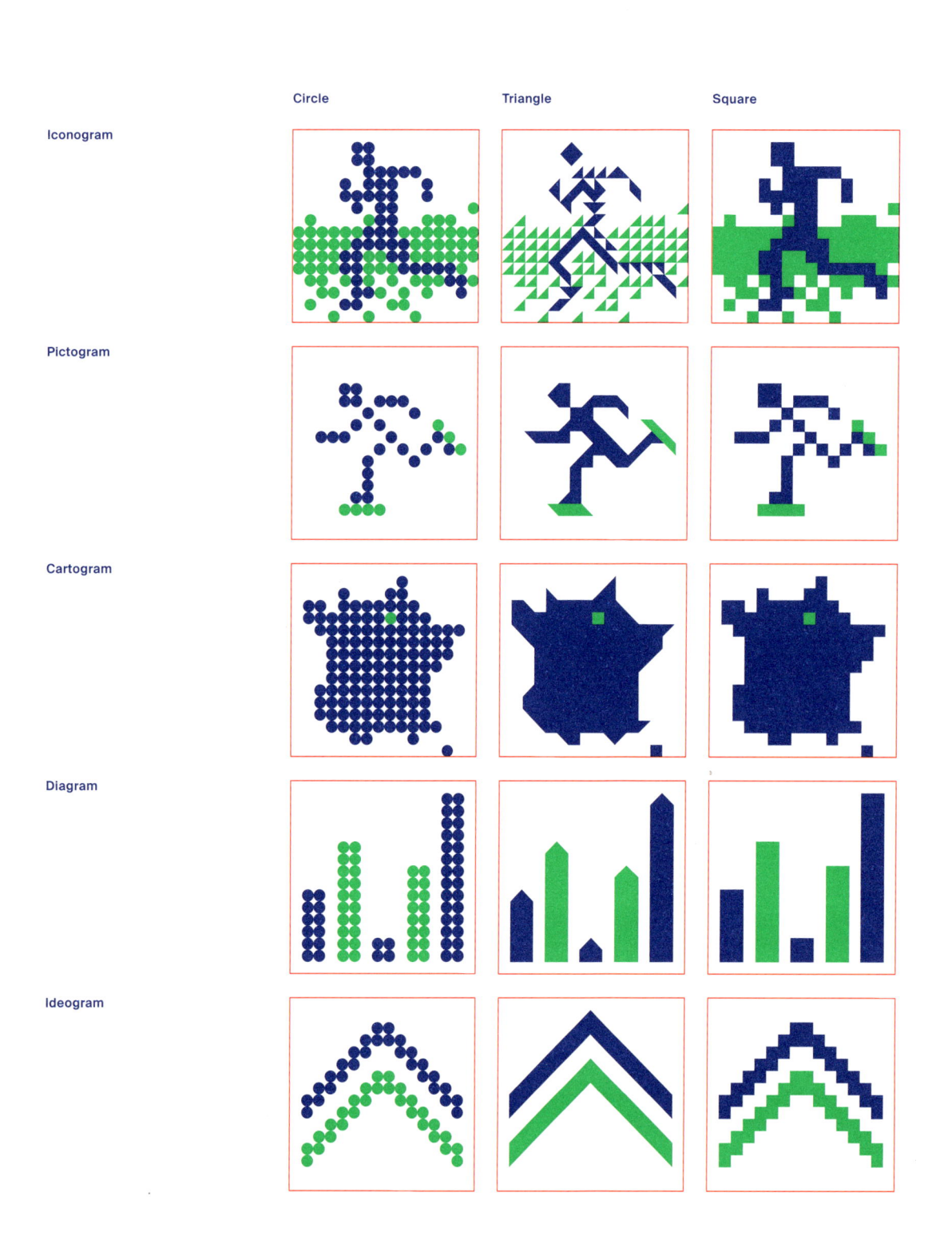

VISUAL LANGUAGE: SYMBOLIC REFERENCES

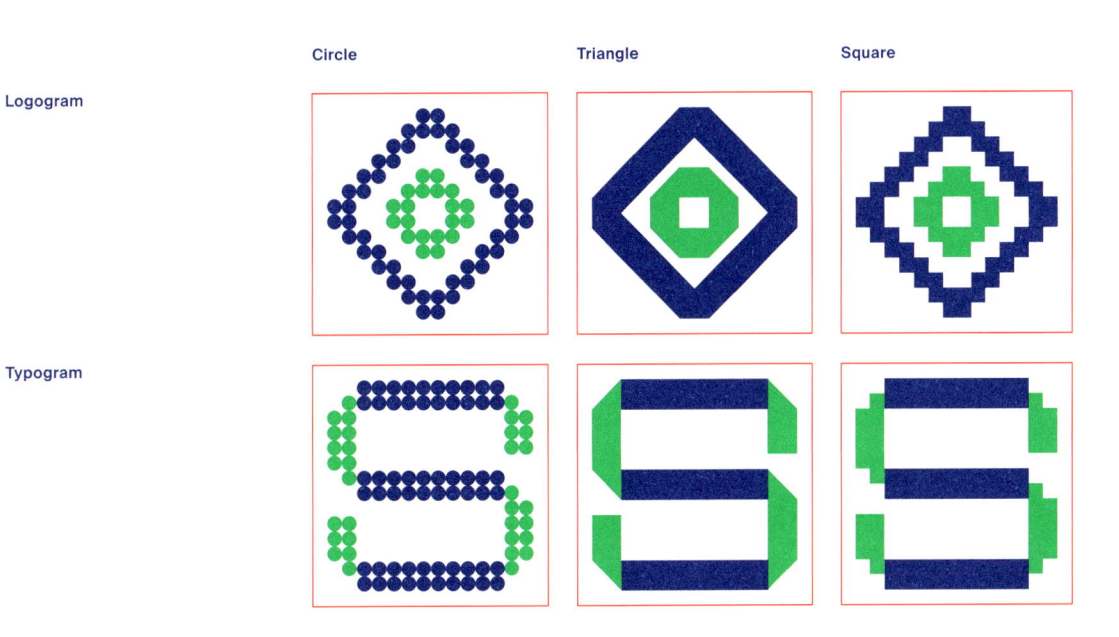

Logogram

Circle | Triangle | Square

Typogram

The examples on this spread show how a circle, triangle, or square and the two colors can create a consistent visual language despite varying forms of visual expression. The examples below show all the available visual variables.

Visual variables

Size | Brightness | Texture

Color | Orientation | Shape

PRECEDENT MODELS FOR VISUAL SYSTEMS

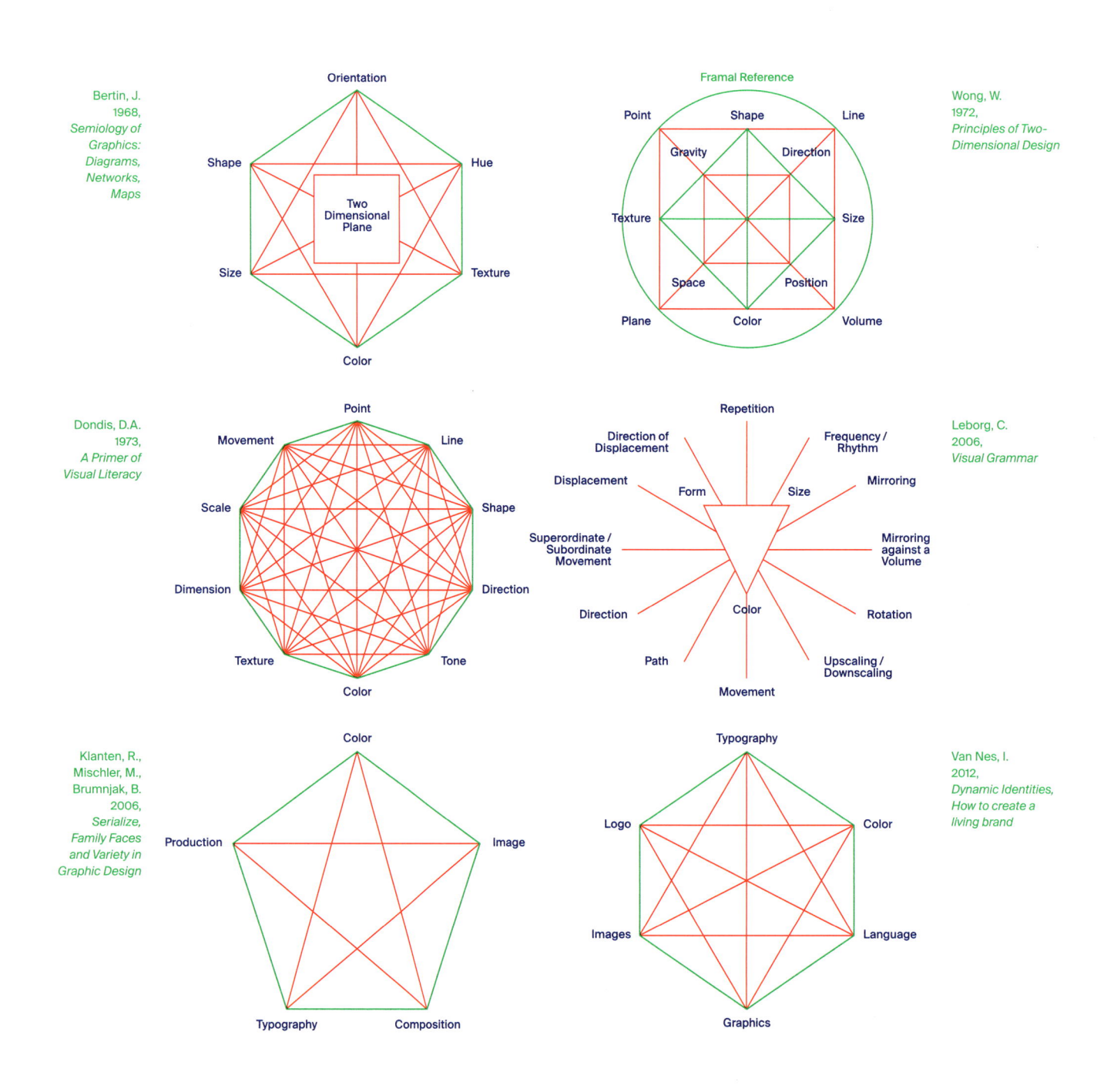

Bertin, J.
1968,
Semiology of Graphics: Diagrams, Networks, Maps

- Orientation
- Hue
- Texture
- Color
- Size
- Shape

Two Dimensional Plane

Wong, W.
1972,
Principles of Two-Dimensional Design

- Framal Reference
- Shape
- Line
- Direction
- Size
- Position
- Volume
- Color
- Plane
- Space
- Texture
- Gravity
- Point

Dondis, D.A.
1973,
A Primer of Visual Literacy

- Point
- Line
- Shape
- Direction
- Tone
- Color
- Texture
- Dimension
- Scale
- Movement

Leborg, C.
2006,
Visual Grammar

- Repetition
- Frequency / Rhythm
- Mirroring
- Mirroring against a Volume
- Rotation
- Upscaling / Downscaling
- Movement
- Path
- Direction
- Superordinate / Subordinate Movement
- Displacement
- Direction of Displacement
- Form
- Size
- Color

Klanten, R., Mischler, M., Brumnjak, B.
2006,
Serialize, Family Faces and Variety in Graphic Design

- Color
- Image
- Composition
- Typography
- Production

Van Nes, I.
2012,
Dynamic Identities, How to create a living brand

- Typography
- Color
- Language
- Graphics
- Images
- Logo

Before drawing my own model, explaining the components of flexible systems for visual identities, I illustrated theories of other authors who deconstructed visual language.

Lorenz, M. (2016). *Sistemas visuales en identidades dinámicas*. (Visual Systems in Dynamic Identities) [Doctoral dissertation, University of Barcelona] Retrieved from http://hdl.handle.net/2445/96603

HOW DO FLEXIBLE SYSTEMS FOR VISUAL IDENTITIES WORK?

If you have read the chapter "Are visual systems a new thing?," you will remember that a historic survey of typographic systems from 1400 until 2000 can draw some parallels to a modern visual identity.

To be able to detect all relevant functions of a modern flexible visual identity I analyzed over one hundred identities. The result was a peer reviewed analytical model of flexible systems for visual identities.[1]

Let's start with Karl Gerstner, who I already mentioned in the part about historic systems and consider the most influential person in the field of flexible systems for visual identities.

In 1964, when Gerstner published *Designing Programs*, it was still unusual for graphic designers to program, and it wasn't until 1970 that Gerstner wrote his first computer program with the help of Klaus Thomas from IBM Stuttgart. A program that generated a huge number of permutations of graphics. Although the use of the computer might have seemed very innovative at that time, it is Gerstner's interdisciplinary approach that makes him interesting to communication designers today. In fact, when using the term "Program" Gerstner does not explicitly refer to computer programs, but to a set of rules that define how a visual identity is applied, a text is written, a photograph is taken or even a building is built.

The Swiss grid design was not as versatile and far-reaching as Gerstner's vision of a programmed design, but easier to learn and use and probably therefore more often implemented. For Gerstner, the grid was the ultimate program. Gerstner wrote in *Designing Programs*: "Is the grid a program? Let me put it this way: If the grid is used as a regulator for proportions, then it is a program par excellence." Gerstner also developed extremely versatile grids, such as the grid for the financial magazine Capital. It helped the magazine strike a harmonious balance between diversity and coherence in the layout. One of the best-known advocates for grid systems was Josef Müller-Brockmann. In his book *Grid Systems*, Müller-Brockmann explains how to develop and use grids. Most of the grid systems presented in this book were used for magazines, brochures, catalogs, and books. Müller-Brockmann also shows how three-dimensional grids can be used for exhibitions and how grids can become an all-encompassing design tool. The most interesting chapter is, in my opinion, the last chapter. Not only because Müller-Brockmann shows grids from other disciplines, such as architecture, construction, urban planning, painting, sculpture, facade design, guidance systems, pictograms, signposting systems, and signets, and compares new examples with old ones, but because he shows examples from nature. Müller-Brockmann manifests an almost religious relationship to grid systems here. Müller-Brockmann writes "Working with grids means submitting to universal laws." Universal laws that are omnipresent through his examples in nature and culture, both then and now.[2]

In 1967 Jacques Bertin published *Sémiologie Graphique. Les diagrams, les réseaux, les cartes* (Semiology of Graphics. Diagrams, Networks, Maps). The book is a classic in cartography, but it is also often quoted by information designers. It might come as a surprise that a book on cartography offers an interesting proposal on how to design flexible visual systems. Even if Bertin designs systems that are used

---

[1] Lorenz, M. (2016). *Sistemas visuales en identidades dinámicas*. (Visual Systems in Dynamic Identities) [Doctoral dissertation, University of Barcelona] Retrieved from http://hdl.handle.net/2445/96603

[2] It was really helpful to me that Gerstner mentioned so many sources in his books. I want to follow his example and recommend three more books to you: The systematic approach to a visual communication problem can also be found in Armin Hofmann's book *Graphic Design Manual: Principles and Practice* from 1965. In this book Hofmann presents systematic experiments with form. The works shown, partly abstract, partly applied to a specific product, were created in collaboration with his students. You can also read about systematic design in Wucius Wong's *Principles of Two-Dimensional Design* from 1972 and Donis A. Dondis' *A Primer of Visual Literacy* from the same year.

MODEL FOR FLEXIBLE SYSTEMS FOR VISUAL IDENTITIES

INPUT(S) → FORM → OUTPUT(S)

INPUT(S) → TRANSFORM → OUTPUT(S)

FORM → TRANSFORM

Systems based on form and transformation can be open or closed. Both types need an input (texts, images, etc.) and an output (application). The output can be used as input.

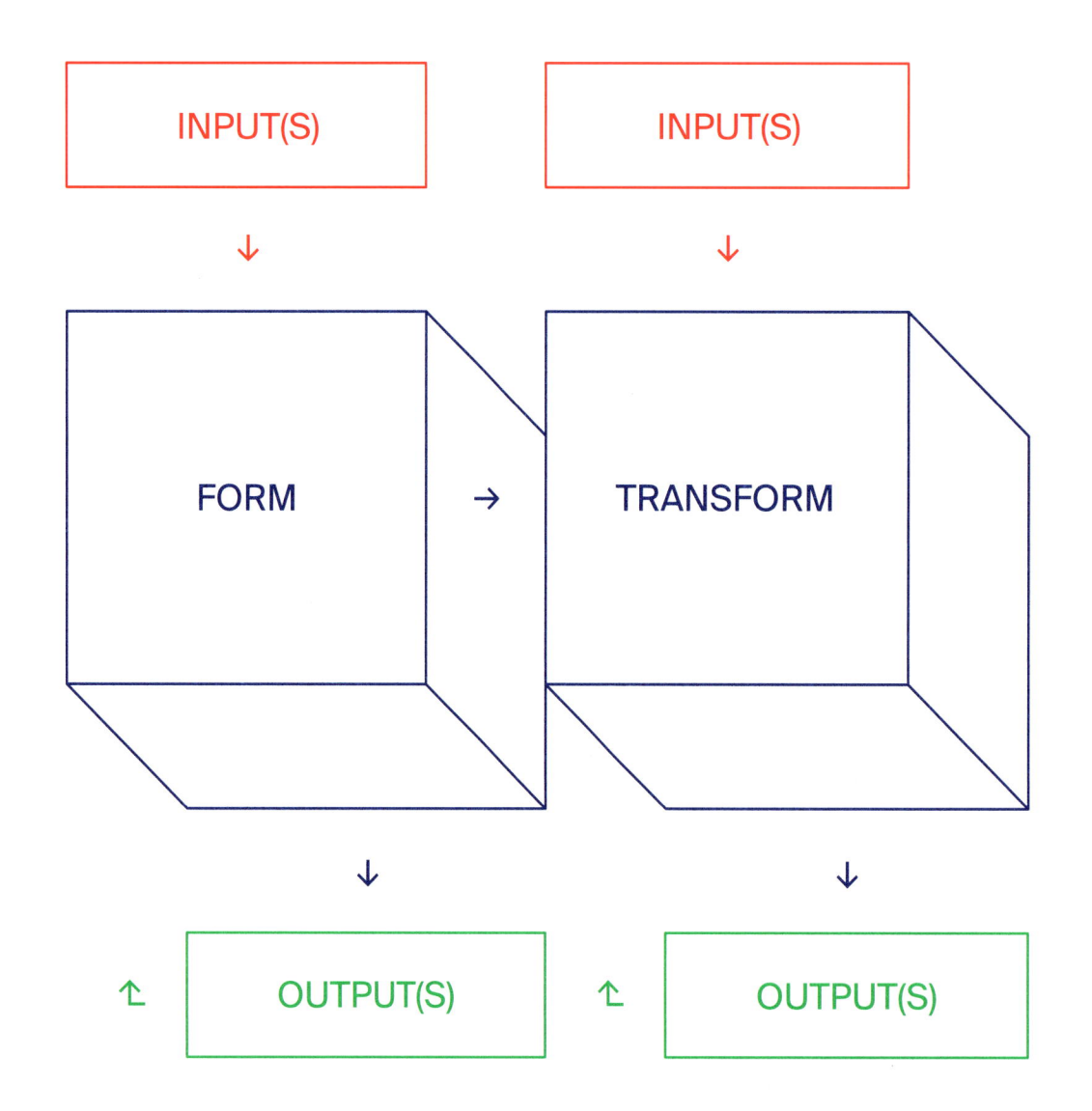

The difference between an open and a closed system is that an open system is able to react, adjust and evolve, while a closed system repeats the same rules it was designed with. Both systems can be flexible but open systems are better at allowing room for evolution in the future.

Evolution of the analytical model for flexible systems in visual identities, developed, peer reviewed, and applied in my doctoral dissertation *Sistemas visuales en identidades dinámicas* (Visual Systems in Dynamic Identities), University of Barcelona, 2016.

There are basically two types of flexible visual systems. Those based on forms and those based on transformation. Any flexible visual system needs to be able to display or process an input to produce an output that can be responsively applied.

as diagrams, statistics, and maps, Gerstner would call them "programs par excellence." In the 1983 edition, Bertin writes about the first edition: "... it was the time of the confrontation between information theory and communication theory that inspired research in graphics. How should we draw? What should be printed in order to facilitate communication, i.e. to explain to others what we know without suffering a loss of information? Ten years later, we see things differently. Of crucial importance today are the properties of the visual variables and the processes behind the graphic classification and permutation. We are beginning the era of operational graphics."

Bertin's graphic system, as you can see on the previous spread, has eight visual variables. The vertical and horizontal position of the element on a surface, as well as the size, tone value, texture, color, orientation, and shape of the element. Depending on the kind of information he wants to visualize, he uses a different combination of variables. The variables always have a range from 0 to 100 to be able to visualize values measured in percentages. If, for example, he wants to draw a map of France, visualizing the population density, he would use the variables "position" and "shape" to visualize the location and "size" to represent the density.

In visual identities variables are used differently. They could, but don't need to visualize data. The main function of a flexible system for a visual identity is to keep constants and variables in balance. The constants are necessary to make the system easy to recognize and remember, i.e. to make the identity identifiable. The variables are needed to react to the changing formal and semantic contexts. Each component of a system can therefore be constant or variable.

Returning to the initially asked question: Are there different types of flexible systems for visual identities? Yes, and I can name them. Comparing theories of authors deconstructing visual language and analyzing hundreds of flexible visual identities published in between 2000 and 2011, I came to the conclusion that there are basically just two main approaches to design visual systems:

1. Visual systems based on form
2. Visual systems based on transformation

Form-Based Visual Systems
I am pretty sure you have seen many. It is the most used type of flexible system for a visual identity. Take a couple of shapes, assign properties, like this shape can contain this color, text, or image and combine the shapes in different ways. The simplicity makes this type of system so powerful. It is easy to build and use.

Transformation-Based Visual Systems
There are not as many visual systems based on transformation as on form, but this does not mean that this type does not have great potential. While a visual system based on form focuses on which shapes to use, a visual system based on transformation concentrates on the design of a specific treatment. I give you an example: take whatever shape, image, or typeface and print it with a Riso printer or an old photocopy machine. The imperfection of the print will create a texture that you will always recognize. If this is too subtle for you, make a lino print, etching, or wood print. The tool and production technique leaves a visible and most importantly, identifiable mark. Today's design and production tools, such as coding, gives us even more possibilities to create visible transformations.

Open vs. Closed Systems
Imagine a box. A closed system is like a closed box. You can shake it and get new variations of the existing elements, but you can not add new ones. If the box or system is open you can add new elements or modify the old. Open system can process external data, evolve over time or be adjusted continuously.

Applications
Don't underestimate the power of a smart application system. Applying the elements of your visual system to a multitude of different mediums with their own particular properties and formats requires a smart system by itself. A simple visual system, even just one single shape, applied cleverly looks great, but a great visual system applied poorly always looks bad. The application system's basic requirement is a responsiveness to aspect ratio and scale, but the more data we can obtain about who is looking where, when, on what to what, the better the visual system can adjust to its application.

FORM-BASED FVS

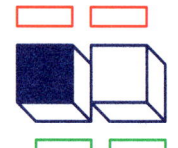

* In reference to format or grid.

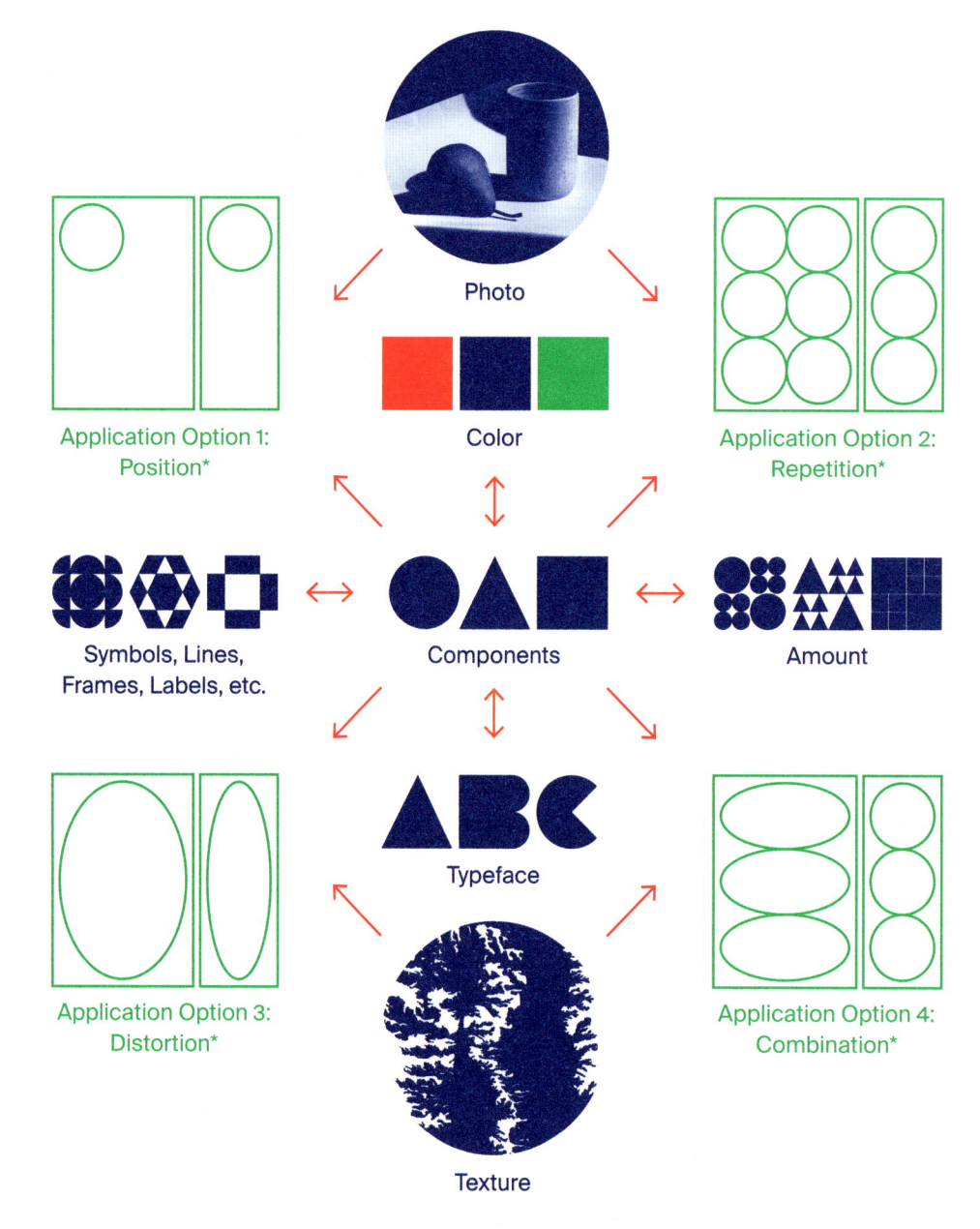

Photo

Application Option 1:
Position*

Application Option 2:
Repetition*

Color

Symbols, Lines,
Frames, Labels, etc.

Components

Amount

Application Option 3:
Distortion*

Typeface

Application Option 4:
Combination*

Texture

Systems based on form start with a component, preferably one that combines with itself. Additional rules about how to combine the components, if they should be mirrored or rotated are added to obtain forms that are more distinctive and therefore easier to recognize. Also, rules about quantities and scale of the shape can add distinctiveness to an otherwise indistinctive geometric form. Properties, such as colors and fonts are added. The fonts could be even custom made with the basic shapes. The forms are applied to the final deliverable and can be used as containers for images or texts.

TRANSFORMATION-BASED FVS

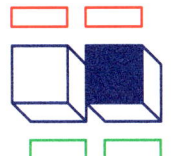

* In reference to format or grid.

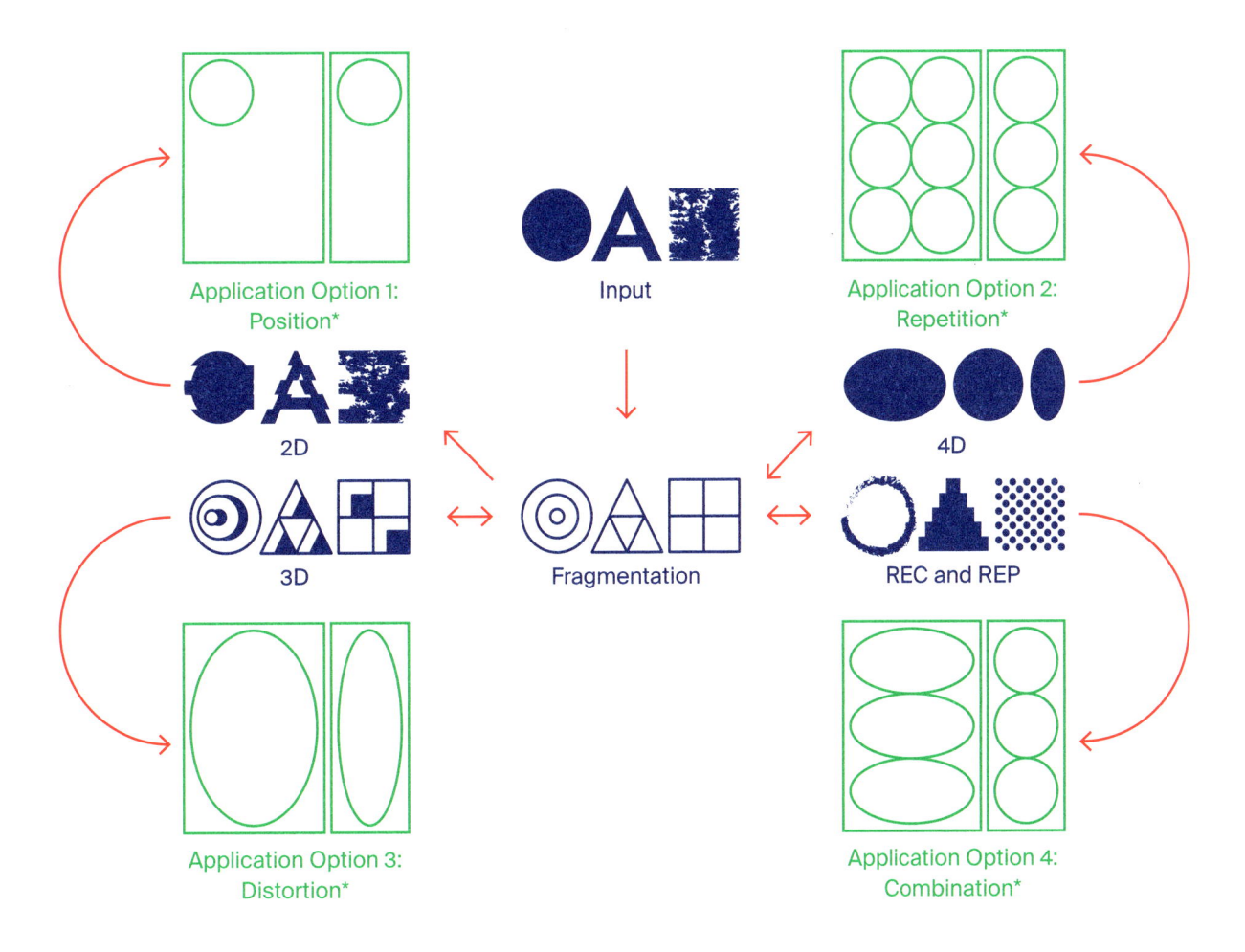

Application Option 1: Position*

Input

2D

3D

Fragmentation

Application Option 2: Repetition*

4D

REC and REP

Application Option 3: Distortion*

Application Option 4: Combination*

While a system based on form concentrates on a recognizable form, the system of transformation concentrates on a recognizable design process. Systems based on transformation can start with shapes too, but they don't have to. In this example I used shapes to cut a form, typography, or photo in pieces and then either transform them by two-, three-, or four-dimensional distortion. A distinguishable recording (REC) or reproduction (REP) technique can be a transformation process too. At last an application system defines how the produced images are applied to the deliverables.

MAPPING THE KEY VARIABLES IN A SYSTEM CAN HELP YOU FOCUS

Visual Systems based on Form

Shape	Circle	Triangle	Rectangle	Pentagram	Hexagon	Heptagon	Octagon	...	Geometric Forms	Organic Forms
Color	Yellow	Orange	Red	Purple	Blue	Green	Black	...	Flat	Gradient
Material	Paper	Wood	Stone	Fabric	Metal	Crystal	Water	...	Photo	Illustration
Different Sizes	1	2	3	4	5	6	7	...	Combination	Concrete Amount
Design Element	Symbol	Edge	Type	Pattern	Line	Frame	Illustration	...	3D	4D
Application on Format	Position (Center, Left, Right, Up, Down)	Filled by distortion	Filled by repetition	Height with distortion, width with repetition	Width with distortion, height with repetition			...	Whole Format	Partial

Visual Systems based on Transformation

Shape	Form	Photo	Illustration	Type	Pattern	Material		...	Defined	Open
Cut up Grid	Circle	Triangle	Rectangle	Pentagon	Hexagon	Heptagon	Octagon	...	Geometric Forms	Organic Forms
2D Distortion	Rotation	Repetition	Reflection	Offset						
3D Distortion	Through objects	Through projection								
4D Distortion	Through time	Through movement								
Recording	Photo	Film	Drawing	Scan						
Reproduction	Offset	Silkscreen	Stamping	Embossing	Die cut	Riso print	Photocopy	Linoleum	Screen	LED
Application on Format	Position (Center, Left, Right, Up, Down)	Filled by distortion	Filled by repetition	Height with distortion, width with repetition	Width with distortion, height with repetition			...	Whole Format	Partial

TOO MANY OPTIONS?
DO YOU NEED HELP TO FOCUS?

Teaching system design for over 15 years made me realize that one of the blockages in the design process comes from the sheer unlimited amount of possibilities that open up once you understand that anything can be systemized.

When I am with my students, I can guide them, motivate them when I see that they are on a good path, and make them aware of the difficulties ahead if they take a bad path. I can help them to combine my systemic approach with their own individual creative path. I feel I have succeeded with my teaching when I see students exploring their own individual interests, skills, and knowledge, while applying a systemic process.

When you will learn with this book or one of my online courses, you will need to guide yourself through the process. Something that can help you to not get lost in the universe of unlimited options is to reduce your options.

The morphological box, invented by the astrophysicist Fritz Zwicky and applied to visual communication by Karl Gerstner, is a way to limit your options and keep an overview about them at the same time. I prepared on the left page a box for form-based systems and a box for transformation based systems. As you can see, it is a list of all the key variables in the left hand column, and an itemization of the ways in which you may fill in those variables in the columns to the right. Just pick one cell from each row and use them to design your visual system. You can do that by chance or choice. It can be a source of inspiration or concentration. Feel free to add or remove cells.

In contrast to Gerstner,[1] I recommend not only selecting one component per row, but also specifying whether the selected component should represent a constant in its visual identity that creates recognition or whether it should be a variable that makes the visual identity flexible.

[1] In his books *Designing Programmes* and *Compendium for Literates*, Gerstner played with Fritz Zwicky's morphological box. Gerstner tried to list all possible aspects of a word mark. He divided the aspects into four main areas: "Basis," "Color," "Appearance," and "Expression." Each of these areas was in turn subdivided and assigned different properties. By choosing one property from one area, different combinations were created. Gerstner writes in the *Compendium for Literates* that the morphological box can be used to create random solutions or to get an overview of the possibilities the designer has when designing a word mark.

FVS: FORM-BASED

CONSTRUCTION OF COMPONENTS AND ASSETS

Component

Choose the elements you want to work with. I chose a circle, divided into four quarter circles, which are easy to combine to new forms.

The new combination of the four quarter circles is repeated four times, so that a square of 16 modules is appears.

Instead of repeating the rearrangement of the four quarter circles, you can also use the vertical ...

... or the vertical and horizontal middle axis to mirror. One of the resulting graphics could be your identification element.

Asset

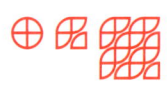

A circle, divided into four quarter circles, reassembled and repeated three times.

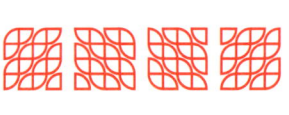

Rotation to create the four corner pieces.

Separation of the last column, the upper left corner module to create a connecting part through horizontal mirroring and repetition.

Rotation to create the four connecting parts.

Frame made of corner and connecting parts

Line made of connecting parts

Line made of corner parts

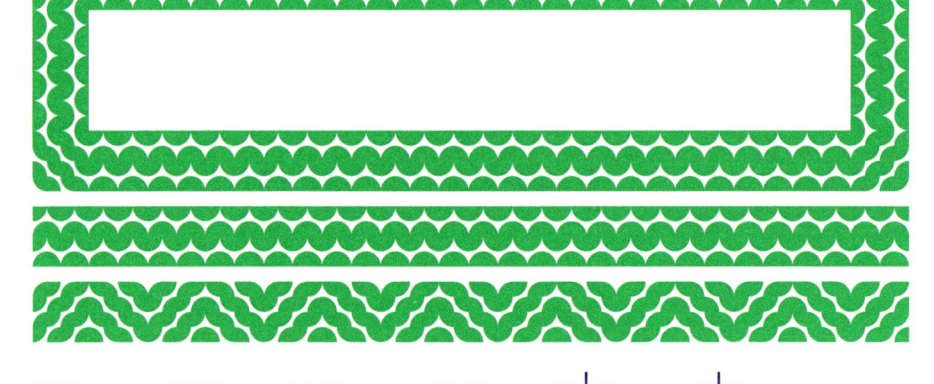

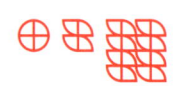

Labels

Repetition

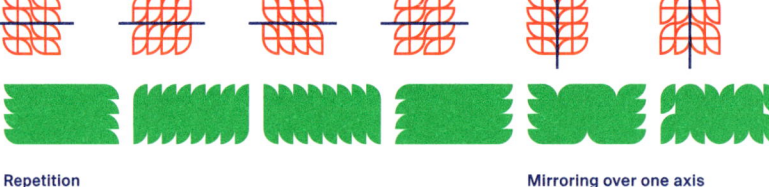

Mirroring over one axis

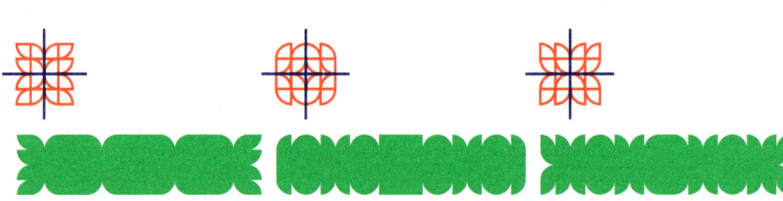

Labels

Mirroring over two axis

HOW TO DEVELOP YOUR COMPONENTS AND ASSETS

Component A simple division and rearrangement of a geometric shape, in this case a circle, can create a small identification element that can be used as a logo. It cannot be stressed enough that a logo alone does not constitute a visual identity and that its primary function in a flexible visual identity is to be identifiable on a small scale. The logo is part of a bigger visual language and should not be relied upon to be a transmitter of a specific message. Apart from being able to be used as a logo, the component can be used to create lines, frames, or patterns.

Asset Assets like lines, frames, or patterns made with the same shape can be very useful for the application of the visual system, which I demonstrate in this book. Apart from being helpful design tools to structure content, being based on the same shape, they are consistent and reinforce the memorization of the identity. Complexity can be increased or decreased by using more or fewer components.

Components can also be used to design "labels," which is the term I use to refer to elements in which texts or images can be placed. They can also be used as interactive buttons, fields in forms, or even as shapes of physical devices such as smartphones, tablets, laptops, or computers. Think of the rounded corners of Apple's hardware and software. A very simple and effective idea inspired by Braun's identity, which again inspired others and therefore lost some of its distinctiveness. However, the simple examples do not play a major role in this book. Not because they don't work per se, but because it's almost impossible to create nowadays a distinctive brand with rounding corners and only using untouched geometric shapes.

USING THE ASSETS

Symbols

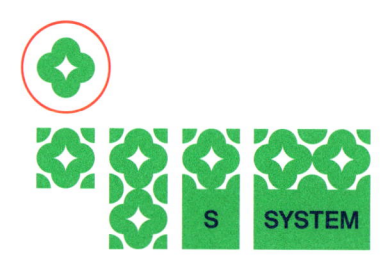

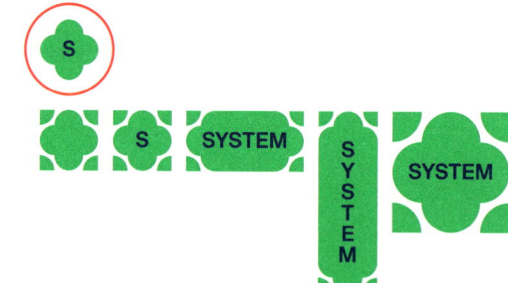

Lines

SYSTEM

Frames

SYSTEM

Patterns

SYSTEM

Labels

SYSTEM   SYSTEM   SYSTEM

SYSTEM

HOW TO USE YOUR ASSETS?

Apart from the explanation of how symbols, lines, frames, patterns, and labels are developed, you will find examples how these can be applied. I will show you how to add text and images to convert them into functional design tools. There are nearly infinite possibilities if you work with this approach. You will find examples in the following chapter "FVS: Form-based."

REGULAR APPLICATION ON DIFFERENT FORMATS

Modules

Repetition

Vertical repetition and horizontal distortion

Horizontal repetition and vertical distortion

Horizontal and vertical distortion

Horizontal repetition and distortion applied to section

Horizontal and vertical distortion applied to section

HOW TO APPLY ASSETS TO DIFFERENT FORMATS?

How a visual system is applied to a format is as important as the visual system itself. If the application is not flexible, the system will be limited. Using many different components can create a sense of complexity that might go against the communication goal. In contrast, using only one component might oversimplify the aesthetics and not be distinctive enough. The application process offers a lot of possibilities and needs to be well designed.

In order to achieve a well balanced application system, it needs to be constantly tested. You need to test the whole range of articulations of your visual language. The first step is to test it on the different formats and then move on to very different types of applications, such as big, small, wide, narrow, subtle, expressive, still, and moving.

If your system is based on motion, it might be best to start with the animation and use stills for the non-moving applications. It is much harder to animate a still than to take a still from an animation.

On the opposite page I demonstrated different ways to apply the component in a regular and format filling manner to different formats. You have basically four options how to apply your shape:

1. Position
Decide where the assets should be placed (center, up, down, left, right, or a combination of the mentioned) and apply that rule to every format.

2. Distortion
Let the assets stretch to the size of the format or a segment of the format. In the example on the left page, the design adapts to the entire format, but using a grid you could decide that the asset only fills a specific row, column, or module.

3. Repetition
Repeat the asset until the format is filled. Again, if you are using a grid, you could decide on just filling a specific row or column, which creates an empty space you can use for text or image.

4. Combination
You could combine all three ways of applying your assets.

It is important to mention that the aesthetics of the examples might deceive. Using a component to make patterns, which actually is already a pattern by itself, creates a specific look that you might or might not want to achieve. If you do not want to achieve the pattern look you simply need to avoid repetition. Use less elements and do not repeat them regularly. On the following page you will find two more examples with different aesthetics. Many more are possible.

This book is about approaches to how to design flexible systems for visual identities, not about showing you all the possible aesthetics, which by the way would be impossible anyways and in my opinion not good for your learning process and not true to your own individual path. The beauty of flexible systems is that any aesthetics can be systemized, even ones that appear to be unsystematic.

IRREGULAR APPLICATION ON DIFFERENT FORMATS

Modules

Repetition of the asset

Vertical repetitio and horizontal distortion of the asset

Horizontal repetition and vertical distortion of the asset

Horizontal and vertical distortion of the asset

Mix of application systems

Horizontal and vertical distortion of the asset, minimal version.

SAME PRINCIPLE, DIFFERENT AESTHETICS

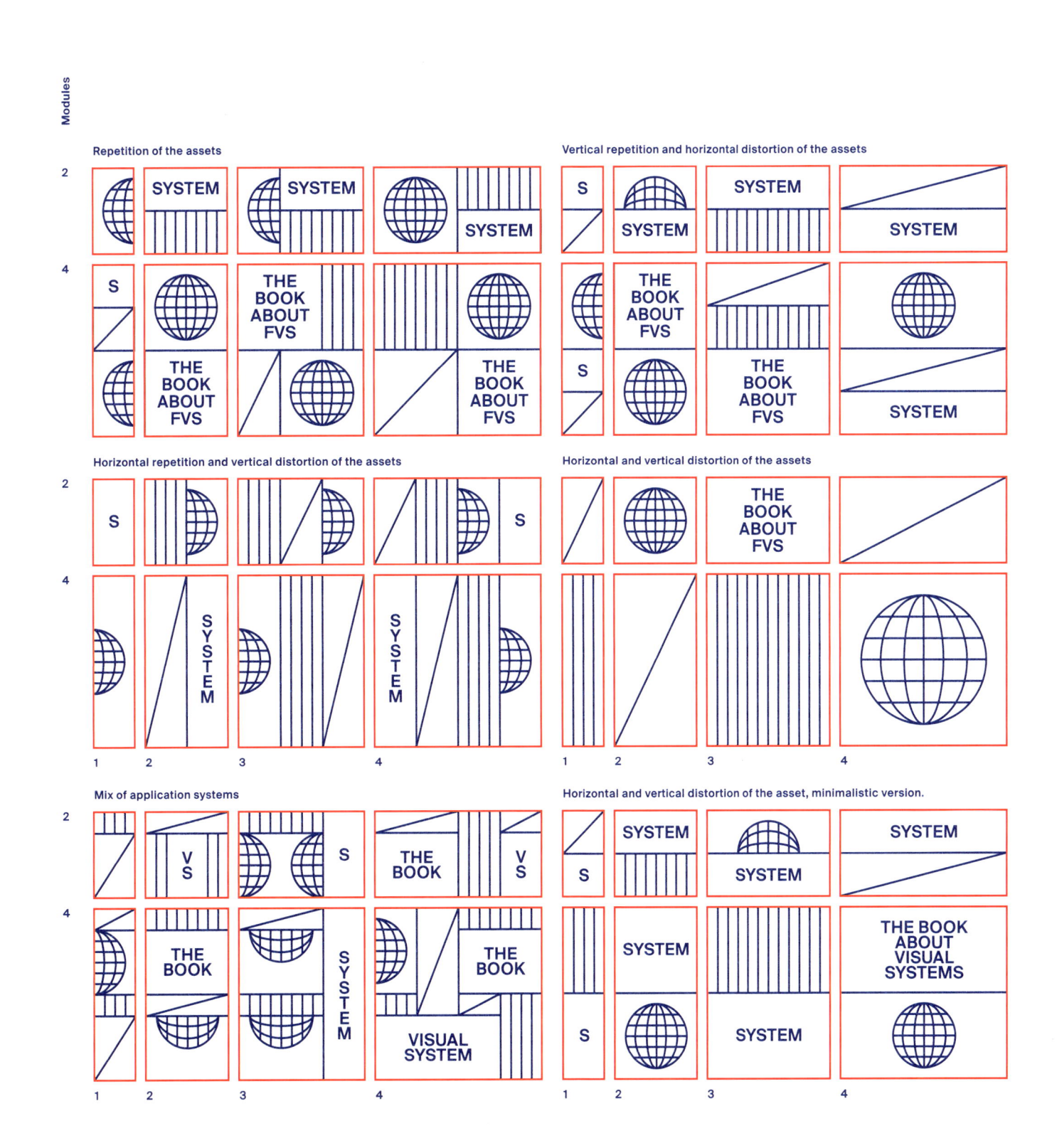

Modules

Repetition of the assets

Vertical repetition and horizontal distortion of the assets

Horizontal repetition and vertical distortion of the assets

Horizontal and vertical distortion of the assets

Mix of application systems

Horizontal and vertical distortion of the asset, minimalistic version.

IDENTIFICATION THROUGH COMPOSITION, COLOR AND / OR FONTS.

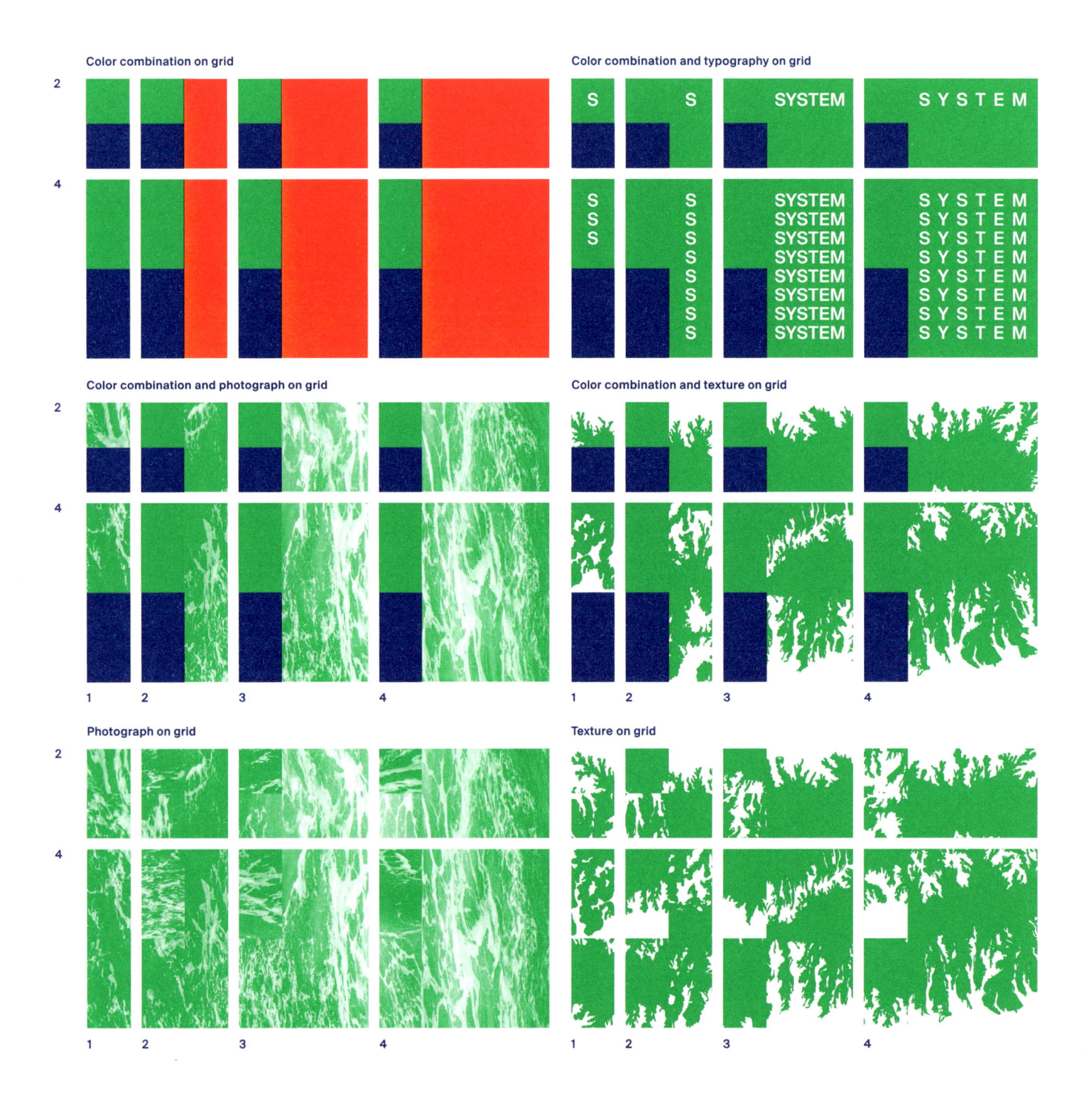

Color combination on grid

Color combination and typography on grid

S S SYSTEM SYSTEM

S SYSTEM SYSTEM
S S SYSTEM SYSTEM
S S SYSTEM SYSTEM
  S SYSTEM SYSTEM
  S SYSTEM SYSTEM
  S SYSTEM SYSTEM
  S SYSTEM SYSTEM
  S SYSTEM SYSTEM

Color combination and photograph on grid

Color combination and texture on grid

1 2 3 4

1 2 3 4

Photograph on grid

Texture on grid

1 2 3 4

1 2 3 4

WORKING WITHOUT ASSETS

Even if you want to work without assets, you still need visual systems. A big part of this book shows how to generate and apply graphics based on geometric shapes. This might evoke the impression that visual identities always need visible graphics. Far from the truth. Geometric shapes, such as rectangles can be used as invisible containers for colors, textures, photos, or text.

 Although at some point geometric shapes will probably be present in your designs through formats, grids, picture, and text frames, they do not need to be the identification element of the identity. A characteristic layout, a special color scheme or a distinctive font can be sufficient to make an identity identifiable.

 Whether a graphic, typographic, or photographic system is appropriate depends to a large extent on the product, the culture of the country, the industry, and the target group. While graphics might be perceived in one occasion as a neutral design element in another they might appear too playful. I will not go into the semantics of the form in this book, as this is a highly context-dependent matter, and should be addressed for each of the projects individually.

 Making shapes invisible does not necessarily mean getting rid of them. Shapes are very helpful to describe a visual system. Many shapes repeatedly form a grid which makes it even easier to describe and work with a system. If you want to make these shapes invisible, think of unusual, but repeatable shapes, apply them irregularly or make the edges blur by not completely filling them.

 Shapes, as in the example on the opposite page are also helpful as text and image containers. Organized in a controlled way they can create identification and establish information hierarchies.

THE COLORS OF THIS BOOK

WHAT ABOUT COLOR?

In this book I have deliberately avoided the topic of color because it's choice is very much context related. It depends on time, place, and culture like no other design element. But I don't want the misunderstanding to arise that color doesn't play any role in the creation of visual identities. On the contrary, color plays an essential role. Color supports the recognizability of an identity to a large extent. Just look at the visual identities based on a recognizable color. Often the color chosen for public transport became the color of the city brand. Color is an extremely powerful tool for identification.

Color is also very helpful to transmit the emotion you want to evoke, the tone of voice of the visual language. Karl Gerstner wrote in *Die Farbe der Form*: "If the form is the body, then color is the soul." The sentence expresses how subtle, but also multi layered color communicates.

In order to sensitize yourself to colors, I recommend the book *Interaction of Color* by Josef Albers. Don't just read it, mix the colors yourself. You will be surprised how much more you learn by doing than just reading.

A few recommendations when picking colors for visual identities:

1. Choose Two or Three Colors for Your Identity
Color combinations of two or three colors work best for visual identities. Choosing only one main color has worked for a long time, but soon there was no single color to pick anymore, because the big companies legally protected their corporate colors, so no company in the same market would be able to use it. Color combinations augment the possibility to find a unique combination. Combining two or three colors also starts a conversation in between them, which gives the visual language more depth. Why only two or three? We humans are very good in color perception, but very bad in color memorization. Scientific studies suggest that when memorizing colors, the name we give them plays a role. That means conversely if we do not have a name for a color we won't remember it. This might explain why most of the visual identities use primary or secondary colors.

2. Test Your Colors on Different Mediums
There is another explanation why most visual identities use primary or secondary colors. Not all colors are reproducible in every medium. Mint greens for example are beautifully bright on screen or printed with Pantone, but very dull when printed with CMYK. That does not mean automatically that you cannot choose mint green for your visual identity. It just means that you need to test your colors in all color systems your client will use in the future. The bigger the company, the less choice you have. Big companies use all kinds of mediums. But smaller companies might use one color system more than another and therefore give you the opportunity to make a unique color choice.

3. Give Your Color Scheme a Logic
Our eyes intuitively perceive harmonies in colors and associate them with the content or identity. You can use that. Think of the effect you want to achieve and choose your colors accordingly. Johannes Itten, the Swiss painter, designer, teacher, writer, and theorist, associated with the Bauhaus, distinguishes between seven color contrasts. The contrast of hue, saturation, light and dark, warm and cool, the complementary contrast, the simultaneous contrast, and the contrast of proportion. If you want to create tension, choose one contrast. Too many contrasts at once will weaken the effect. If you want harmony, don't choose contrasts, but similarities, like for example tones of the same color or colors of a similar warmth or hue. Adobe proposes the following color systems: Analogous, Monochromatic, Triad, Complementary, Split Complementary, Double Split, Complementary, Square, Compound, and Shades. Each color contrast or similarity has its inherent logic and therefore for the viewer comprehensible relation in between colors.

IDENTIFICATION THROUGH RULES AND TOOLS

1. TAKE A RED PEN
2. DRAW A LINE
3. TAKE A BLUE PEN
4. DRAW A LINE WHICH IS AS LONG AS THE RED LINE, STARTING FROM ONE END OF THE LAST DRAWN LINE
5. REPEAT UNTIL YOUR DRAWING IS FINISHED

WORKING WITHOUT GRIDS

Even if you want to work without grids, you still need visual systems. Grids are one of the most helpful inventions since communication designers had to design more than one deliverable. By limiting the options where to place text or images and in which size, so much time has been saved. Apart from being an efficient design tool, they also establish a comprehensible order that makes reading easier. Having said that, you are not obliged to use them.

A visual system is nothing else than a set of rules, an instruction manual for humans and/or machines. By inventing rules, similar to the ones on the left, you can design processes that lead to distinctive visual identities. The instructions you are giving are actually code that can be executed by humans (usually slowly) or by machines (usually more quickly). When you let these rules be executed by machines instead of humans, you gain a lot of new possibilities. Not just that your design can become more complex, you can instruct any machine that is manageable with code. Even a remote-controlled spray can installation,[1] drone, or car can be used to visualize the applications of your system.

But not everything programmable needs to be executed by machines. The imperfection coming from humans can create interesting details a machine would avoid. Suprematism, Constructivism, and De Stijl would have been extremely boring if not painted by humans but printed by machines. Executing programs by humans also have a collaborative dynamic that can add interesting interpretations within the parameters of the rules.[2] We see and remember only the things that make sense to us. Based on our experience some things appear to be comprehensible and some don't. Not everything that is logical to us is logical to someone else, because the other person has different experiences in life. The more people with different backgrounds we want to reach, the more universal the language we use has to be. Maths and physics are such universal languages. If you show a person from the other side of the world an animation using physics, this person will intuitively understand it because they've lived with the same physics on the same earth.

---

1   Jürg Lehni programmed a tool to spray paint vector images to walls. He called his machine "Hektor." The perfection of vectors and the imperfection of the spray paint create an interesting contrast and a distinctive visual language that could serve as a visual identity.

2   Studio Moniker's "Conditional Design" workshops are a good example for programmed design, executed by humans. They imposed on themselves rules, which they then executed together. The execution of Sol le Witt's murals come to mind also, who instructed his assistants how to draw his huge murals with tiny pencils. From far the murals appear to be perfect, but from close you notice the imperfection of the human stroke.

THE ADVANTAGES OF A GRID

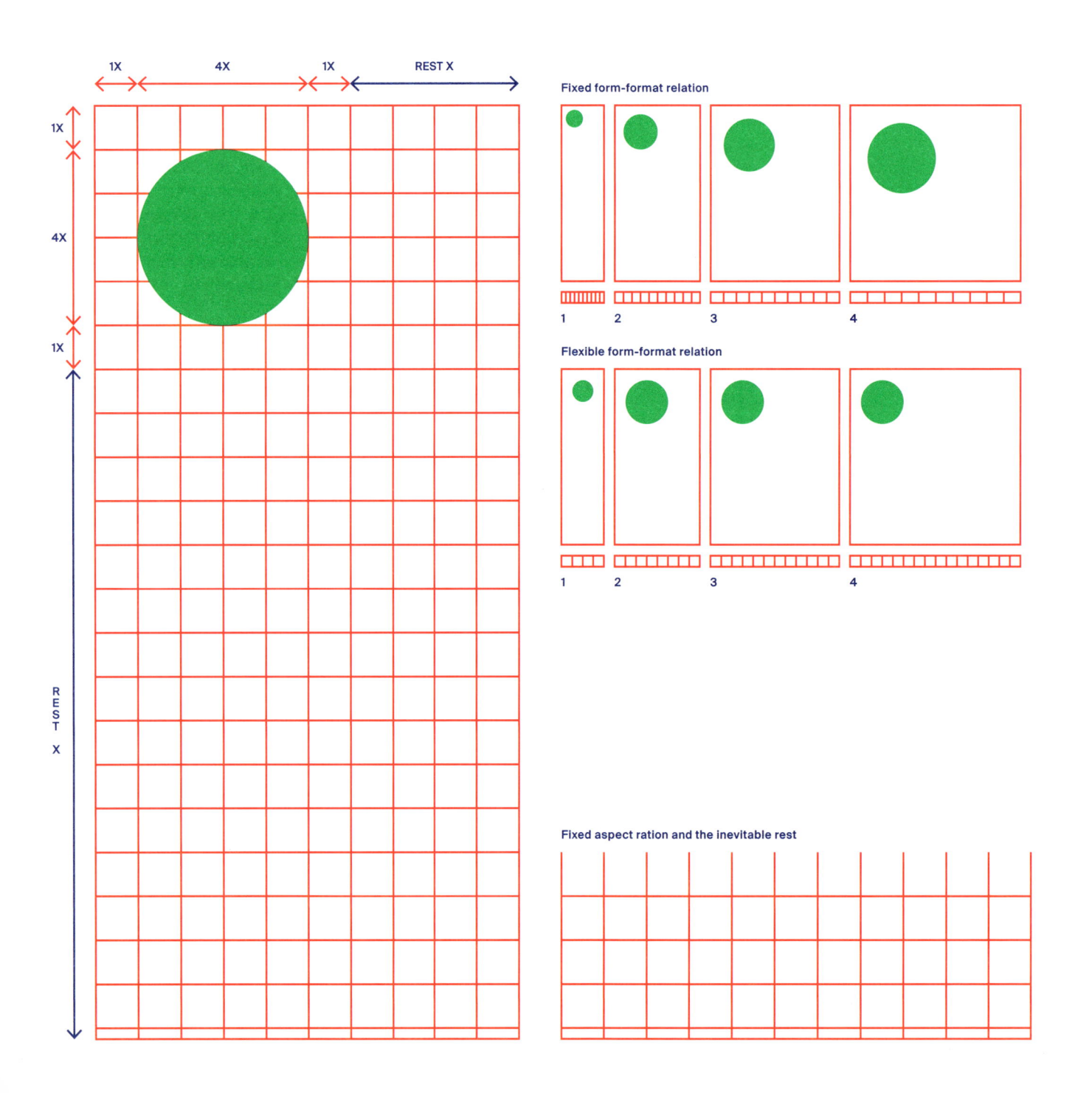

1X 4X 1X REST X

1X
4X
1X
REST X

Fixed form-format relation

1 2 3 4

Flexible form-format relation

1 2 3 4

Fixed aspect ration and the inevitable rest

WHICH ADVANTAGES DOES USING A GRID HAVE?

While you do not need a grid, this book is full of them because grids make it easier to determine the positions and sizes of the assets. Just as the assets can react to formats, grids can also adapt to different formats by repeating or distorting its modules.

Designing with grids has several advantages:

1. Structure
Grids create a comprehensible visual structure that can help to distinguish different information types from each other. For example, three columns can be used for three different languages or the top row can always be used for headings.

2. Aesthetics
Grids can create the feeling of order and harmony, but also of dynamism. Through the interaction between positive and negative spaces or the irregular and regular placement of elements tension can be built up.

3. Efficiency
At first glance, grids look like more work for the designer. In fact, they save us a lot of work. By reducing the options for positioning assets, the number of decisions to be made when designing is also reduced. If, in addition to the grid, you have found a system for distributing the various types of information, you only have to make a manageable number of design decisions on each page. With a book of 48 pages or more, you will quickly see how much time this saves you.

4. Harmony
After a number of pages you will also see that the design decisions influenced by the grid make the book a harmonious whole, even if each page looks different you will always notice the underlying logic.

5. Identification
In the context of this book the possibility of creating a recognizable visual language with grids is very interesting. If the grid, and/or the system on how to apply the assets on the grid, is distinctive it serves as an identifiable design element.

6. Instructions / Design Manual
The description of how something is designed is often disregarded as a non-essential part of the design process. I consider it as one of the most important phases. If a system is easy to understand and apply it will most likely be used for a long time. If a system is highly complex and there is a human applying it, it will most likely be wrongly interpreted. A grid helps to visualize rules. Everybody understands what it means to divide the width of the format by ten and use a tenth of the format as a space around an object, as shown on the left page. The modules resulting from the division of the format help to define position and size of objects and spaces and the best thing about them, they are scalable and adapt to the size of the format.

At the risk of mentioning the obvious, I would like to point out that there is a difference between graphic and typographic grids and that these must be coordinated with each other. While typographic grids need space in between columns and rows, also called gutter, graphic grids can work perfectly without the gutter. In fact, they are easier to manage and calculate without the gutter. When working with graphic-heavy visual systems I usually start with a graphic grid and place a typographic grid inside the sections which have text. If I am working on a book or any other text-heavy application I start with the typographic grid and place the graphic grid inside of the modules of the typographic grid. Another option would be to place a format-spanning typographic grid on top of a graphic grid, but to this date design software does not make this easy.

CREATE GRIDS WITH GEOMETRIC SHAPES

Acute triangle

Hexagonal pattern

Right triangle

Square pattern

Acute triangle

Hexagonal pattern

Right triangle

Hexagonal pattern

HOW TO CREATE A GRID WITH DIFFERENT GEOMETRIC FORMS?

Reset
Forget about the software you are working with and the possibilities they offer you at the moment, and you will see that you are very limited and that there are countless other ways to develop grids. You only need to look at centuries old Islamic patterns. These seemingly complex patterns are based on simple grids based on different geometric shapes and their intelligent use. Even the much simpler posters for Musica Viva by Josef Müller-Brockmann, designed on a grid rotated by 45 degrees, look very innovative for a today's designer adapted to today's software. Not to mention Müller-Brockmann's circular grids. All of these are quite complicated to realize with today's software.

Starting Points
Begin your experiments with alternative grid systems with a geometric shape that is not the rectangle. For example, take a triangle or hexagon and put them together. Use the resulting characteristics to design shapes and patterns, but also to design or arrange fonts.

Adaptation
Today's software favors the grid based on horizontal and vertical guidelines. Adapting the grid based on other shapes is complicated. This is why in this book I have worked with triangles, pentagons, and hexagons that fit into a rectangular grid.

USING GRIDS

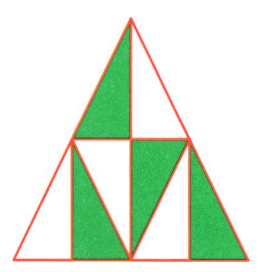

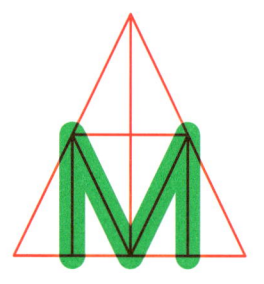

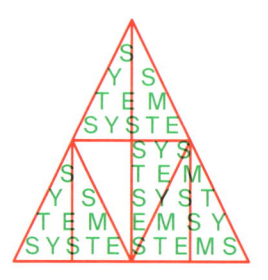

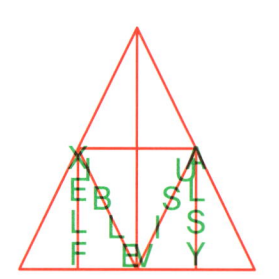

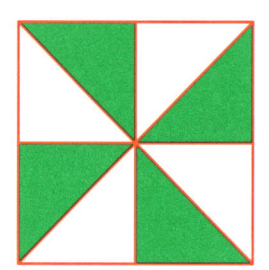

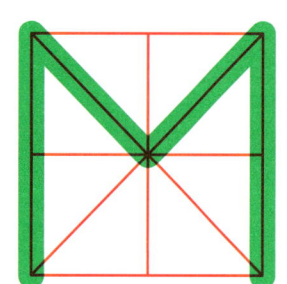

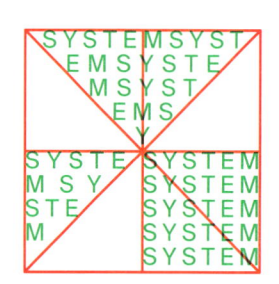

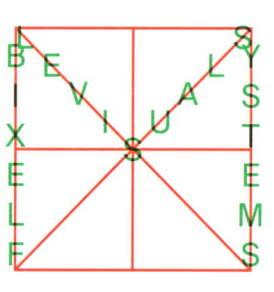

Use of the modules | Use of the nodes | Use of the modules | Use of the nodes

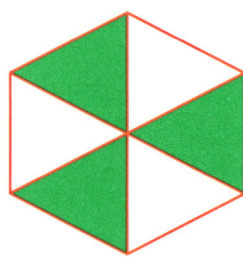

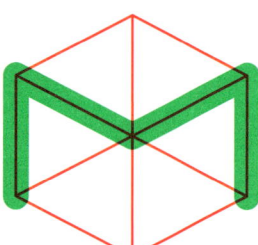

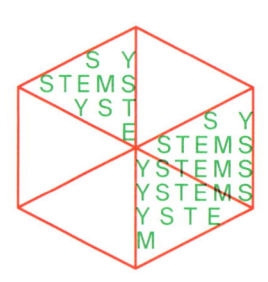

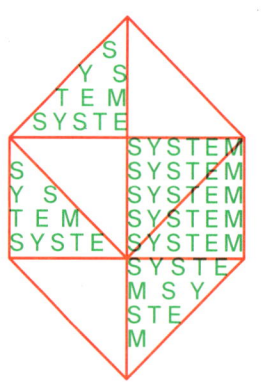

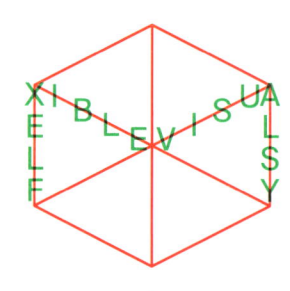

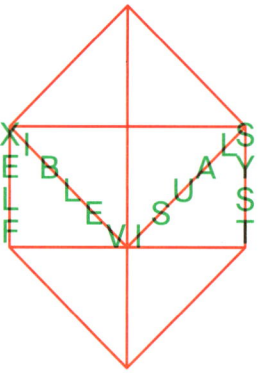

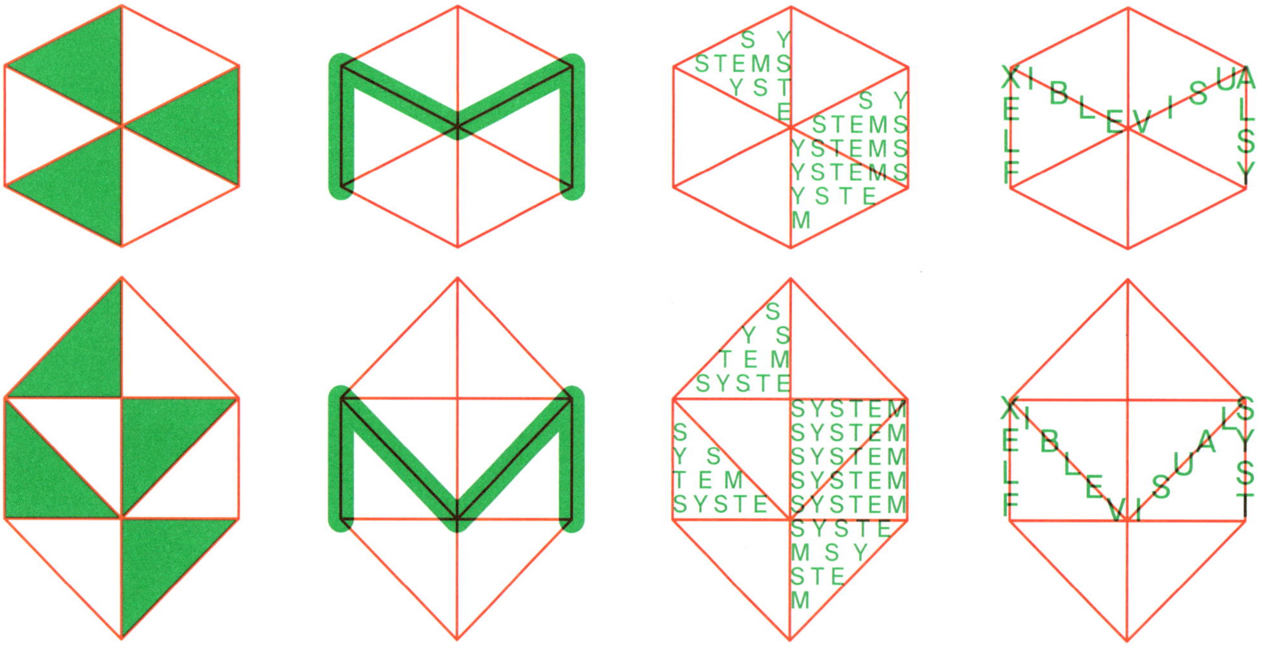

HOW TO USE GRIDS?

There are different ways to use a grid. You can generate shapes by filling modules or their outline. You can also use the module or outline to align text or graphics. The more unusual the grid and its use is the better it serves as a distinctive visual identity. These couple of options give you already sheer unlimited possibilities. You can repeat the modules and use them to create larger patterns, lines, frames, or labels, depending on the need of each deliverable. Adjusting the complexity of the grid needs to be dependent on content and scale of the deliverable. Simple solutions are better suited for small applications. The larger the format, the more complex you can get.

FONT CONSTRUCTION

Adding diagonals to the modular font by connecting the nodes

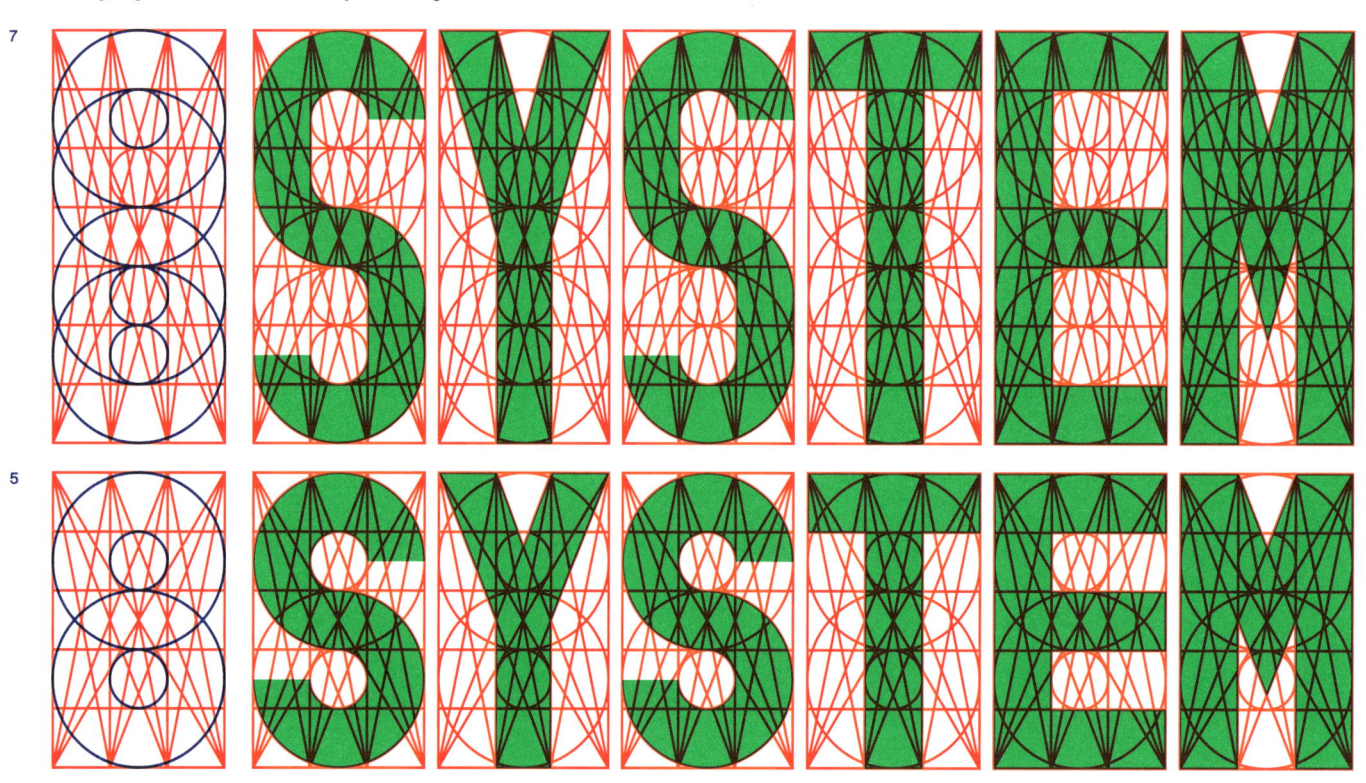

Designing fonts with grids without any optical correction and, as in this case, without adjusting the width, inevitably leads to an irregular distribution of weight. But that doesn't have to be bad thing, it can actually increase the distinctiveness of the design, which in case of identities is key. Obviously not for long texts.

Different grids produce different letter styles. Here is an example of what grids for a light and an italic weight could look like. The letters shown here are low in contrast and have no serifs, which could be added without a problem. The example on the right shows how to make a higher and therefore more condensed font.

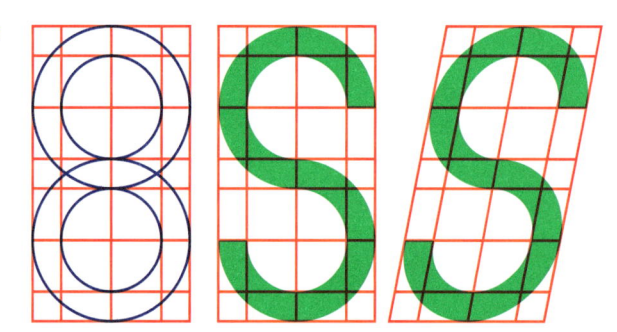

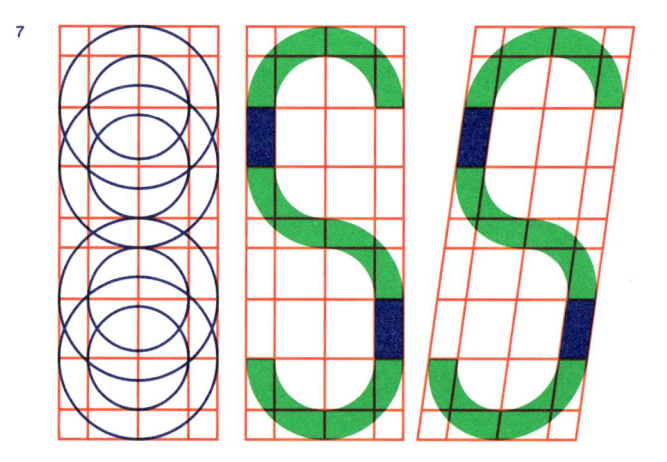

WHAT KIND OF GRIDS DO I NEED TO DESIGN MODULAR LETTERS?

You could use any kind of grid to design letters. In this book I have limited myself to the modular construction of letters like the one on the opposite page. The modules should be versatile, and be used for lines, frames, and patterns, as well as serve as a symbol. Shapes that only work with letters are unsuitable for a flexible visual identity. Nevertheless, on this page I would like to give you a glimpse into the world of the unlimited possibilities of systemic type design.

Different grids produce different font styles. On the opposite page is an example of a grid for a bold, light, and italic weight. The font is low in contrast and has no serifs.

With a modular letter construction, based on a square grid, it is important to use at least two different shapes in order to be able to imitate the curves of letters such as the B, C, D, G, etc. Instead of quarter circles for the curves, triangles can also lead to legible results.

The shape can be used to create symbols, lines, frames, and patterns, but also letters. A modular font is not suitable for typesetting longer texts, but can serve as an identification element due to the constant repetition of the same shape. Characteristic display fonts are also often used as word marks.

FONT CONSTRUCTION

Changing the weight, by changing the grid

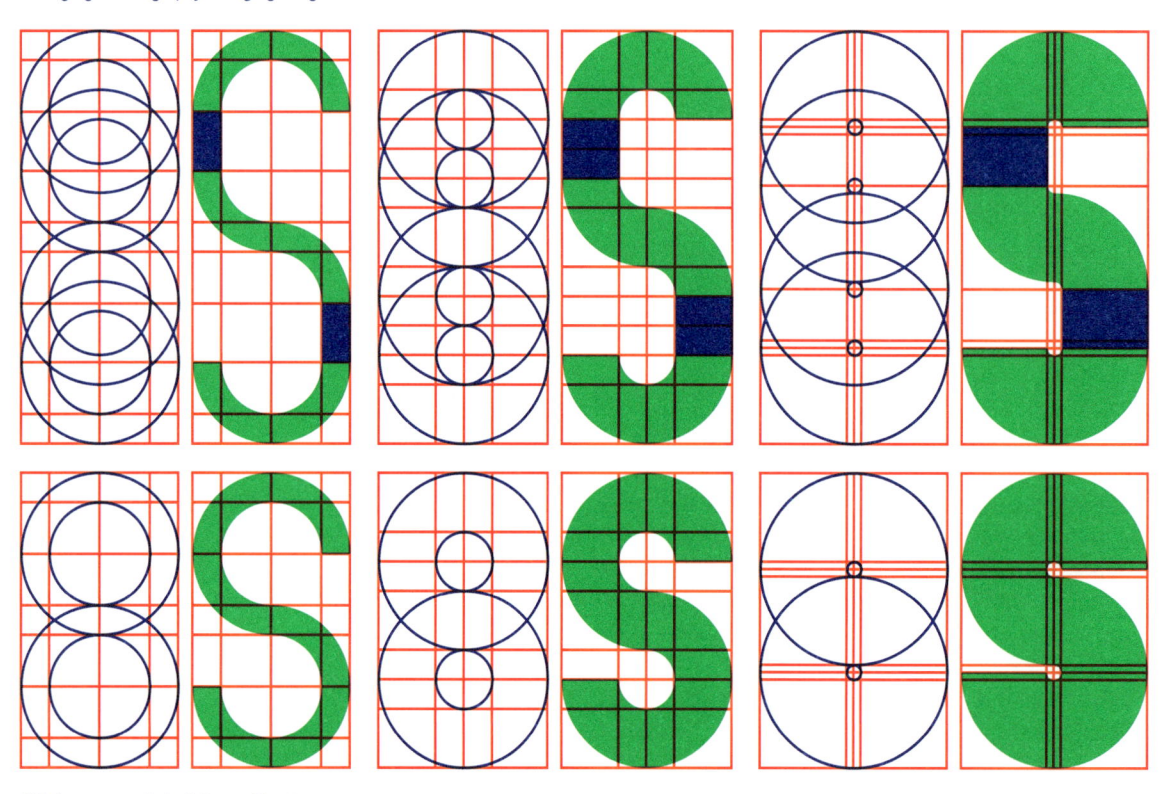

This is an example for letters without contrast. The examples on the bottom show how you can add contrast and still work with a grid.

Broadnip pen inspired construction

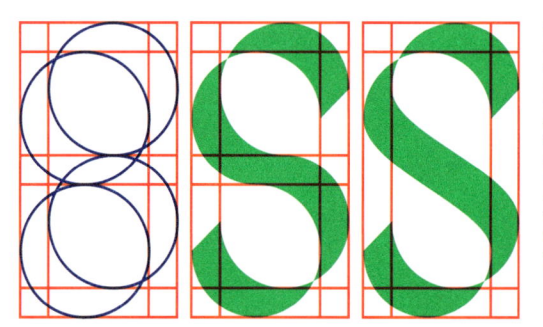

Slight optical corrections such as the removal of the vector points in the middle of the diagonal stroke on the left or adding a serif or dot on the right help to soften the constructed look.

Pointed pen inspired construction

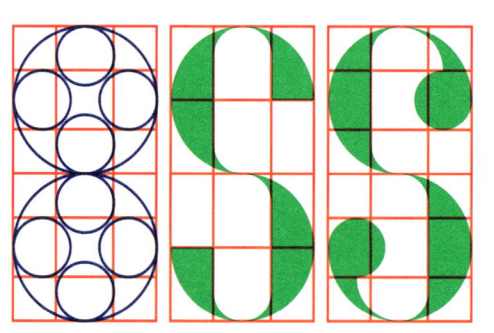

FONT CONSTRUCTION WITH CUSTOM COMPONENTS

Corner elements

Corner elements

Connection elements

Center elements

3 modules wide

7

5

3

5

FONT CONSTRUCTION

Corner and connection elements

2 modules wide   3 modules wide   5 modules wide

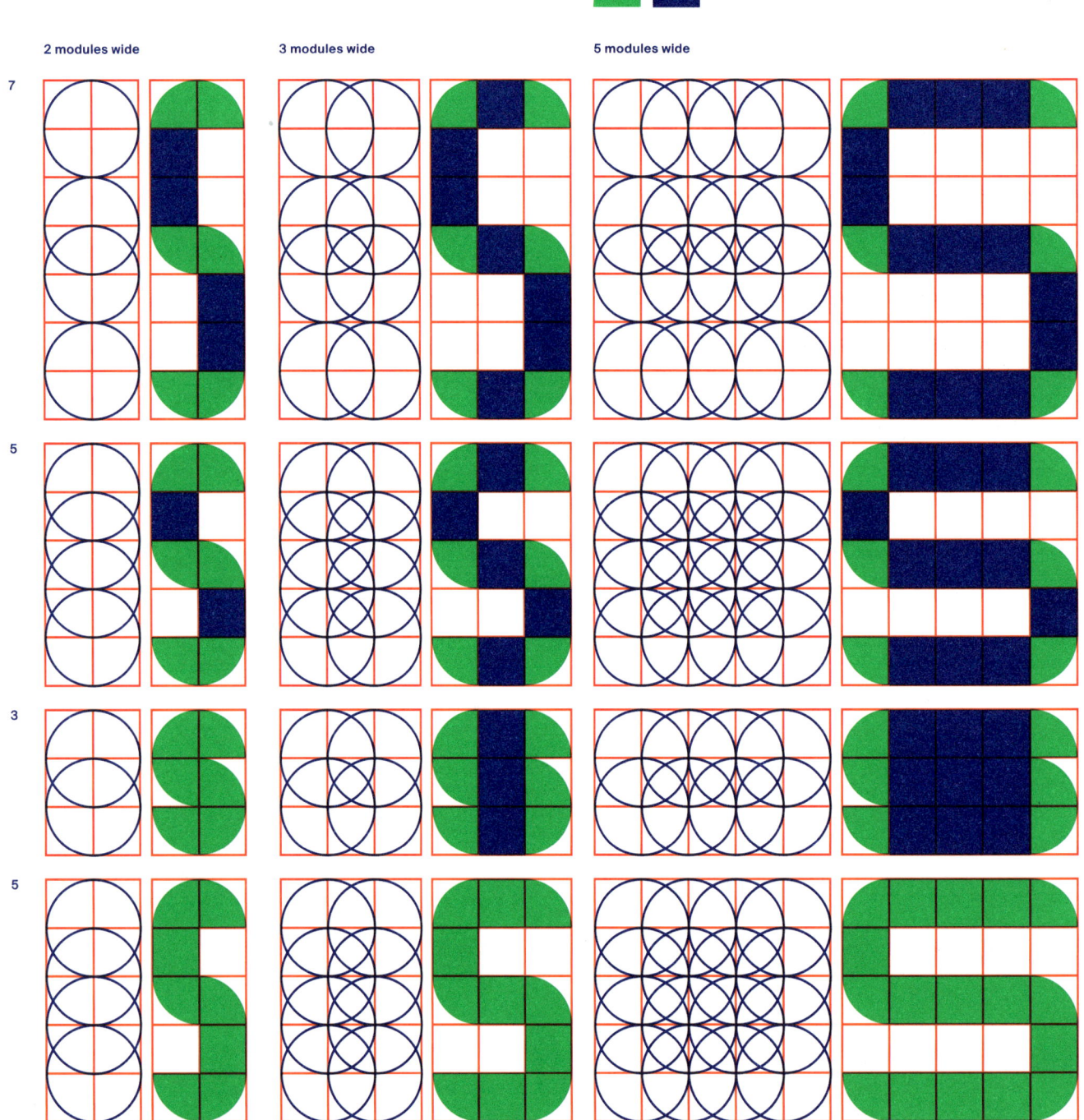

FONT CONSTRUCTION WITH CUSTOM COMPONENTS

Corner and connection elements

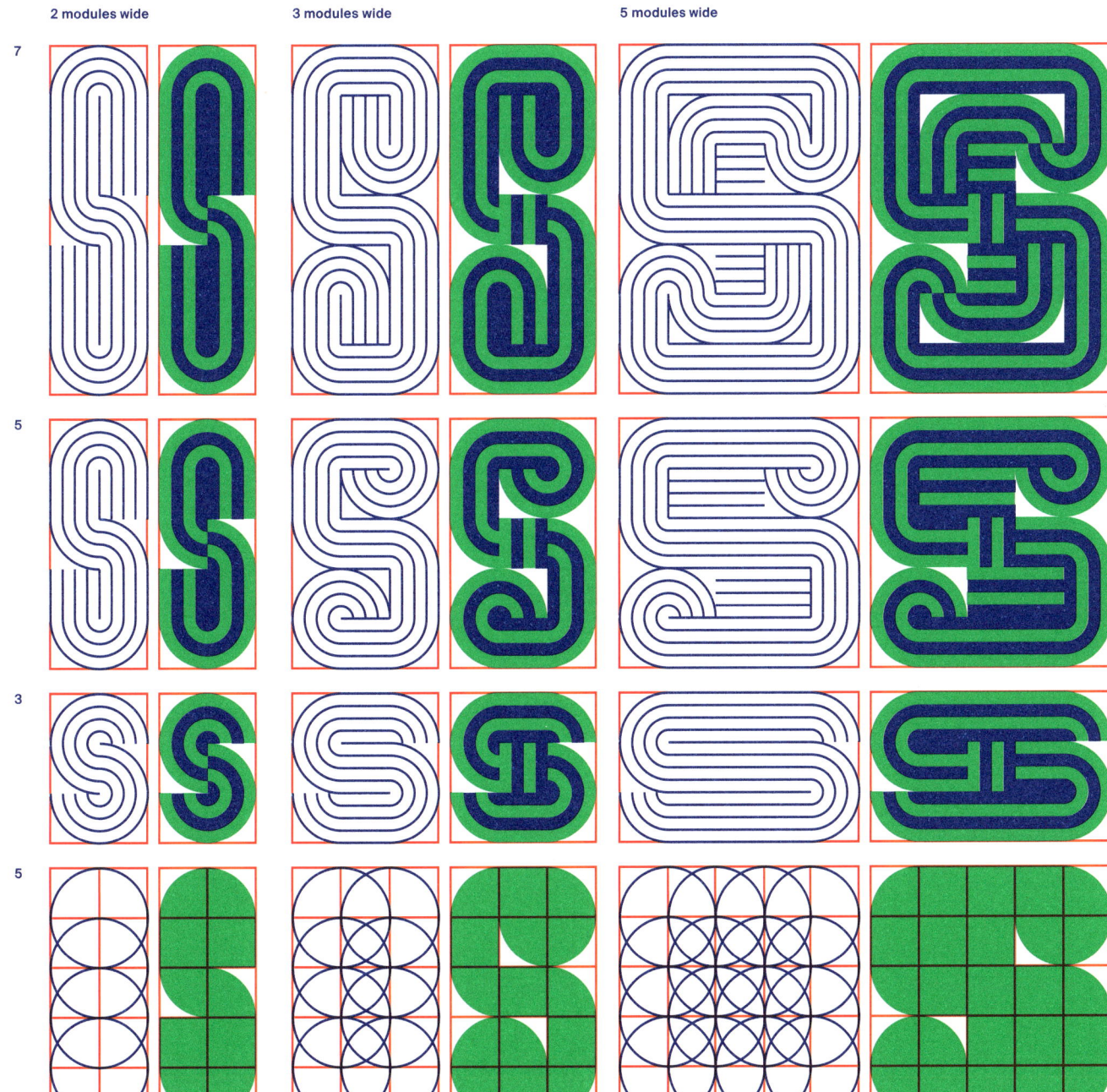

2 modules wide   3 modules wide   5 modules wide

7

5

3

5

FVS:
FORM-BASED

Form-based FVS

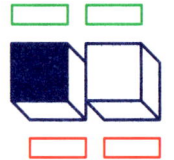

*In reference to format or grid.

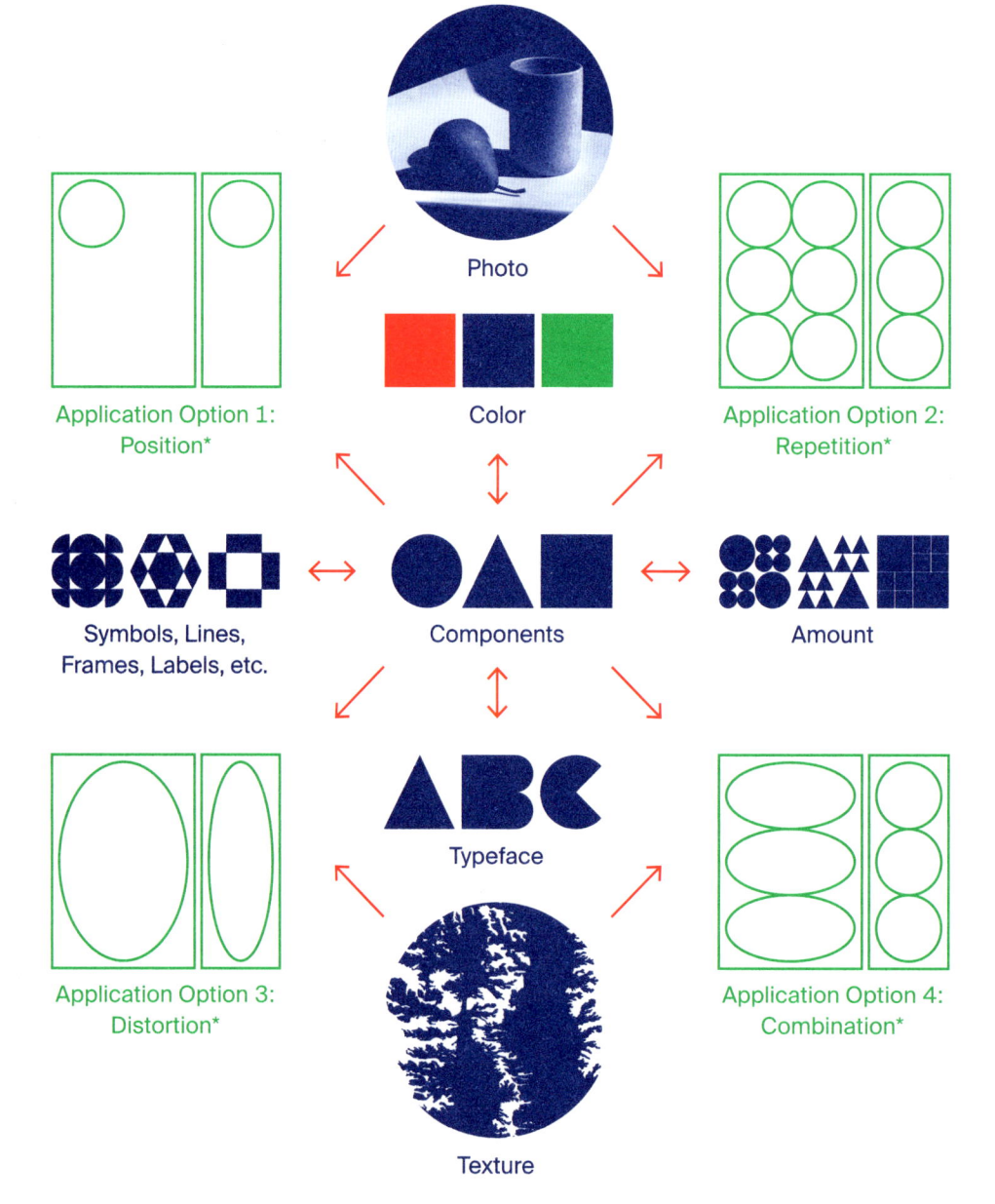

Photo

Application Option 1:
Position*

Application Option 2:
Repetition*

Color

Symbols, Lines, Frames, Labels, etc. ↔ Components ↔ Amount

Typeface

Application Option 3:
Distortion*

Application Option 4:
Combination*

Texture

FORM-BASED FLEXIBLE VISUAL SYSTEMS

I am going to show you in this chapter how to develop a form-based visual system with a circle, triangle, square, pentagon, and hexagon. Just flipping through the pages you might get the impression that the process is complicated. It is not. To give you an overview, have a look at the illustration on the opposite page. It all starts with the most basic element:

Component:
Since geometric shapes are easy to cut up and combine, I will work with circles, triangles, squares, pentagons, and hexagons in this book, but the advanced student could still use my process with more complex shapes. It could be any kind of shape.

Assets:
In order to increase the variety of shapes, I cut up the geometric shapes and assemble them again by rotating and mirroring. The variety of new shapes increases the uniqueness of the visual language and thus the possibility of the visual identity to differentiate itself from other identities. The assembled shapes result in design assets as symbols, lines, labels, frames, patterns, or letters.

Amount:
The number of assets on the format as well as the number of different sizes have an impact on the aesthetics. In a design manual the number is usually defined by a minimum and maximum amount, since the size of the application plays a role. Smaller applications need fewer shapes, larger applications can be more complex.

Color:
Color is one of the key ingredients of a visual system. A well chosen color scheme makes recognition much easier and as Gerstner says, it is the soul of form. The mood that is immediately perceived intuitively. I don't want to give you any advice here on how to pick a color, because neither theory, ideology, nor fashion seem to offer a reliable system to make an adequate color choice in terms of time, geography, and target group. Sensitize yourself to colors and trust your feelings.

Typeface:
It is easier to choose a typeface. There are clear rules for legibility and data to analyze the habits of the target group. Choosing the right font has an effect on visual identity that should not be underestimated. In certain occasions it is the most important identification element.

Application:
You have now defined the basic properties of the visual system. Now you have to decide how to apply the visual system. All of the options for an application system need to be format-responsive.

Application 1: Do you want to place an asset at a specific position on the format?
Application 2: Do you want to fill the format (or column, row, or module) by repeating the asset?
Application 3: Do you want to distort an asset so that it fills the entire format?
Application 4: ...or are you aiming for a combination of positioning, repetition, and distortion?

Photo, Illustration, Texture, Text:
The last step of the design process is adding or placing photos, illustrations, textures, or texts inside of the shapes. It is the last step because the mentioned material needs to be chosen specifically for a specific function of a specific deliverable in a specific context.

FORM: CIRCLE

Part 1 Form-based FVS

Form: Circle
Asset: Symbol

Fragmented components, repeated, mirrored over one axis and mirrored over two axes.

The examples on this page show what is possible with a simple four-part division, repetition and mirroring.

Different subdivisions can create entirely new possibilities. Try drawing symbols from other grids.

Part 1

Form: Circle
Asset: Symbol

Form-based FVS

Fragmented components, rearranged to obtain more variations.

The rearranged shapes can be repeated three times, so that a square of 16 modules is created.

Instead of repeating the assembled shapes, you could also use the vertical or

the vertical and the horizontal middle axis to mirror the elements.

Rearrangement | Repetition | Mirroring over one axis | Mirroring over two axes

Elements have been deleted from the patterns in the first row to create new, lighter patterns.

● Lighter patterns can be used in infographics or cartographies to show lower values.

Part 1

Form:
Asset:

Form-based FVS

Circle
Line

Fragmented shape, rearranged

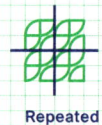

Repeated

Mirrored over one axis

Mirrored over two axes. On this page I only used symbols created with this method to create lines.

Part 1   Form-based FVS

Form: Circle
Asset: Frame and Line

Fragmented components, rearranged and repeated to obtain more variations.

Rotation of the component to create the four corner elements.

The last column of the first corner element, mirrored and repeated can be used as a connection component.

Rotation of the connection element to create all four elements for all four sides.

Corner elements

Connection elements

- In this example, the connecting parts have been matched to the corner parts. A hard contrast with a connecting or corner part that looks completely different can be interesting too.

Line from connecting elements

Line from corner elements

Colored elements

Corner elements

Connection elements

Frame with four corner and connecting elements

Line from connecting elements

Line from corner elements

Part 1

Shape:
Asset:

Form-based FVS

Circle
Label

Part 1   **Form-based FVS**

Form: Circle
Application: on 12 Formats

Repetition of the assets

Vertical repetition and horizontal distortion of the assets

Horizontal repetition and vertical distortion of the assets

Horizontal and vertical distortion of the assets

Part 1   **Form-based FVS**

Form: Circle
Asset: Letters

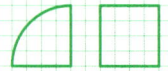

Corner- and Connection element

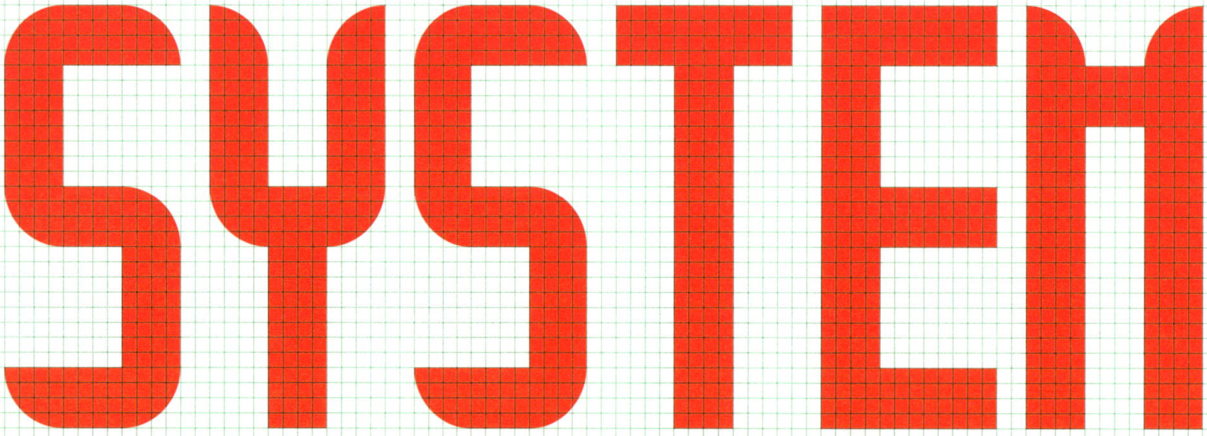

SYSTEM — Monospaced 3×7 modules

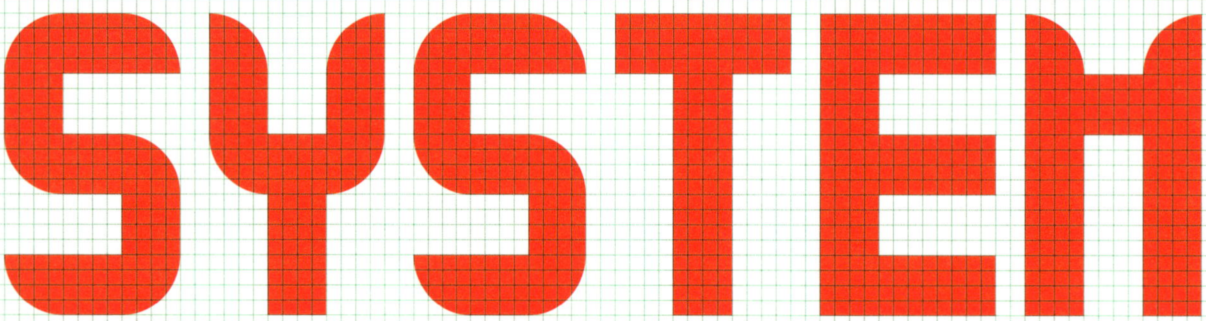

SYSTEM — Monospaced 3×5 modules

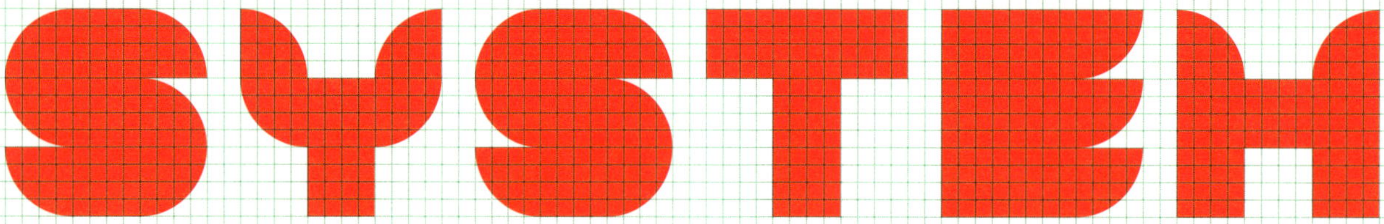

SYSTEM — Monospaced 3×3 modules

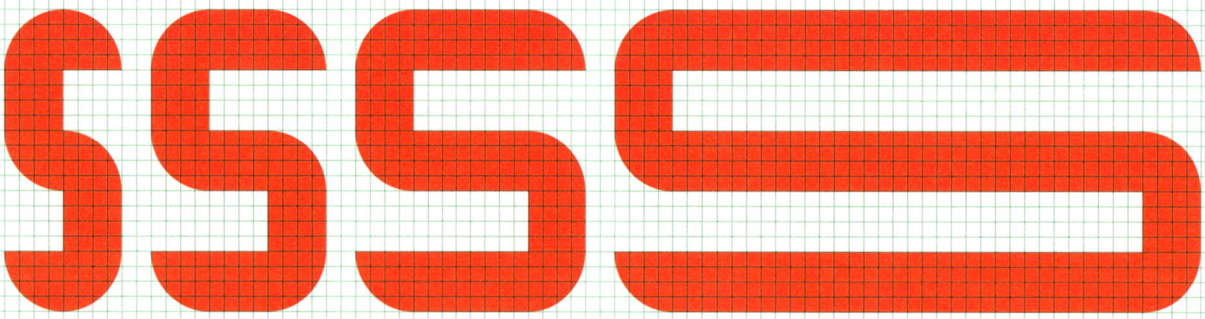

SSSS — Varying widths

2×5 Modules   3×5 Modules   4×5 Modules   10×5 Modules

Part 1

Form: Circle
Asset: Letters

Form-based FVS

Component, rearranged and repeated

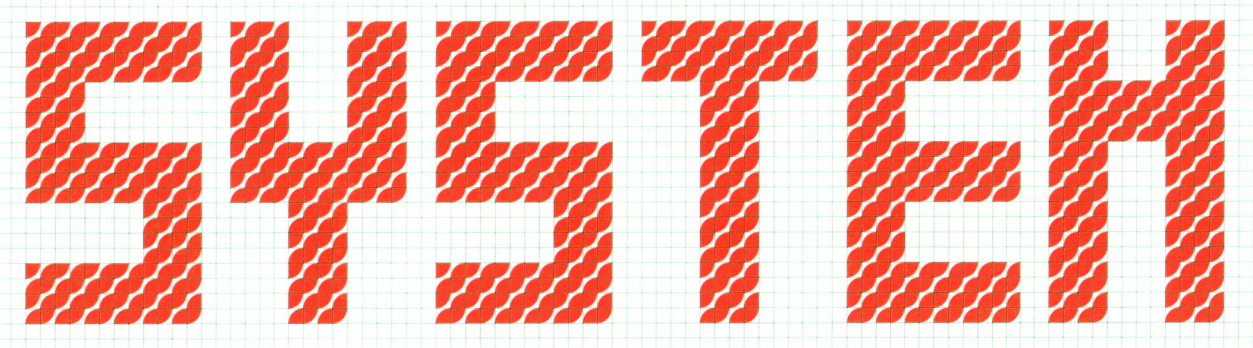

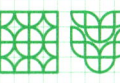

SYSTEM

Monospaced
3×5 modules

Coner elements   Corner elements   Connection elements   Center elements

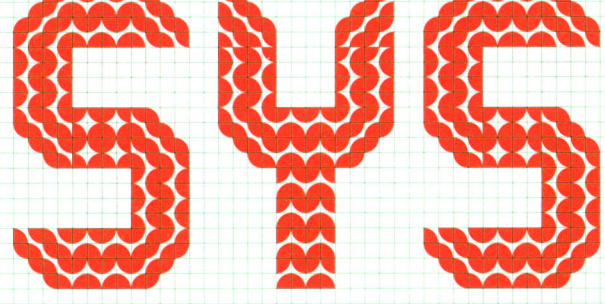

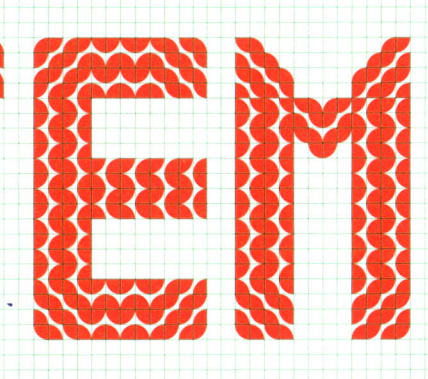

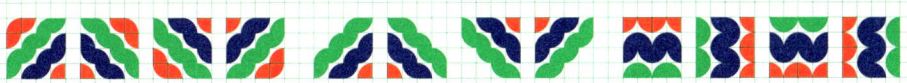

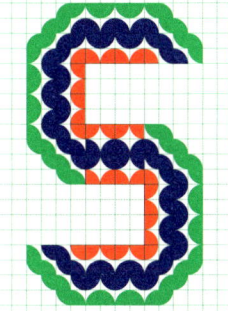

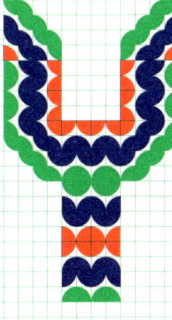

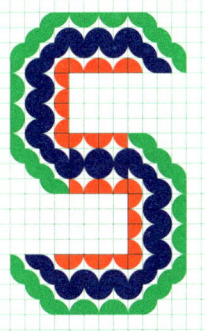

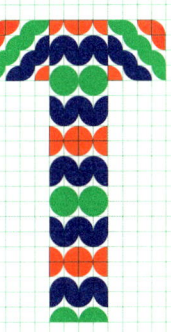

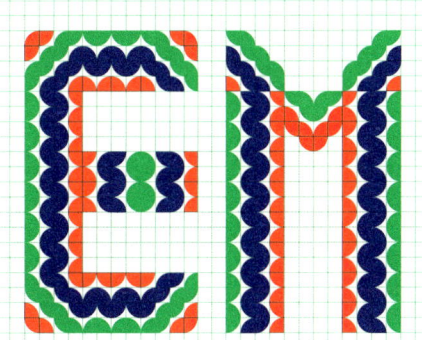

SYSTEM

Monospaced
3×5 modules

Coner elements   Corner elements   Connection elements   Center elements

SYSTEM

Monospaced
3×5 modules

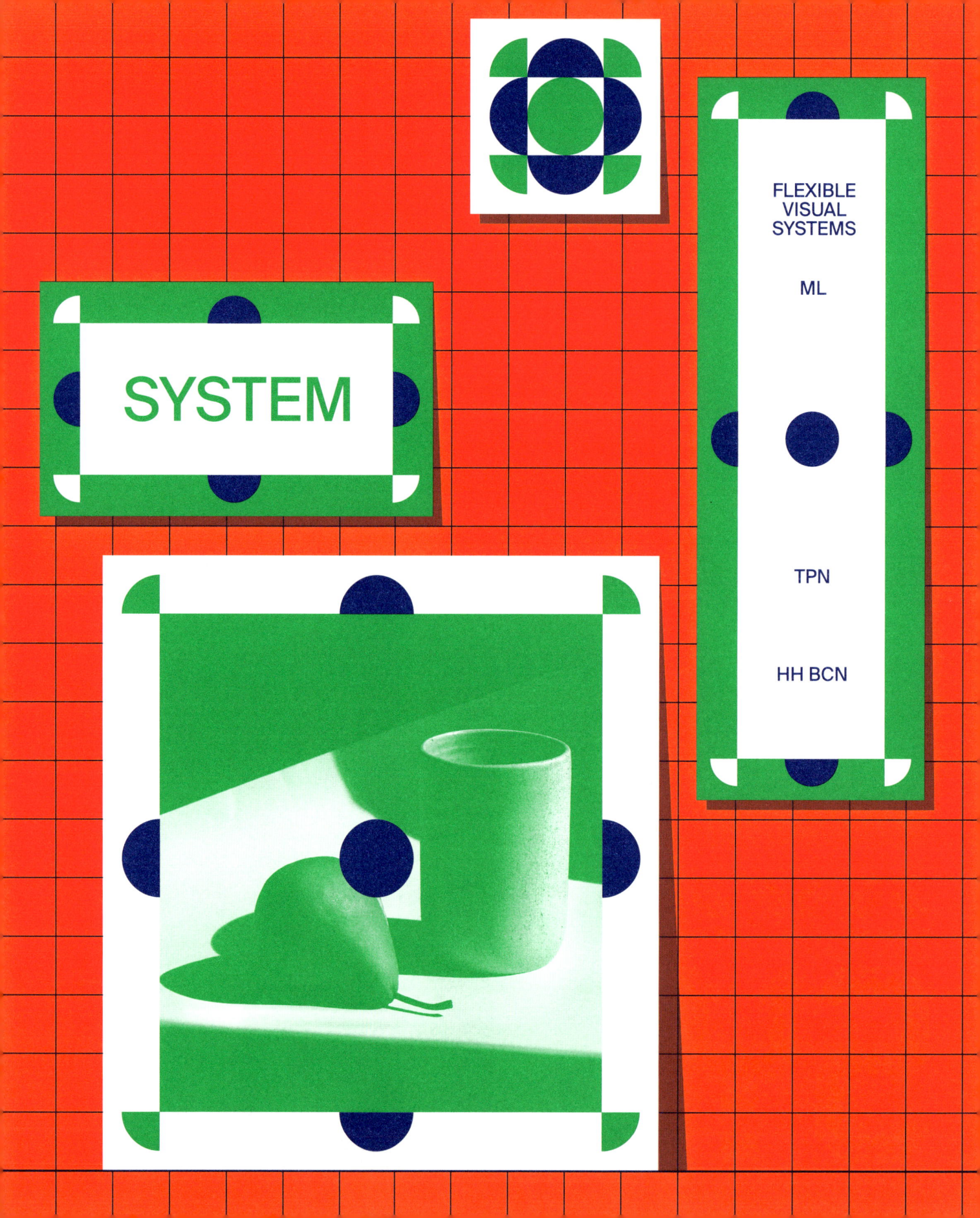

SYSTEM

FLEXIBLE
VISUAL
SYSTEMS

ML

TPN

HH BCN

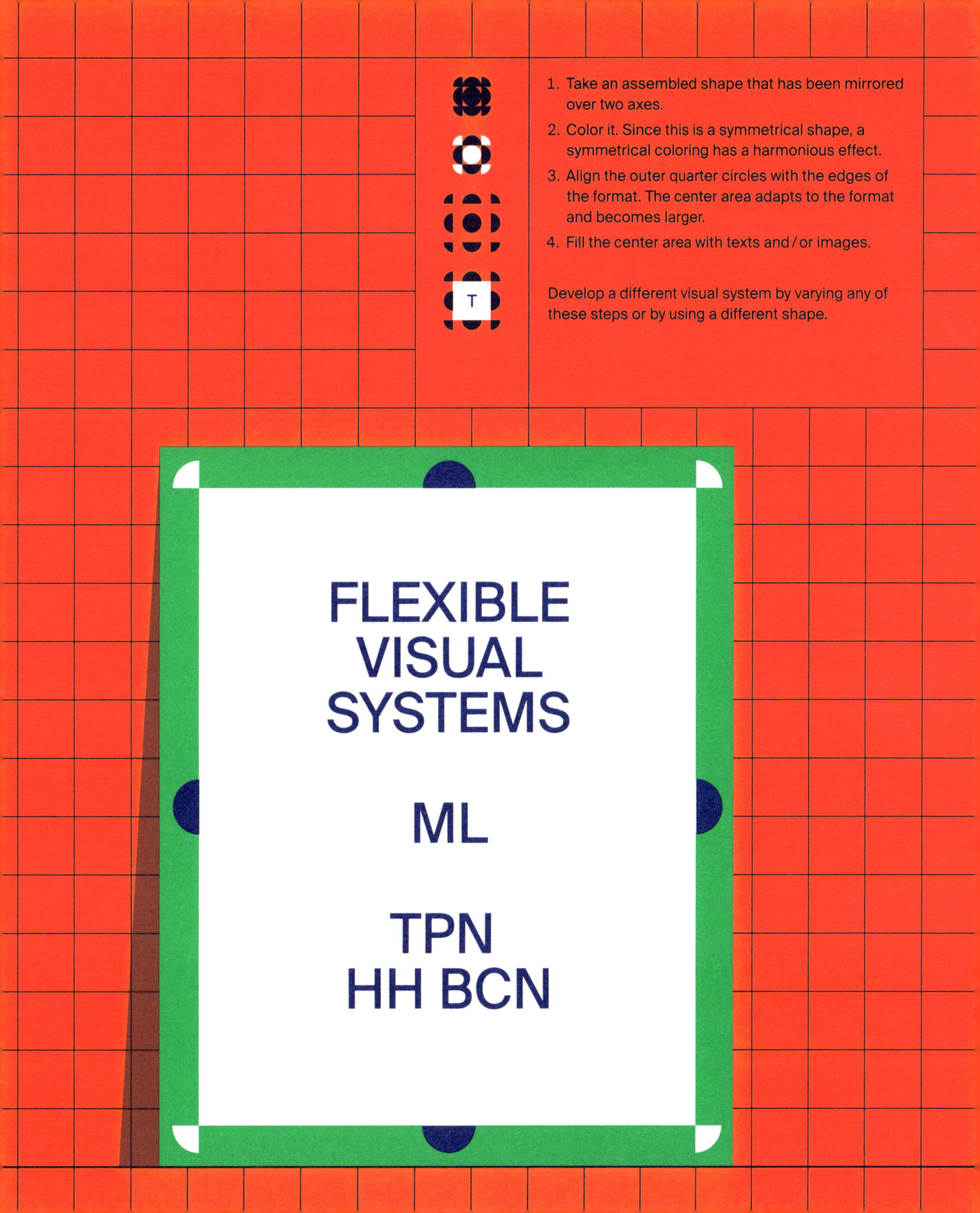

1. Take an assembled shape that has been mirrored over two axes.
2. Color it. Since this is a symmetrical shape, a symmetrical coloring has a harmonious effect.
3. Align the outer quarter circles with the edges of the format. The center area adapts to the format and becomes larger.
4. Fill the center area with texts and / or images.

Develop a different visual system by varying any of these steps or by using a different shape.

FLEXIBLE VISUAL SYSTEMS

ML

TPN
HH BCN

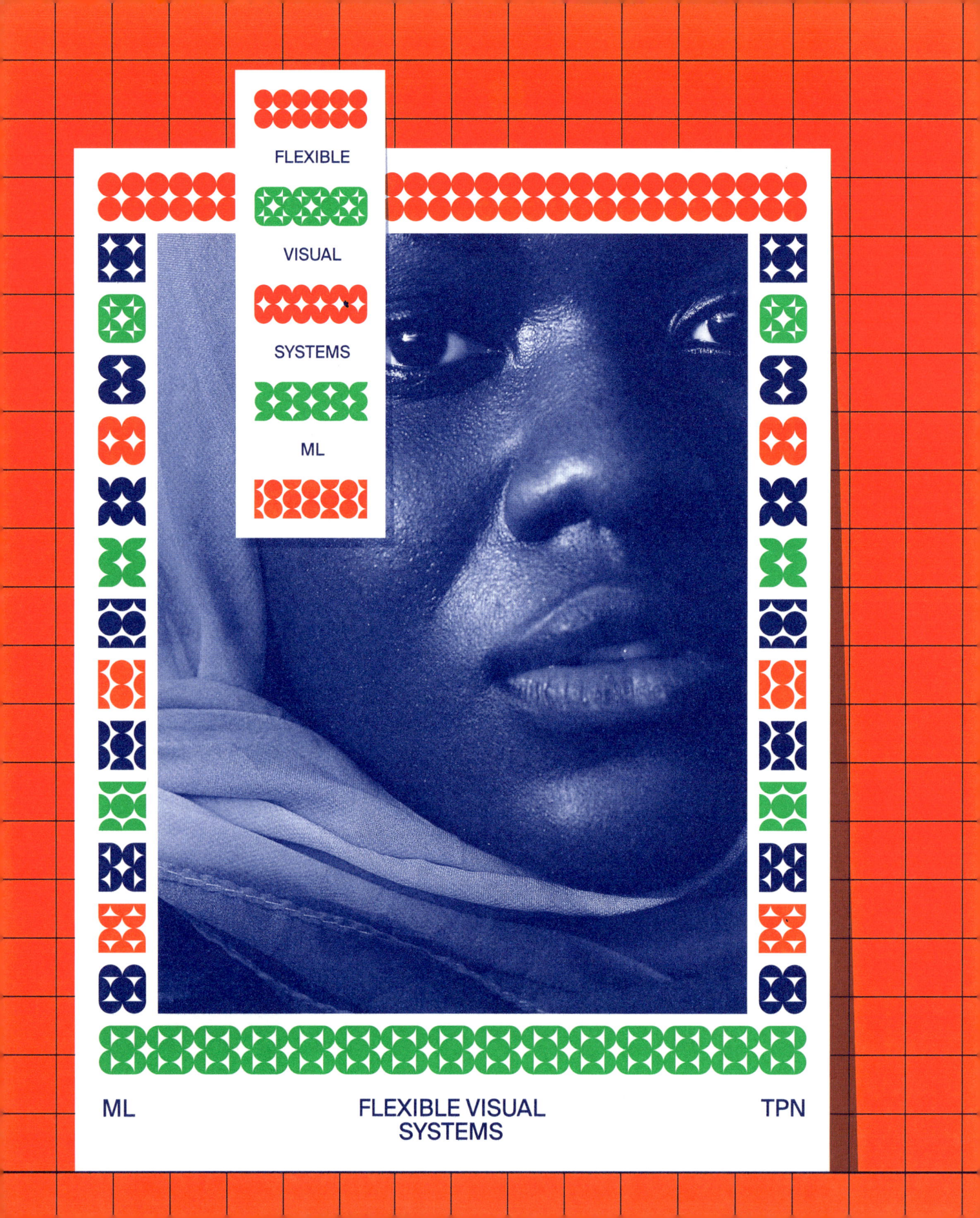

FLEXIBLE VISUAL SYSTEMS ML

ML · FLEXIBLE VISUAL SYSTEMS · TPN

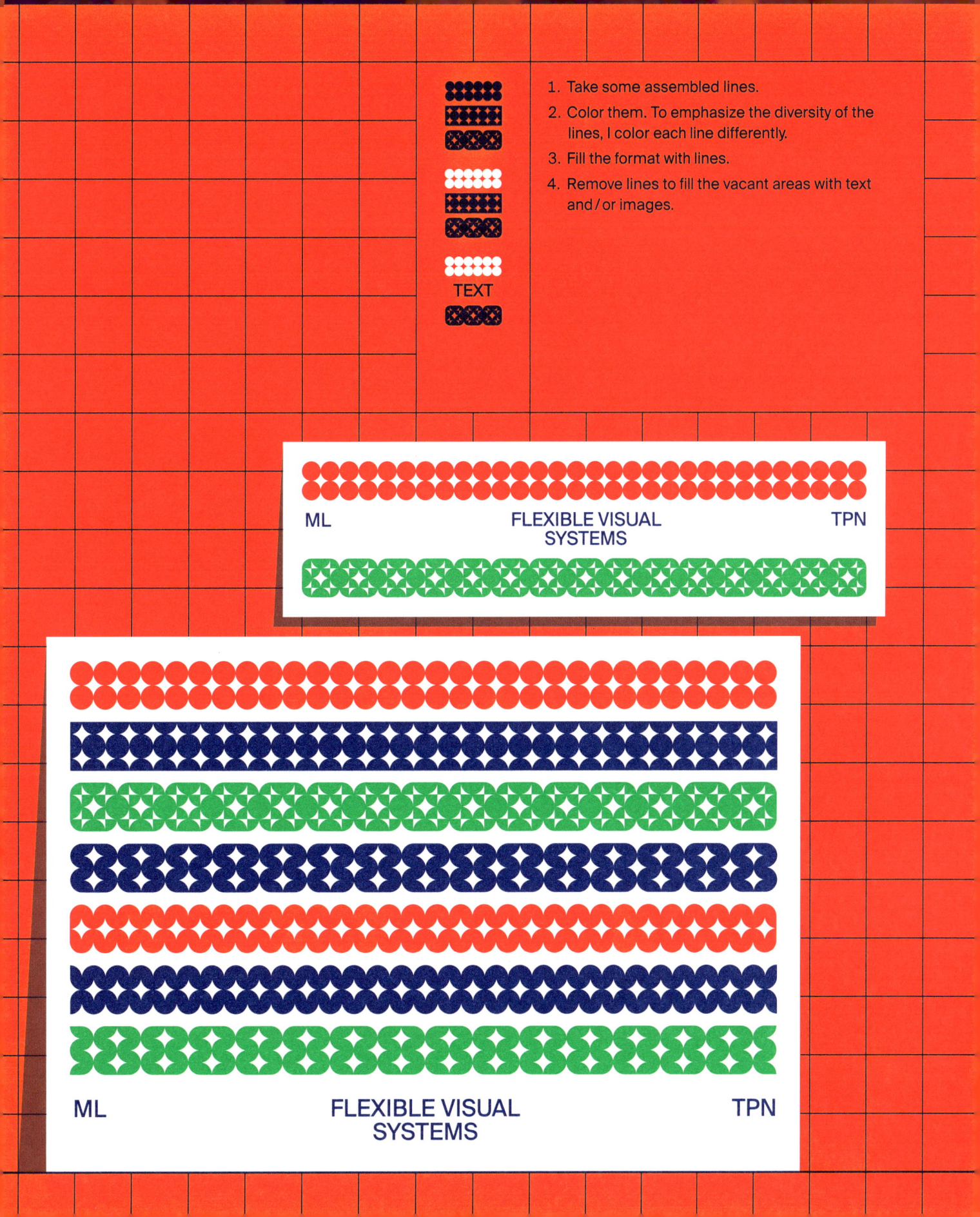

1. Take some assembled lines.
2. Color them. To emphasize the diversity of the lines, I color each line differently.
3. Fill the format with lines.
4. Remove lines to fill the vacant areas with text and/or images.

TEXT

ML FLEXIBLE VISUAL SYSTEMS TPN

ML FLEXIBLE VISUAL SYSTEMS TPN

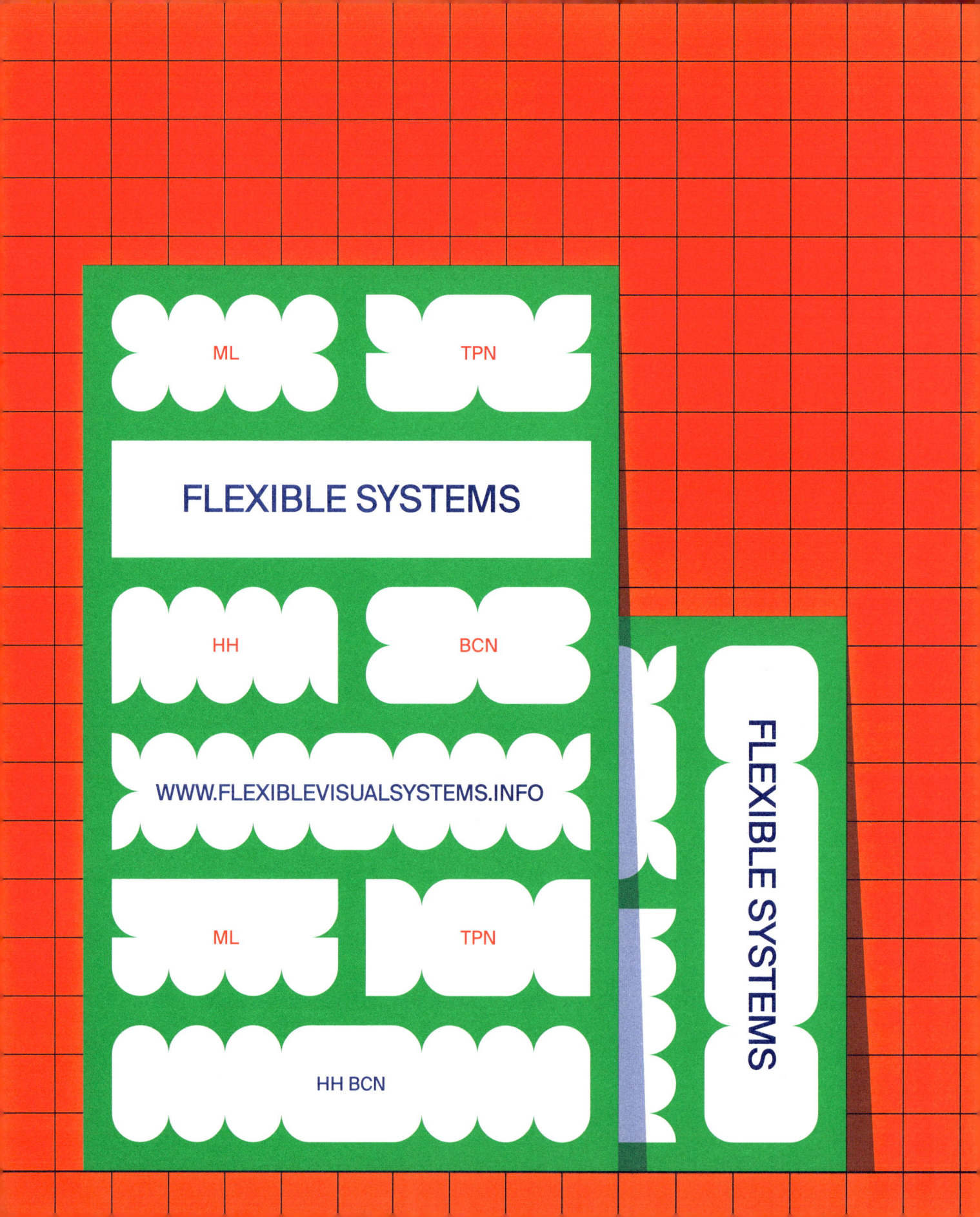

ML TPN

FLEXIBLE SYSTEMS

HH BCN

WWW.FLEXIBLEVISUALSYSTEMS.INFO

ML TPN

HH BCN

FLEXIBLE SYSTEMS

1. Take an assembled shape.
2. Color it. In this example I have colored the shapes white and the background green. An easily to recognize shape also makes color variations possible.
3. Fill the format with shapes to achieve a calm aesthetic. If you want more tension or hierarchy, work with different sizes or more negative space.
4. Place text and/or images in the shapes.

SYSTEM

TEXT

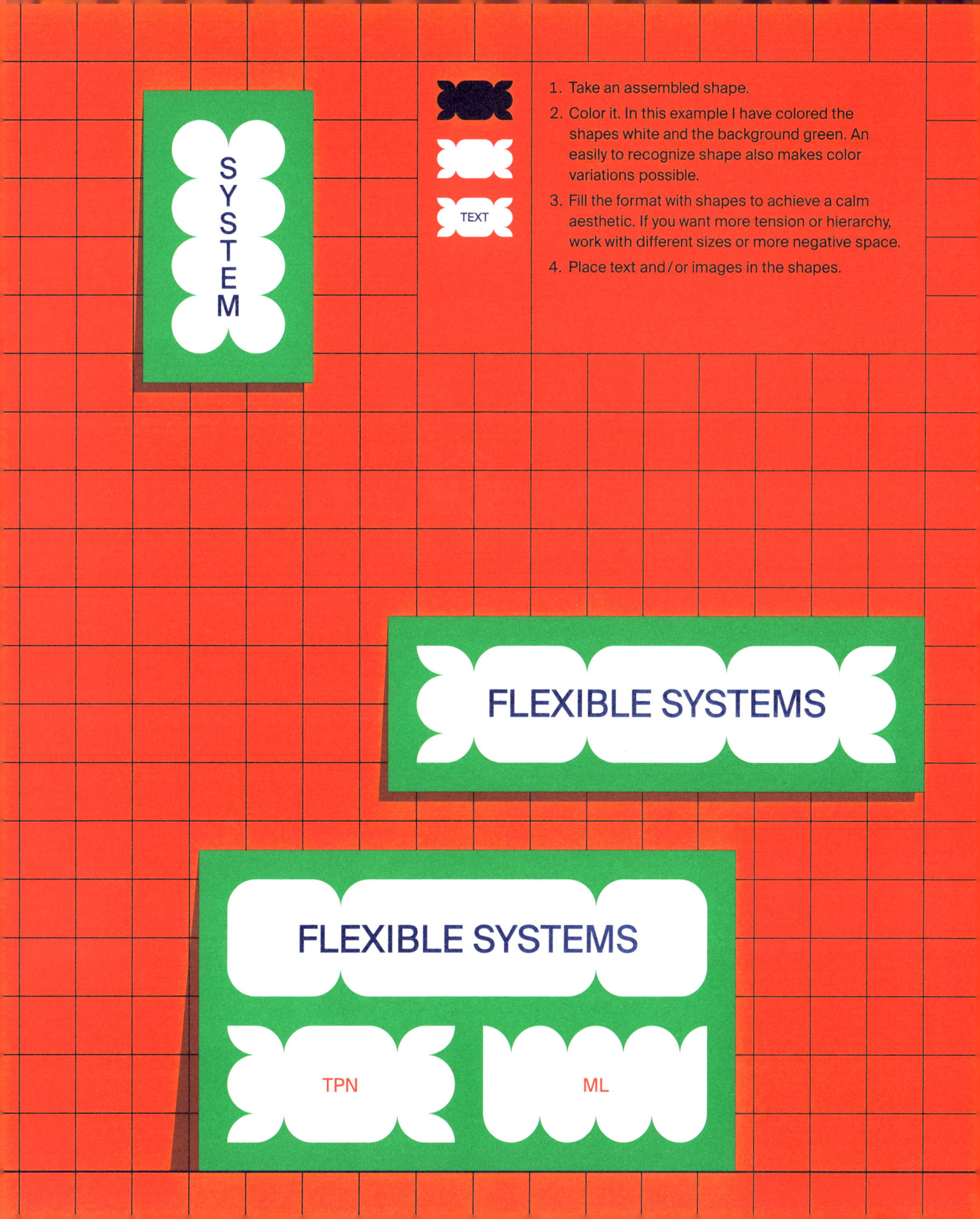

FLEXIBLE SYSTEMS

FLEXIBLE SYSTEMS

TPN

ML

1. Take three assembled shapes.
2. Turn one of them into a corner element and another in a connection element.
3. Use the elements to construct letters. You can rotate the basic pattern however you want.

SYSTEMS

FLEXIIBLE
SYSTEMS

ML TPN
HH BCN

FLEXIBLE
VISUAL
SYSTEMS
.INFO

4. Color an assembled shape.

5. Construct patterns, lines, and frames. The colors and shapes create such a strong recognition that you can apply them more freely.

FLEXIBLE SYSTEMS

ML TPN
HH BCN

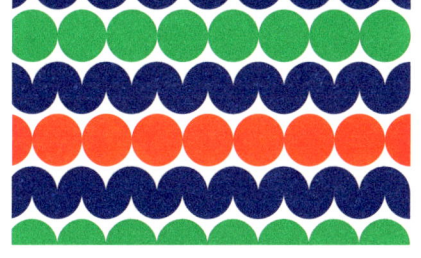

FLEXIBLEVISUAL
SYSTEMS.INFO

FORM: RIGHT TRIANGLE

Part 1

Form: Triangle
Asset: Symbol

Form-based FVS

Component, rearranged, repeated, mirrored over one axis and mirrored over two axes

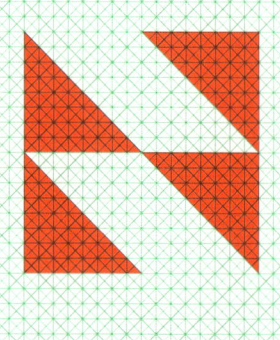

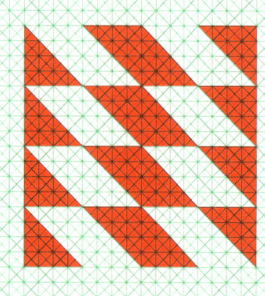

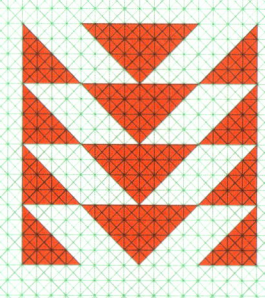

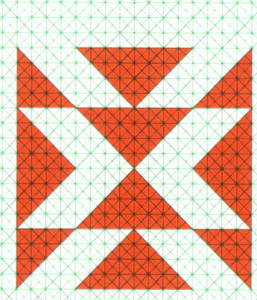

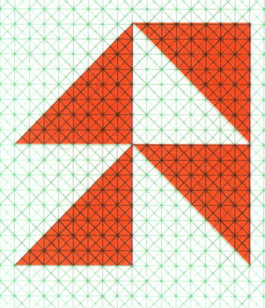

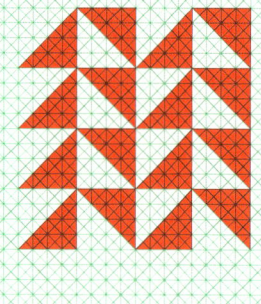

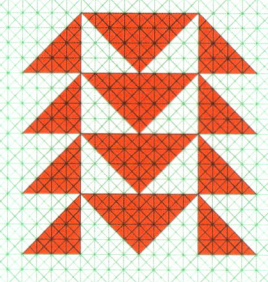

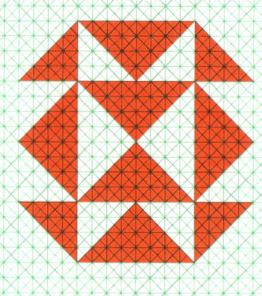

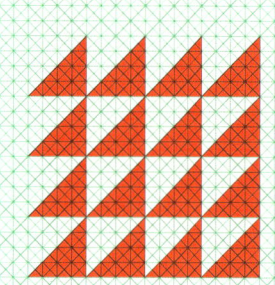

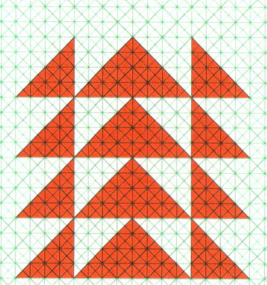

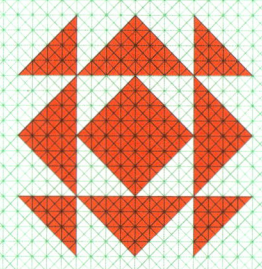

- The examples on this page have been drawn with an Isosceles triangle because they make a perfect square.

However, a grid and pattern construction with equilateral triangles would also have been possible, which can also result in a square if one adds half an equilateral triangle.

Part 1

Form:
Asset:

Form-based FVS

Triangle
Symbol

Four triangles are rearranged in a square and

repeated three times.

Instead of repeating the basic pattern three times, it could be repeated once and then mirrored over one axis or

or over two axes.

Rearrangement

Repetition

Mirrored over one axis

Mirrored over two axes

Elements have been deleted from the pattern in the first row to create new, lighter patterns.

● Lighter patterns can be used in infographics or cartographies to show lower values.

Part 1

Form:
Asset:

Form-based FVS

Triangle
Line

Component, rearranged,

repeated,

mirrored over 1 axis and

mirrored over 2 axes. On this page I only used symbols created with this method to create lines.

Part 1

Form:
Asset:

Form-based FVS

Triangle
Frame

Component, rearranged and repeated.

Rotation of component to create four corner elements.

The last column of the first corner element, mirrored and repeated can be used as a connection element.

Rotation of the connection element to create all four elements for all four sides.

Corner elements

Connection elements

● In this example, the connecting parts have been matched to the corner parts. A hard contrast with a connecting or corner part that looks completely different can also be interesting.

Line from connecting elements

Line from corner elements

Colored elements

Corner elements

Connection elements

Frame with four corner- and connecting elements

Line from connecting elements

Line from corner elements

Part 1

Form: Form-based FVS
Asset: Triangle Label

Part 1 **Form-based FVS**

Form: **Triangle**
Application: on 12 Formats

Repetition of the assets

Vertical repetition and horizontal distortion of the assets

Horizontal repetition and vertical distortion of the assets

Horizontal and vertical distortion of the assets

Part 1

Form:
Application:

Form-based FVS

Triangle
Letters

Corner- Connection element

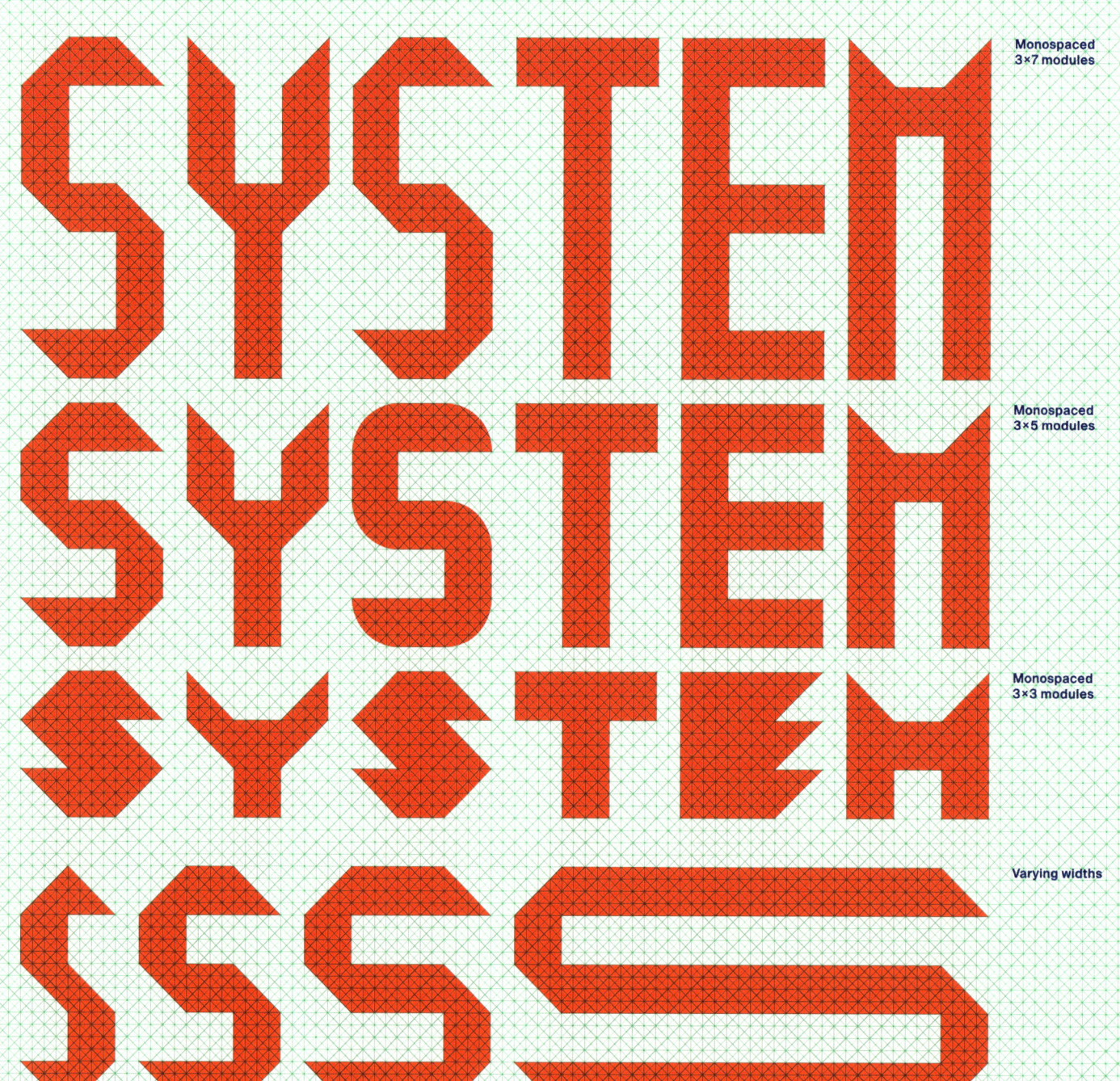

SYSTEM — Monospaced 3×7 modules

SYSTEM — Monospaced 3×5 modules

SYSTEM — Monospaced 3×3 modules

SSSS — Varying widths

2×5 modules   3×5 modules   4×5 modules   10×5 modules

Part 1

Form-based FVS

Form:
Application:

Triangle
Letters

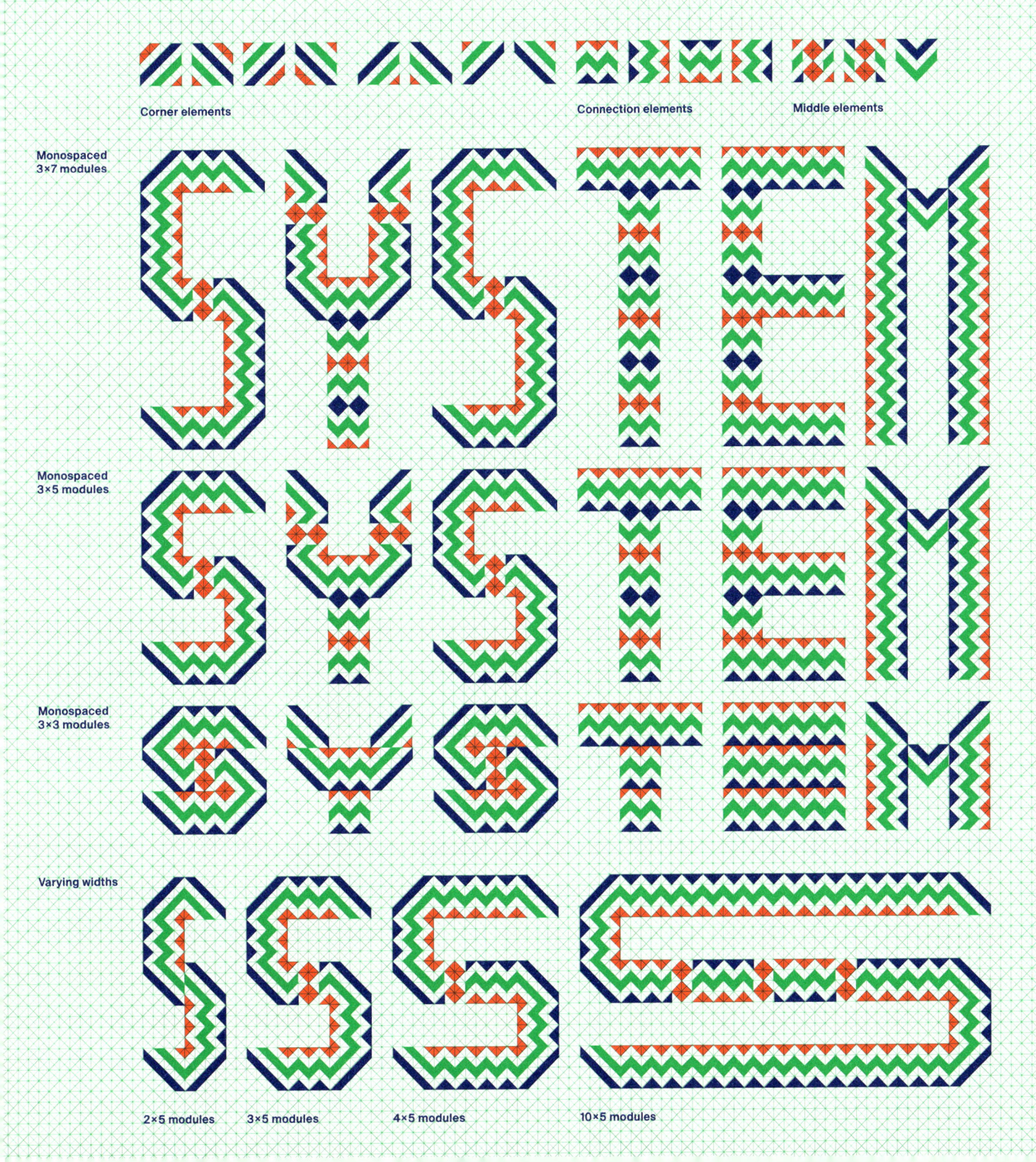

Corner elements

Connection elements

Middle elements

Monospaced
3×7 modules

Monospaced
3×5 modules

Monospaced
3×3 modules

Varying widths

2×5 modules

3×5 modules

4×5 modules

10×5 modules

1. Take an assembled shape.
2. Color it.
3. Cover a part and insert text and / or images in the covered area.

FLEXIBLE ML
VISUAL
SYSTEMS
.INFO

TPN
HH BCN

FLEXIBLE
VISUAL
SYSTEMS
.INFO

ML TPN
HH BCN

FLEXIBLE ML
VISUAL   TPN
SYSTEMS HH
         BCN

1. Take an assembled shape.
2. Color them.
3. Cover a part and insert text and / or images in the covered area.

TEXT

FLEXIBLE SYSTEMS

1. Take an assembled line.
2. Color it.
3. Fill the format with lines, leaving regular gaps in between them.
4. Fill the gaps with text and / or images.

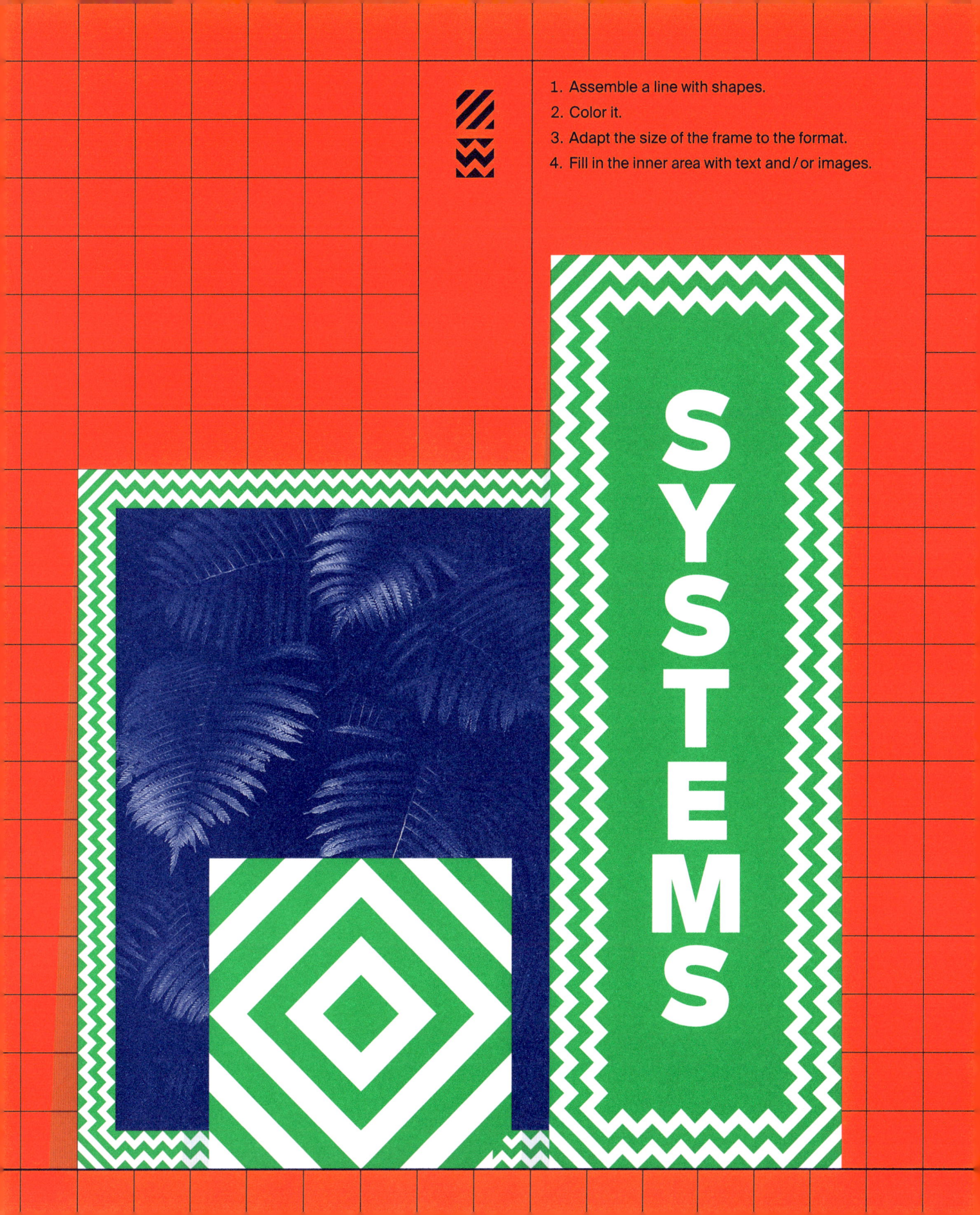

1. Assemble a line with shapes.
2. Color it.
3. Adapt the size of the frame to the format.
4. Fill in the inner area with text and / or images.

SYSTEMS

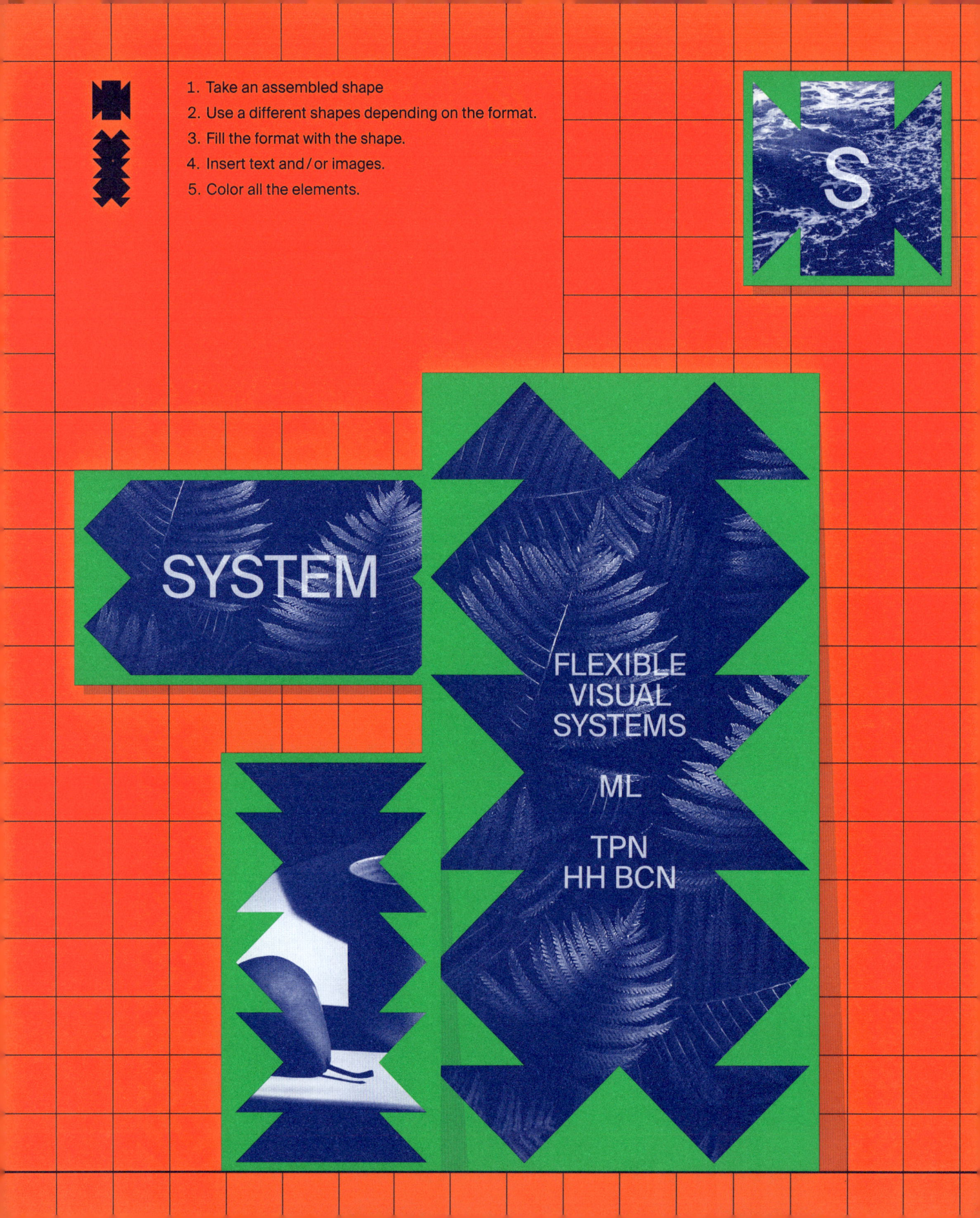

1. Take an assembled shape
2. Use a different shapes depending on the format.
3. Fill the format with the shape.
4. Insert text and / or images.
5. Color all the elements.

SYSTEM

FLEXIBLE
VISUAL
SYSTEMS

ML

TPN
HH BCN

1. Take a assembled shape.
2. Duplicate the shape, place it in the next column or row and change the width or height.
3. Insert text and / or images on top of the pattern.

FLEXIBLE VISUAL SYSTEMS

ML
TPN
HH BCN

FLEXIBLE VISUAL SYSTEMS

ML
TPN
HH BCN

FLEXIBLE SYSTEMS

1. Use assembled shapes to design letters and patterns.
2. Color the outlines.
3. Fill in the format with either letters or patterns.
4. Insert text and / or images in the gaps.

ML

FLEXIBLE
VISUAL
SYSTEMS

TPN

HH
BCN

1. Use assembled shapes to design letters and patterns.
2. Color them.
3. Fill in the format with either letters or patterns.
4. Insert text and / or images in the gaps.

FLEXIBLE SYSTEMS

**TPN
HH
BCN**

FLEXIBLE SYSTEMS

TPN HH BCN

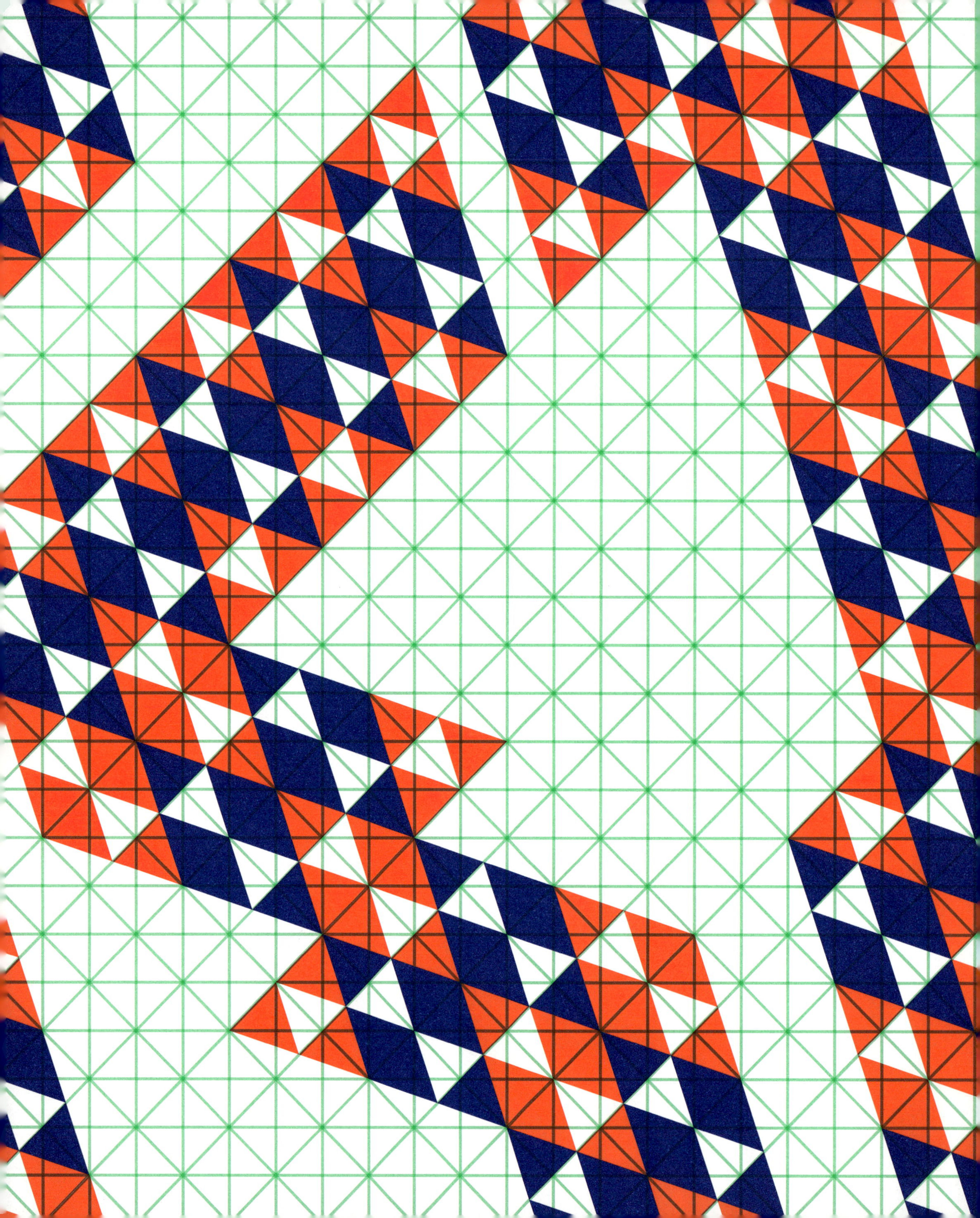

FORM: ACUTE TRIANGLE

Part 1

Form:
Asset:

Form-based FVS

Triangle
Symbol

Component, mirrored,

repeated,

mirrored over one axis and

mirrored over two axes.

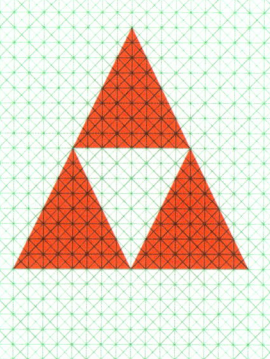

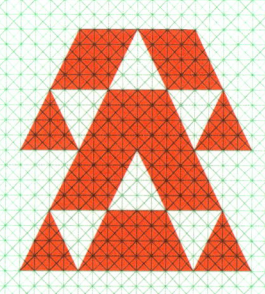

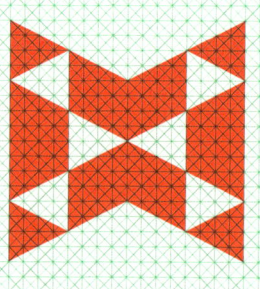

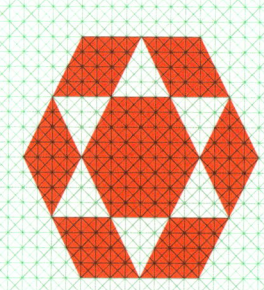

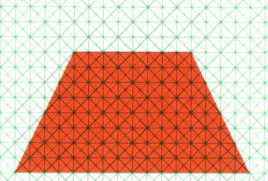

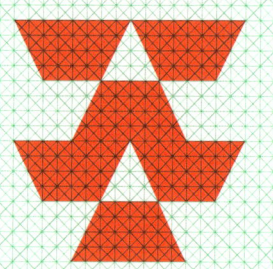

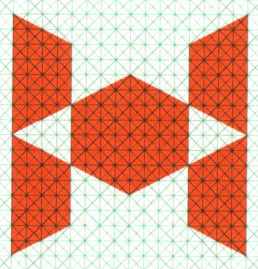

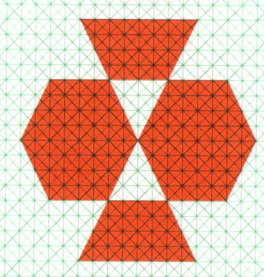

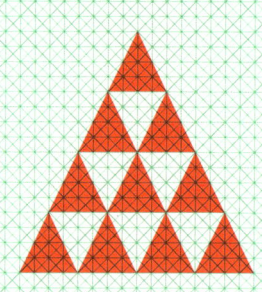

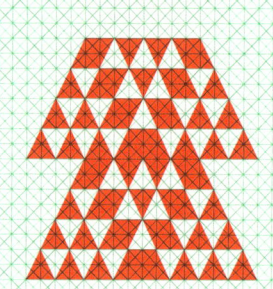

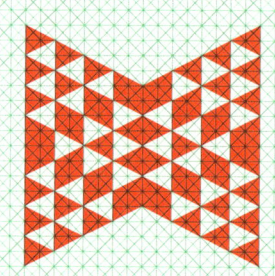

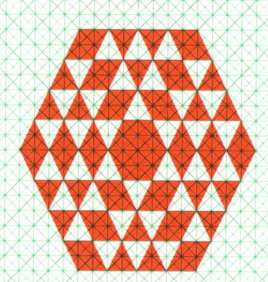

The examples on this page have been drawn with an equilateral triangle because they make a perfect square.

However, a grid and pattern construction with isosceles triangles would also have been possible, which can also result in a square if one adds half an equilateral triangle.

Part 1

Form:
Asset:

Form-based FVS

Triangle
Symbol

Component, repeated and mirrored over three axes to a square composition.

The basic pattern is rotated in all four directions,

mirrored over one axis or

mirrored over two axes.

Rearrangement | Rotation | Mirroring over one axis | Mirroring over two axes

Repetition / Rotation | Rotation | Mirroring over one axis | Mirroring over two axes

Part 1

Form: **Form-based FVS**
Asset:
Triangle
Line

Component, mirrored, repeated, mirrored over one axis and mirrored over two axes.

Part 1

Form:
Asset:

Form-based FVS

Triangle
Frame and Line

A triangle, repeated and mirrored over three axes ...

... to generate two elements that go together perfectly.

Connection elements

• In this example, the connecting parts are matching. A hard contrast with a not matching element can also be interesting.

Line from connecting elements

Line from corner elements

Colored elements

Connection elements

Frame with four corner- and connecting elements

Line from connecting elements

Line from corner elements

Part 1

Form:
Asset:

Form-based FVS

Triangle
Labels

Component, mirrored, repeated, mirrored over one axis and mirrored over two axes.

Part 1 **Form-based FVS**

Form: Triangle
Asset: on 12 Formats

Repetition of the assets

Vertical repetition and horizontal distortion of the assets

Horizontal repetition and vertical distortion of the assets

Horizontal and vertical distortion of the assets

Part 1

Form:
Asset:

Form-based FVS

Triangle
Letters

Construction

Pieces for letters

Pieces for shadows

5 × 12 Modules

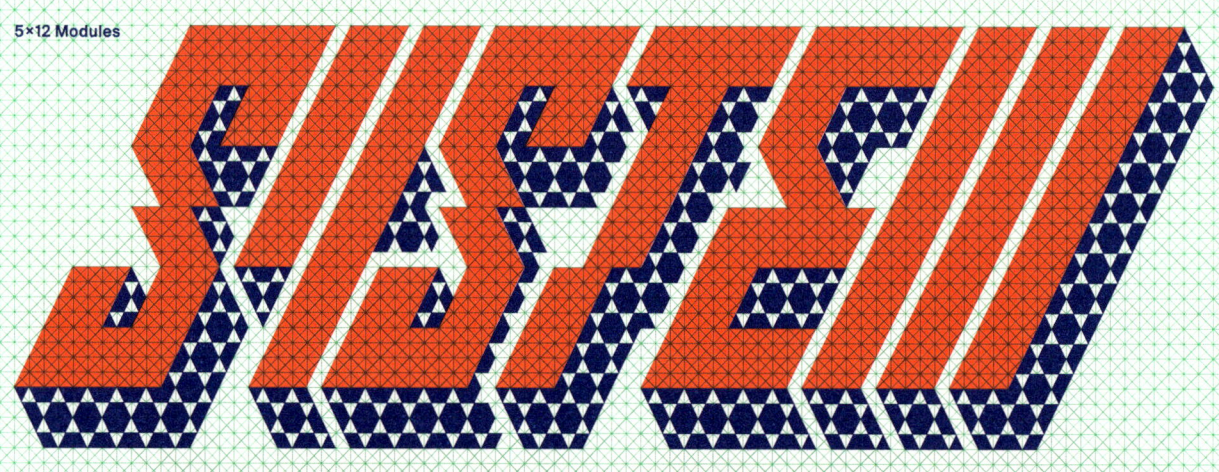

5 × 10

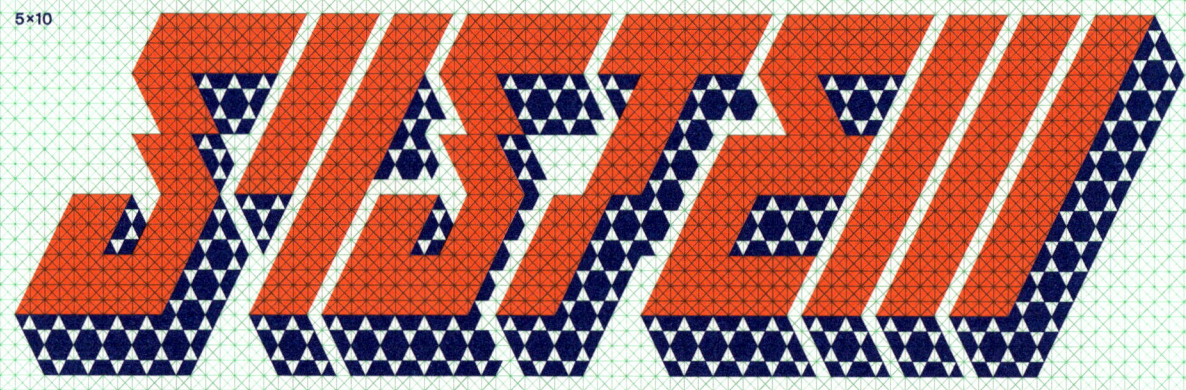

5 × 8

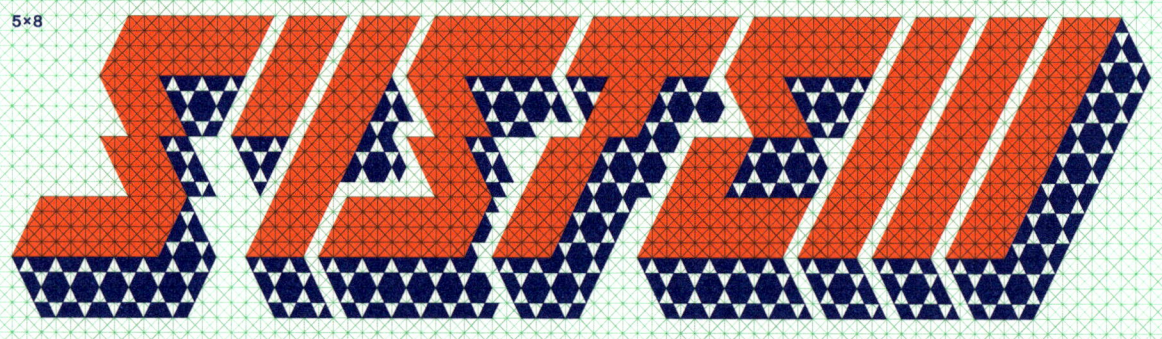

Part 1

Form:
Asset:

Form-based FVS

Triangle
Letters

Construction

Pieces

5×12

5×10

5×8

5×6

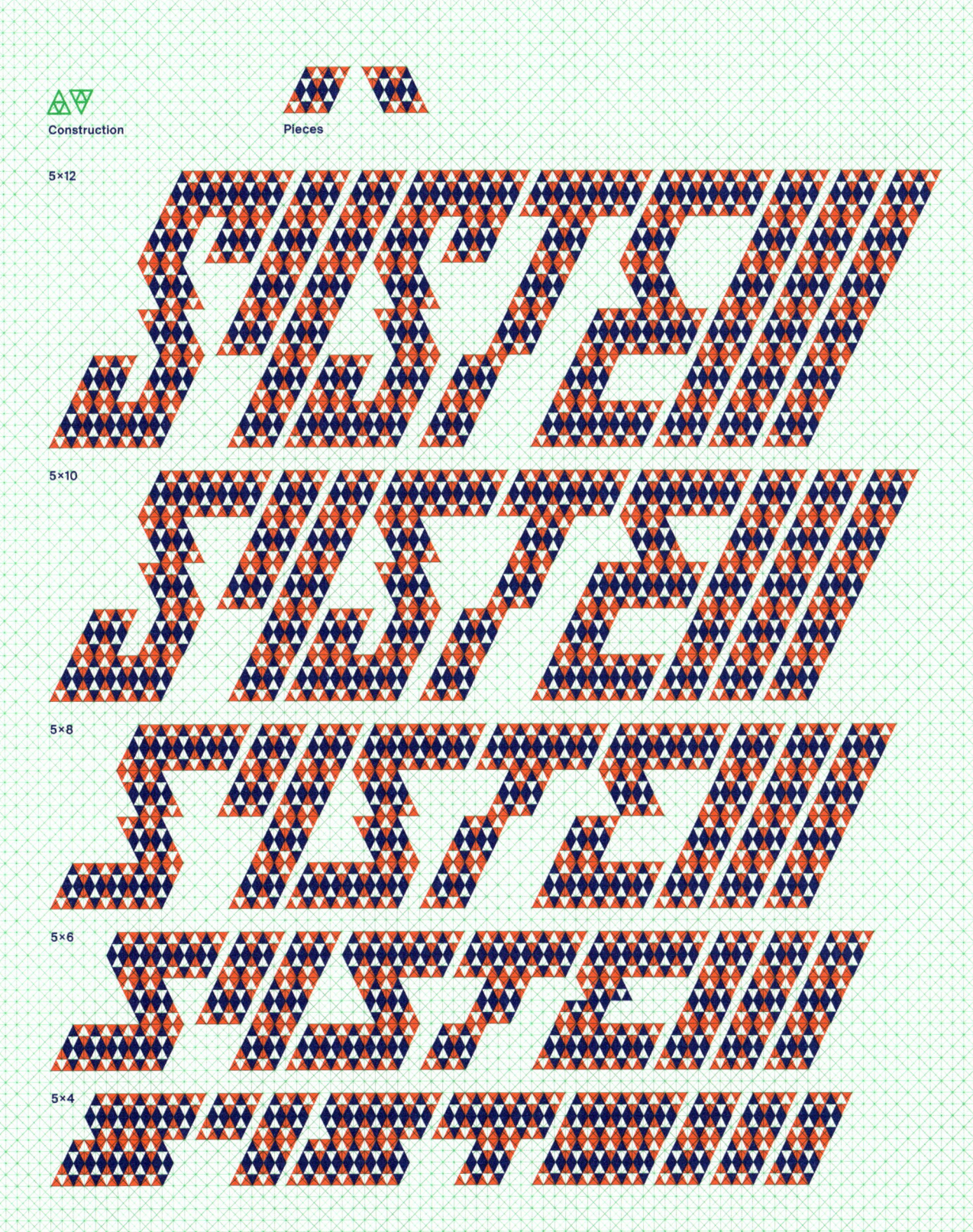

5×4

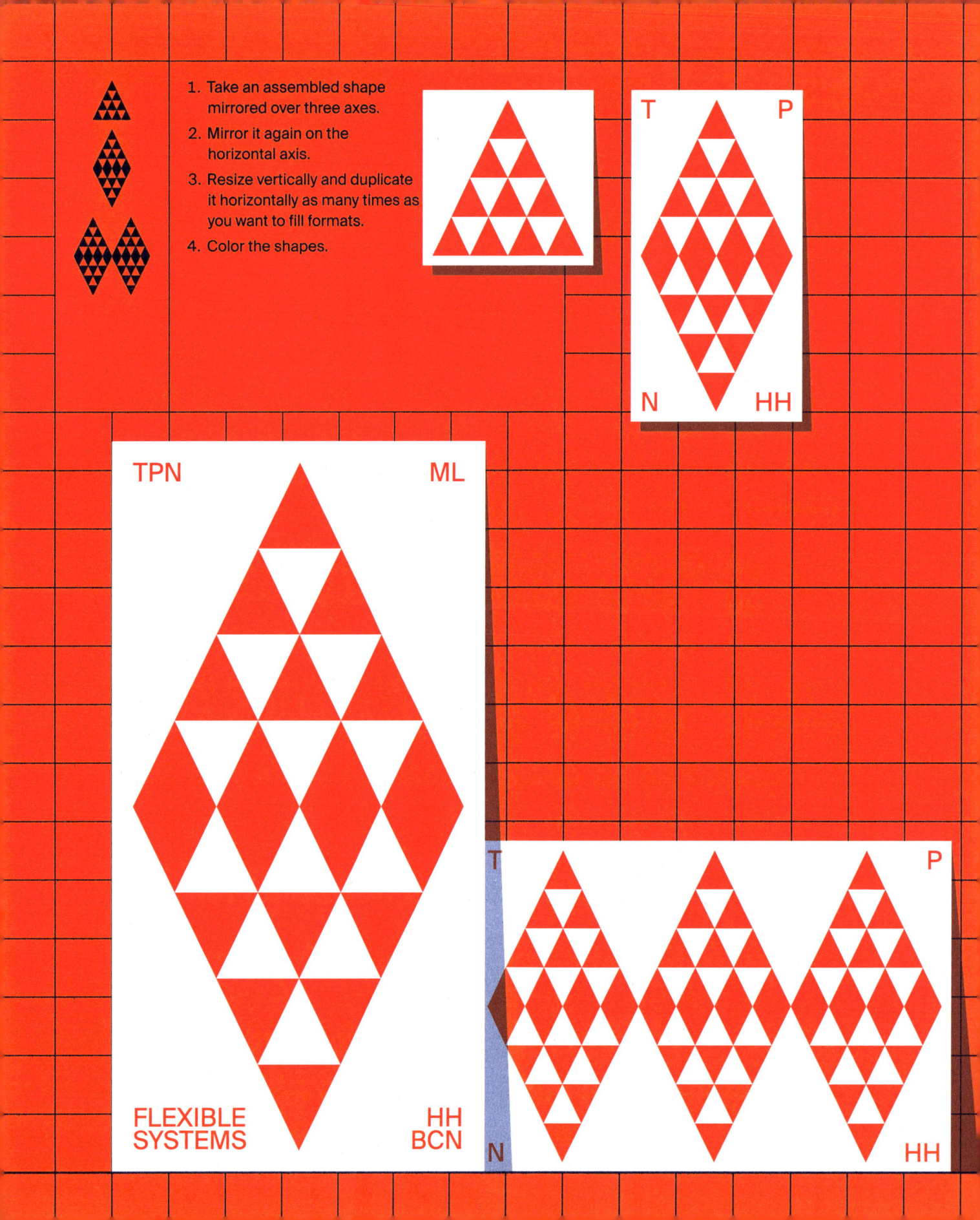

1. Take an assembled shape mirrored over three axes.
2. Mirror it again on the horizontal axis.
3. Resize vertically and duplicate it horizontally as many times as you want to fill formats.
4. Color the shapes.

FLEXIBLE SYSTEMS

1. Take an assembled shape.
2. Distort it so that it fills the format.
3. Color it.
4. Add text and / or images on top of the patterns.

FLEXIBLE VISUAL SYSTEMS

FLEXIBLE SYSTEMS

ML

TPN
HH BCN

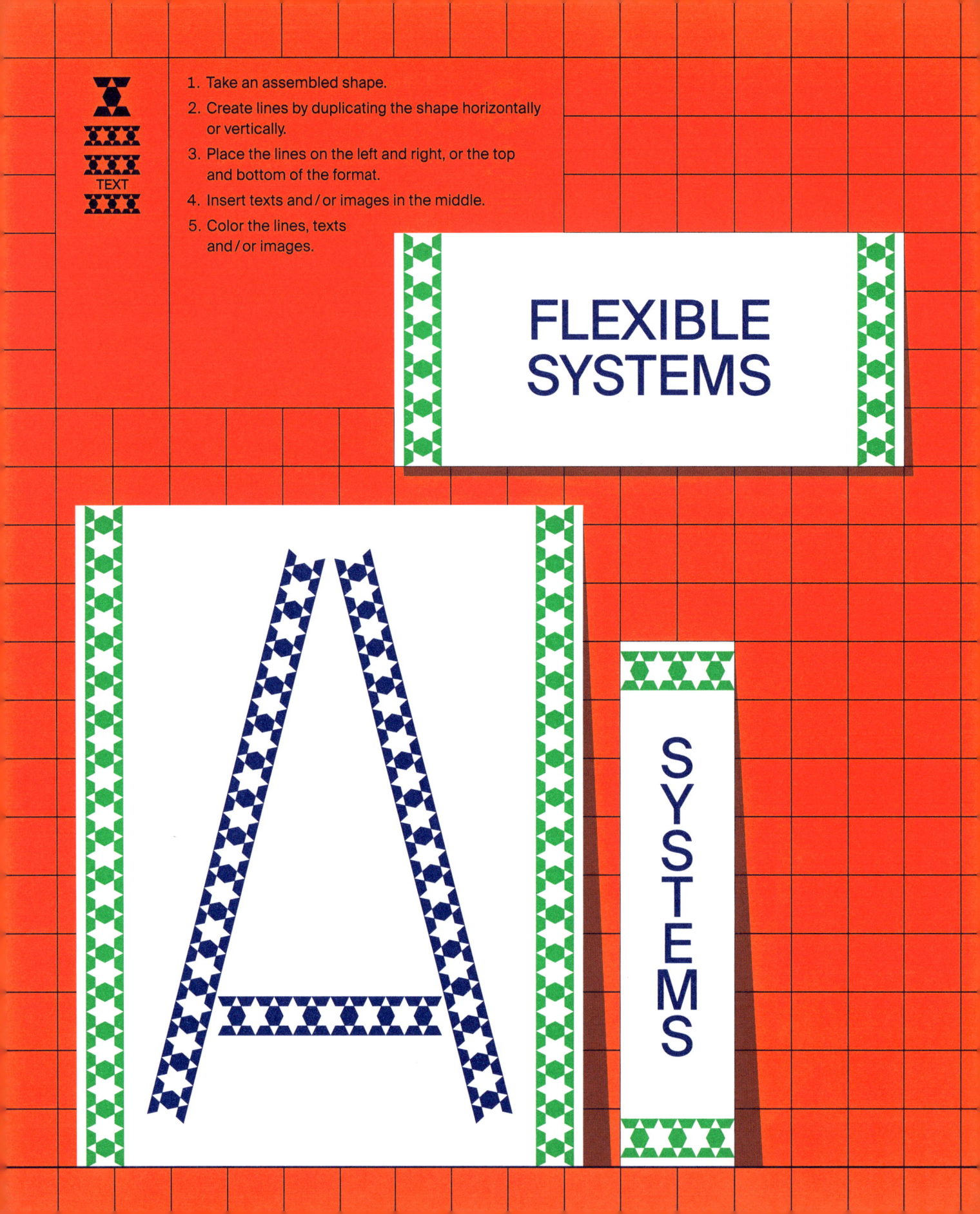

1. Take an assembled shape.
2. Create lines by duplicating the shape horizontally or vertically.
3. Place the lines on the left and right, or the top and bottom of the format.
4. Insert texts and/or images in the middle.
5. Color the lines, texts and/or images.

FLEXIBLE SYSTEMS

SYSTEMS

FLEXIBLE SYSTEMS

ML

TPN
HH BCN

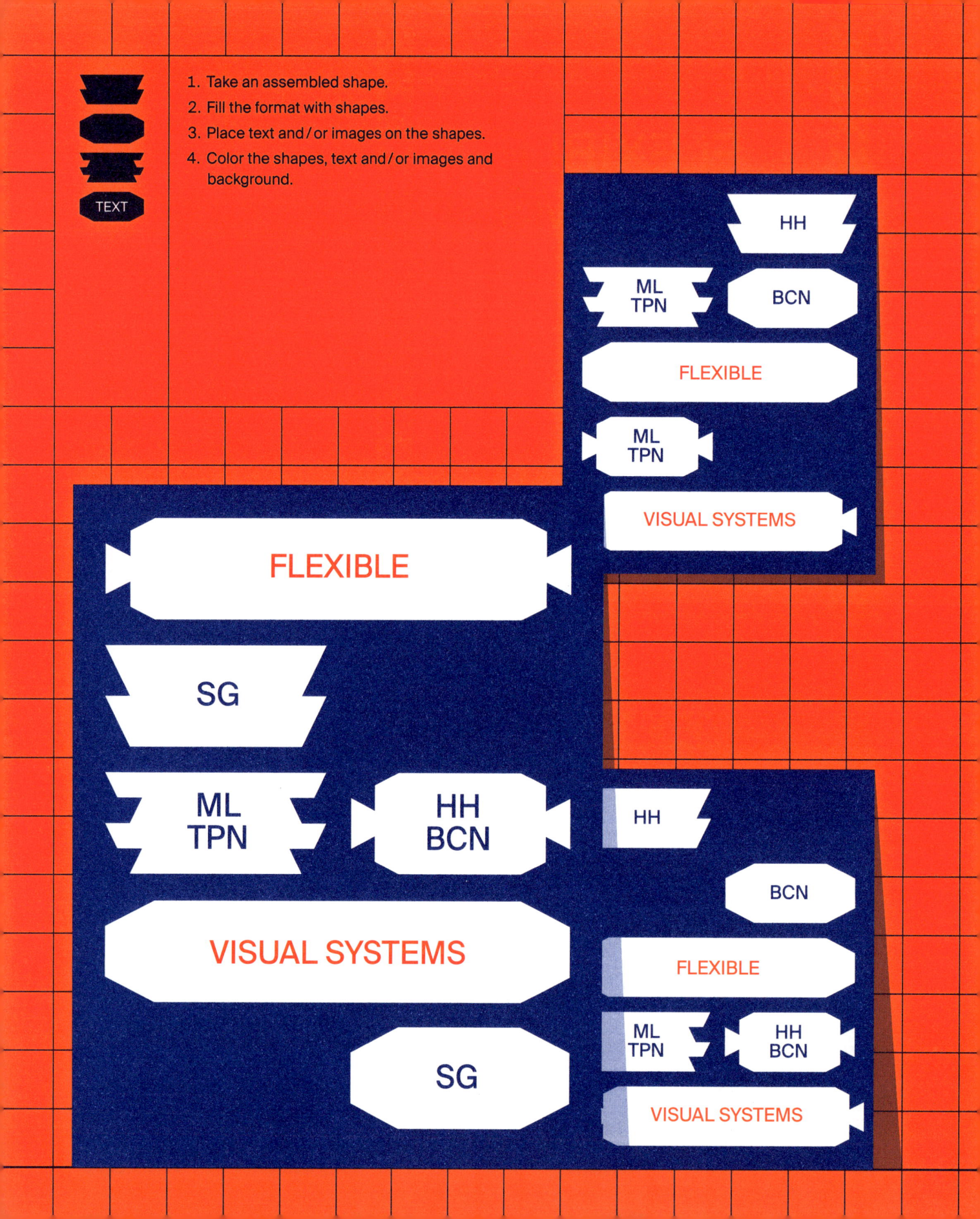

1. Take an assembled shape.
2. Fill the format with shapes.
3. Place text and / or images on the shapes.
4. Color the shapes, text and / or images and background.

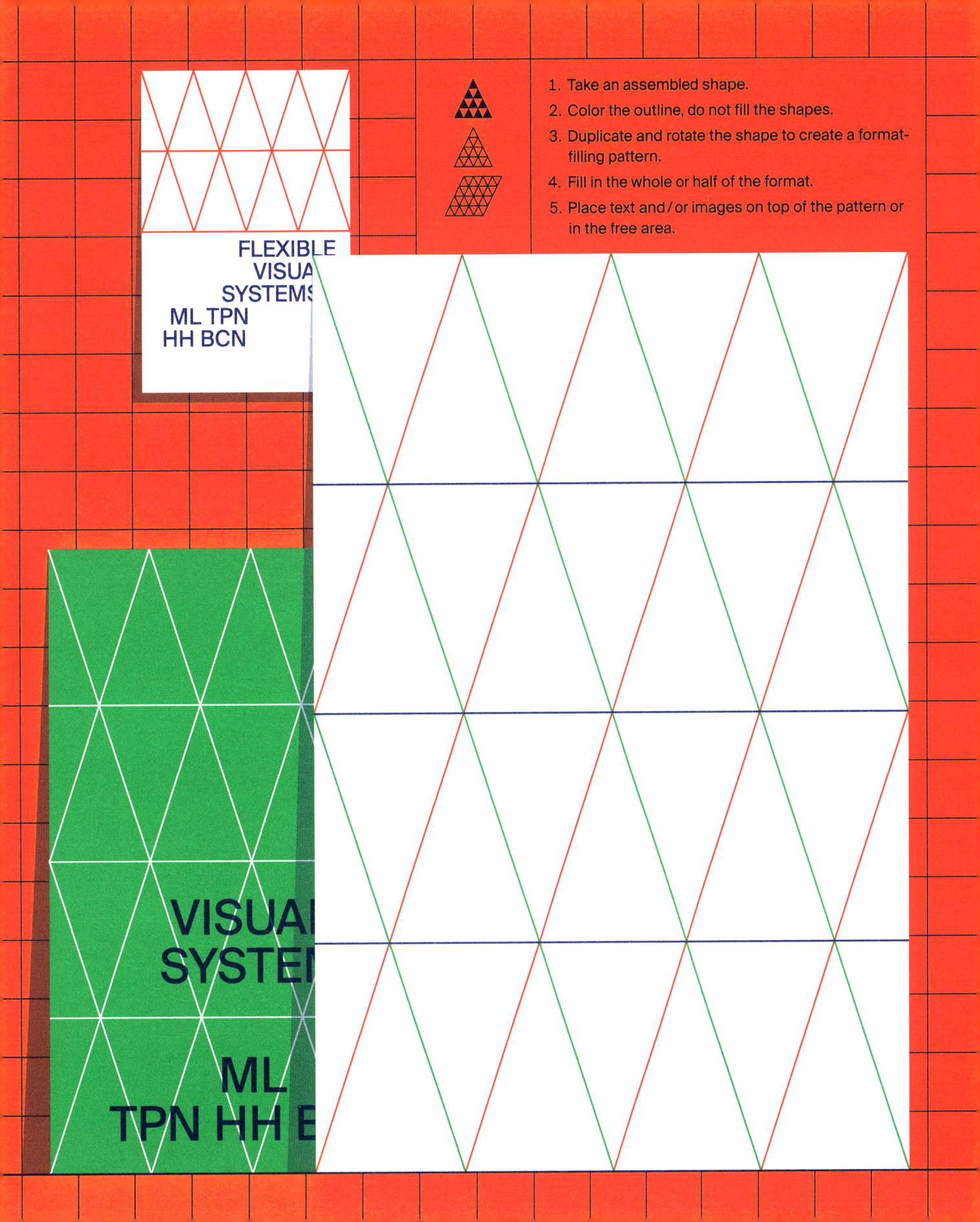

1. Take an assembled shape.
2. Color the outline, do not fill the shapes.
3. Duplicate and rotate the shape to create a format-filling pattern.
4. Fill in the whole or half of the format.
5. Place text and / or images on top of the pattern or in the free area.

FLEXIBLE
VISUAL
SYSTEMS
ML TPN
HH BCN

VISUAL
SYSTEM
ML
TPN HH B

FLEXIBLE VISUAL SYSTEMS
ML TPN HH BCN

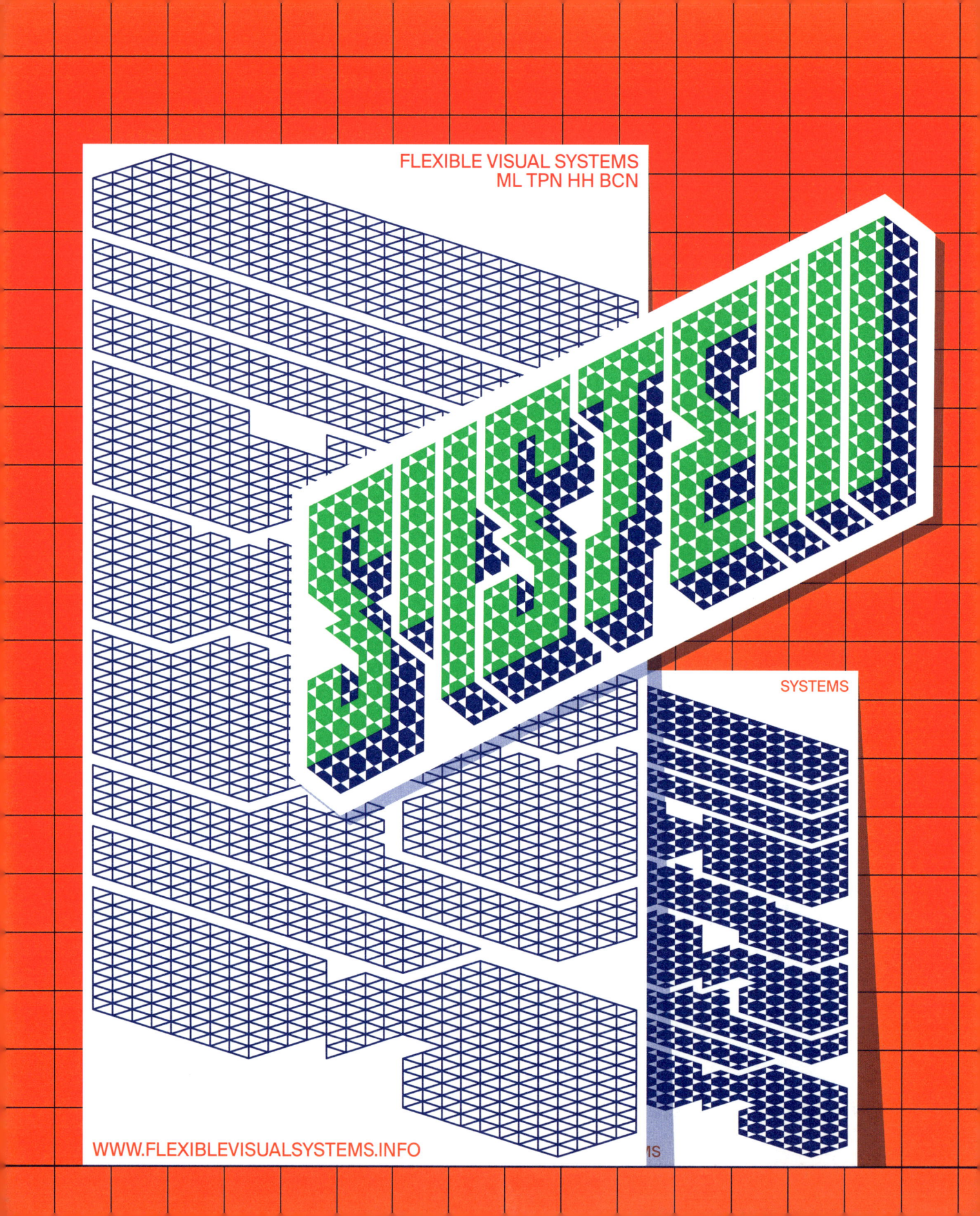

SYSTEMS

WWW.FLEXIBLEVISUALSYSTEMS.INFO

1. Use an assembled shape to construct letters.
2. Color them.
3. Fill the format.
4. Add text to the gaps.

FLEXIBLE
VISUAL
SYSTEMS

ML TPN
HH BCN

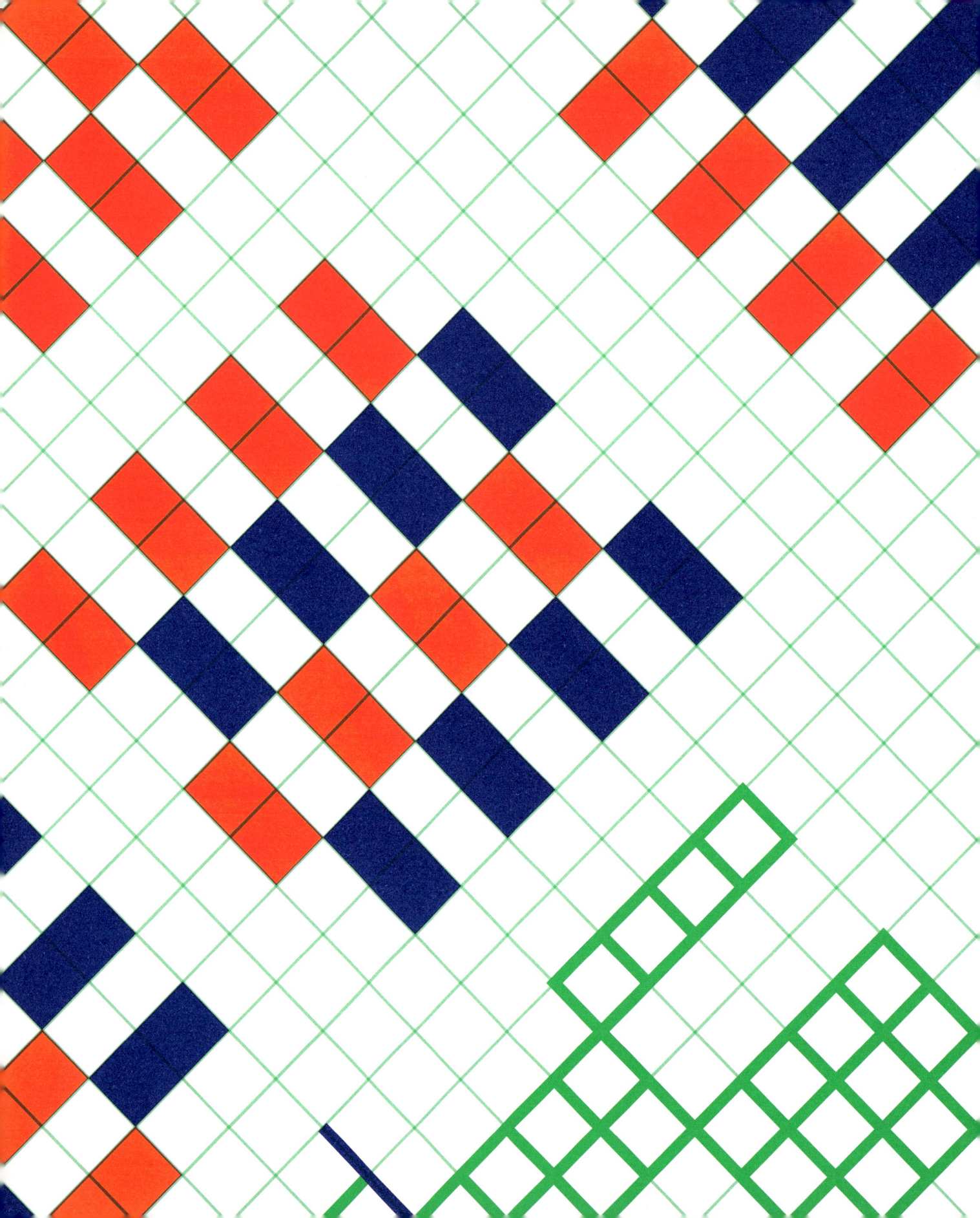

FORM: SQUARE

Part 1

Form-based FVS

Form: Square
Asset: Symbol

A square divided into four squares, of which one to three are deleted.

The one to three squares, arranged in a square of four modules is repeated.

Instead of repeating the arrangement, you can also use the vertical

or the vertical and horizontal middle axes to mirror it.

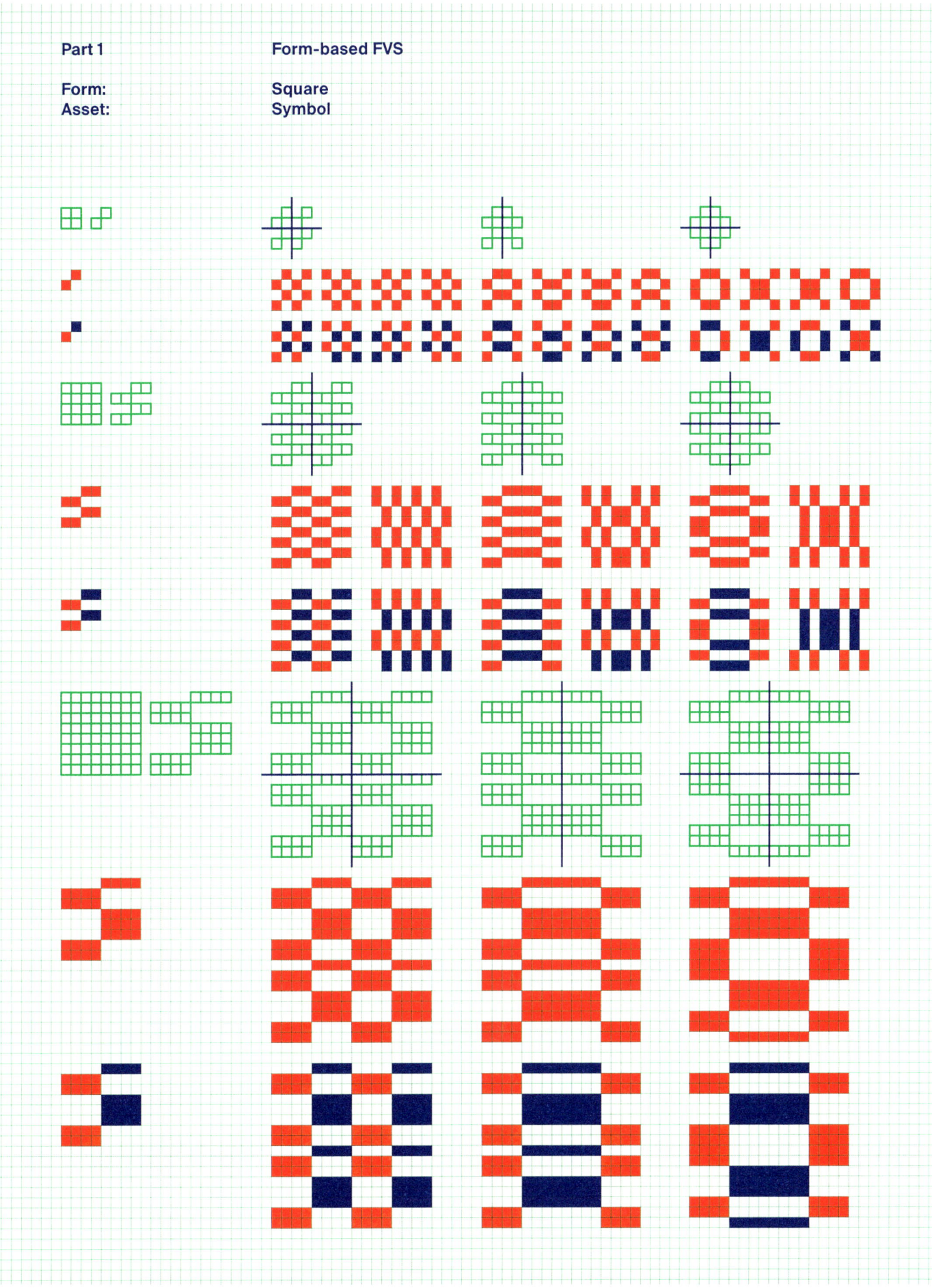

Part 1　　　　　　**Form-based FVS**

Form:　　　　　　Square
Asset:　　　　　　Symbol

Part 1

Form:
Asset:

Form-based FVS

Square
Line

Part 1	Form-based FVS
Form:	Square
Application:	Frame

A square divided into four squares, of which one to three are deleted. The basic element is mirrored over two axes. For the corner element one basic element will be removed.

The corner element rotated four times for every of the corners.

As we started working with a connection element that was already mirrored over two axes the above steps do not need to be taken, but I mention them anyway if you start with a different basic pattern.

Connection element

Corner elements

Connection elements

• In this example, the connecting parts have been matched to the corner parts. A hard contrast with a connecting or corner part that looks completely different can also be interesting.

Line from connecting elements

Line from corner elements

Colored elements

Corner elements

Connection elements

Frame with four corner- and connecting elements

Line from connecting elements

Line from corner elements

Part 1 **Form-based FVS**

Form: Square
Asset: Label

Part 1　　　　　　　　Form-based FVS

Form:　　　　　　　　Square
Application:　　　　　　on 12 Formats

Repetition of the assets　　　　　　　　　　**Vertical repetition and horizontal distortion of the assets**

Horizontal repetition and vertical distortion of the assets　　　　**Horizontal and vertical distortion of the assets**

Part 1   **Form-based FVS**

Form: Square
Asset: Letters

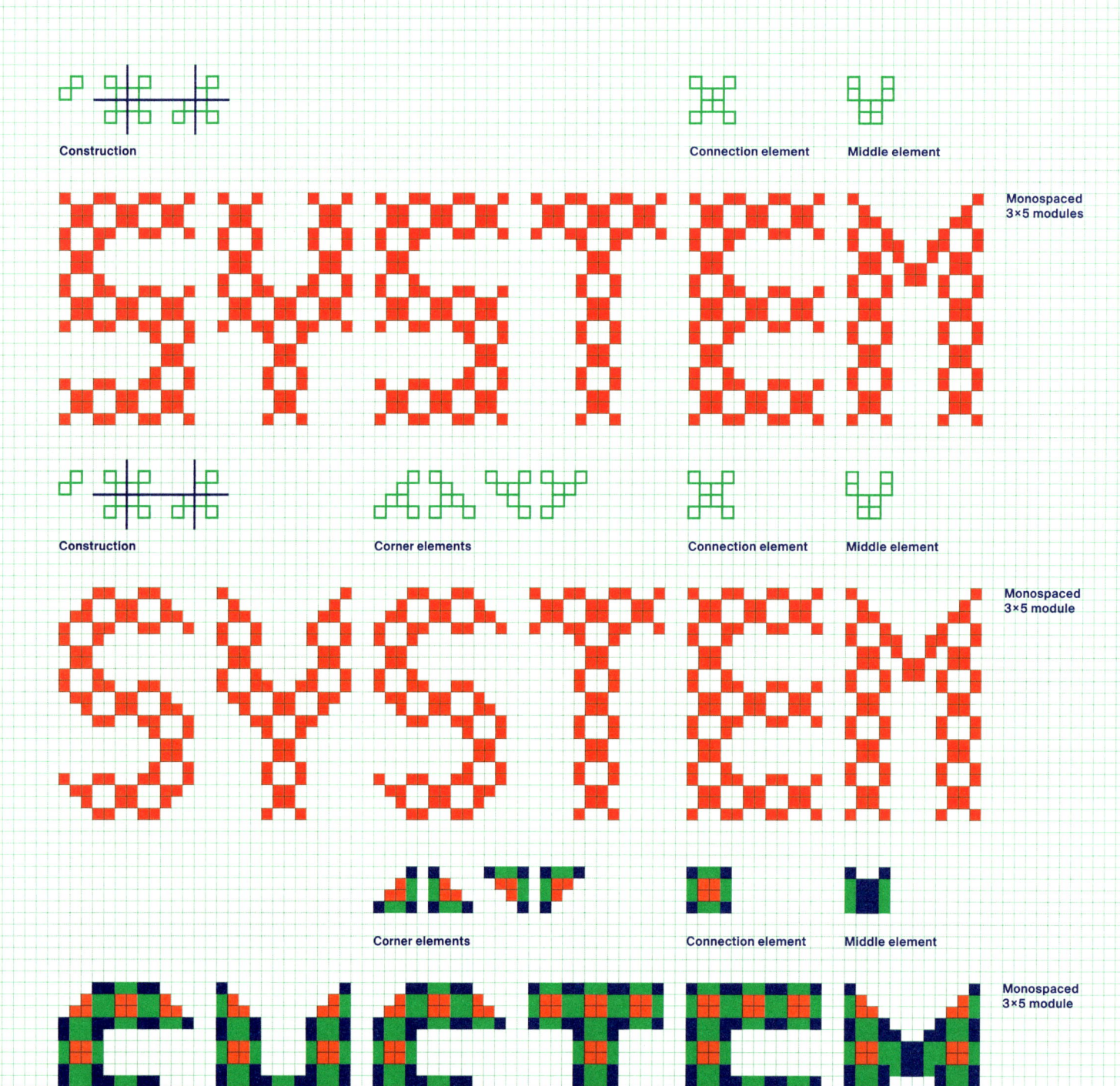

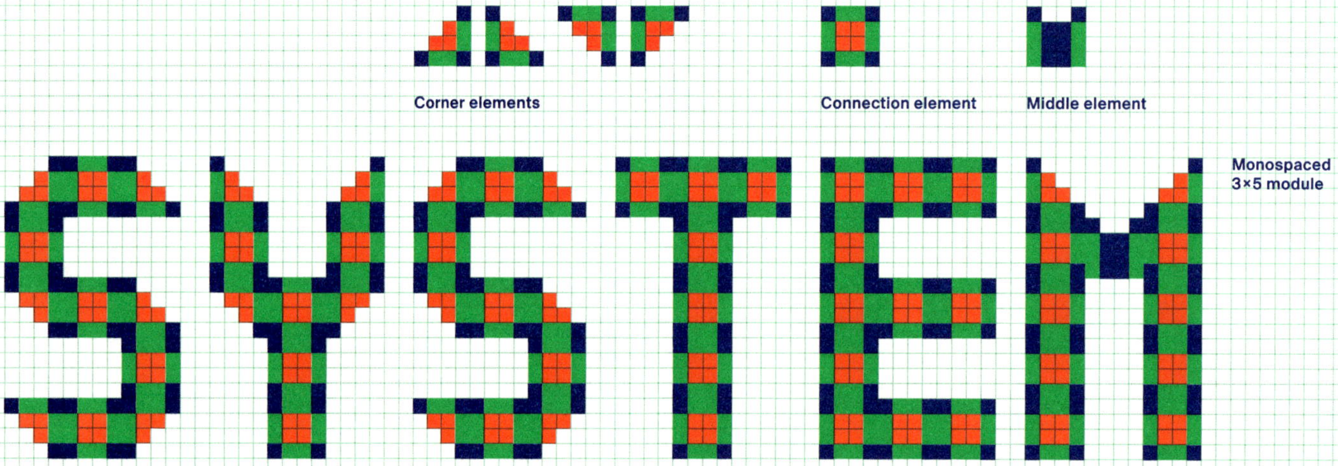

Construction   Connection element   Middle element

Monospaced 3×5 modules

Construction   Corner elements   Connection element   Middle element

Monospaced 3×5 module

Corner elements   Connection element   Middle element

Monospaced 3×5 module

Part 1　　　　　Form-based FVS

Form:　　　　　Square
Asset:　　　　　Letters

Construction　　　　　Corner elements　　　　　Connection element　　　Middle element

Monospaced
3×7 modules

Monospaced
3×5 modules

Monospaced
3×3 modules

Varying widths

2×5 modules　　3×5 modules　　4×5 modules　　10×5 modules

1. Take an assembled shape.
2. Color it. Since this is a symmetrical shape, a symmetrical coloring has a harmonious effect.
3. Enlarge the inner area of the shape until you get a frame.
4. Fill the frame with texts and / or a images.

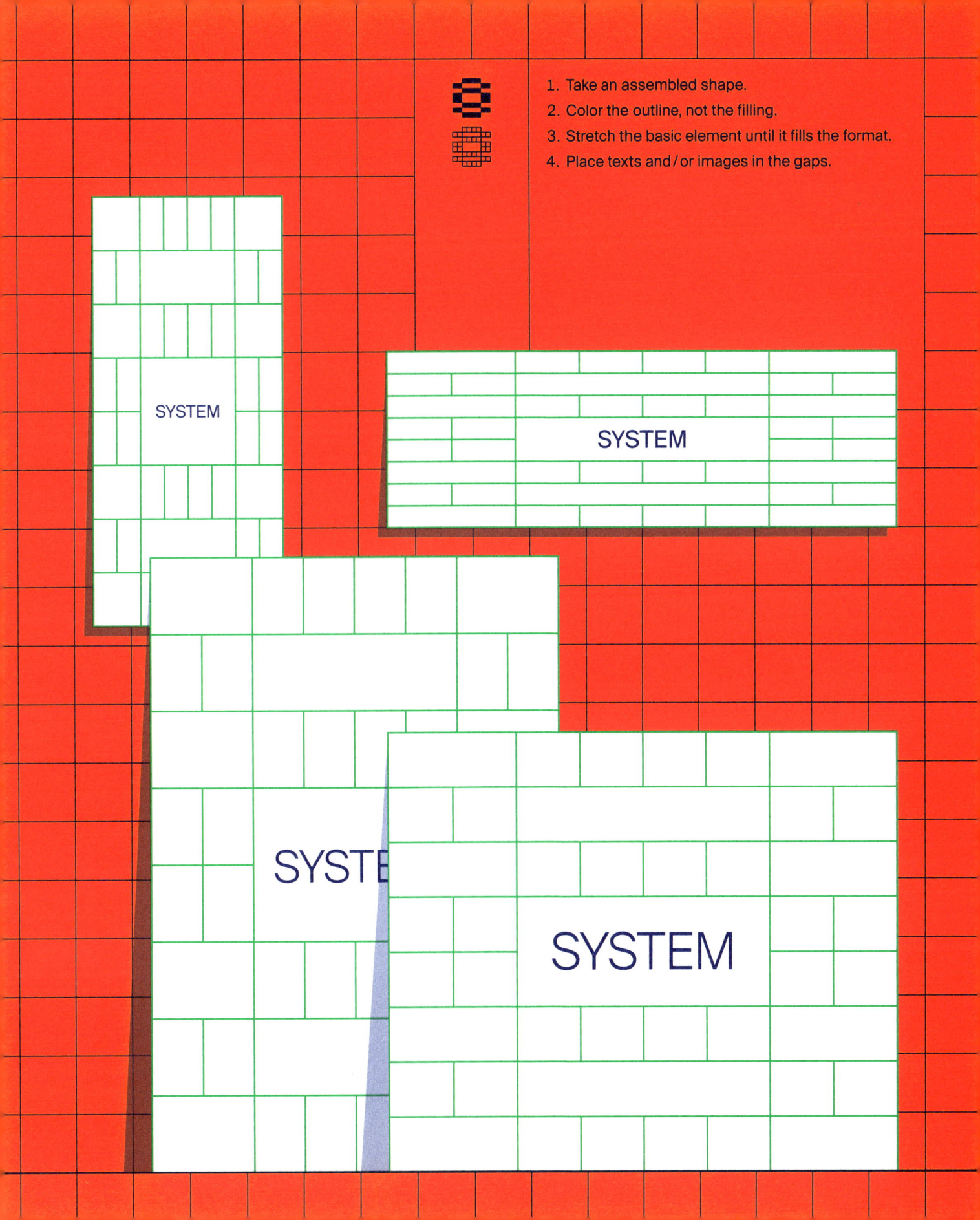

1. Take an assembled shape.
2. Color the outline, not the filling.
3. Stretch the basic element until it fills the format.
4. Place texts and / or images in the gaps.

SYSTEM

SYSTEM

SYSTE

SYSTEM

FLEXIBLE

HH BCN

ML TPN

SYSTEMS

S

1. Take an assembled shape.
2. Duplicate it and delete pieces from the duplicated shape to create corner elements.
3. Combine the two elements to build frames, shapes, and patterns.
4. Place texts and/or images in the middle of them.
5. Color the shapes, texts, images, and/or background.

FLEXIBLE VISUAL SYSTEMS

SYSTEM

SHOP

ML TPN

1. Take an assembled shape.
2. Fill the format with the shape. The inner area can be stretched in width or height.
3. Place texts and/or images on the shapes.
4. Color the shape, text, images and/or background.

SYSTEMS

FLEXIBLE VISUAL SYSTEMS

BLE
AL
EMS

1. Take an assembled shape.
2. Duplicate it.
3. Shrink the height by half.
4. Put all the variations together.
5. Color the pattern.
6. Place rectangles with a different colors on top of the pattern and use it for texts and / or images.

ML   TPN

FLEXIBLE SYSTEMS

HH
BCN

FLEXIBLE SYSTEMS

ML   TPN

HH   BCN

ML   TPN

FLEXIBLE SYSTEMS

HH BCN   WWW
.FLEXIBLE
VISUAL
SYSTEMS
.INFO

ML TPN

HH BCN

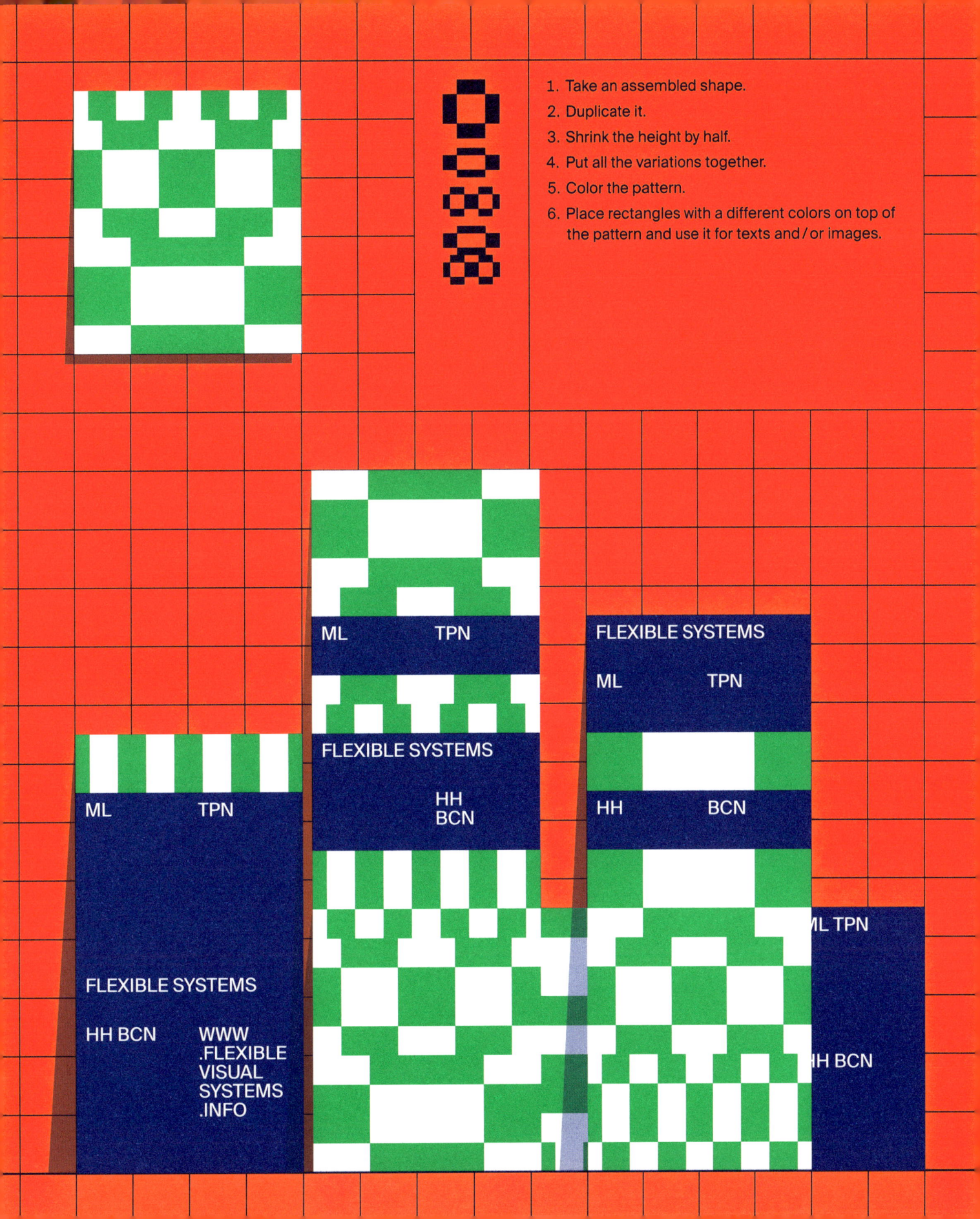

SYSTEM
SYSTEM
SYSTEM

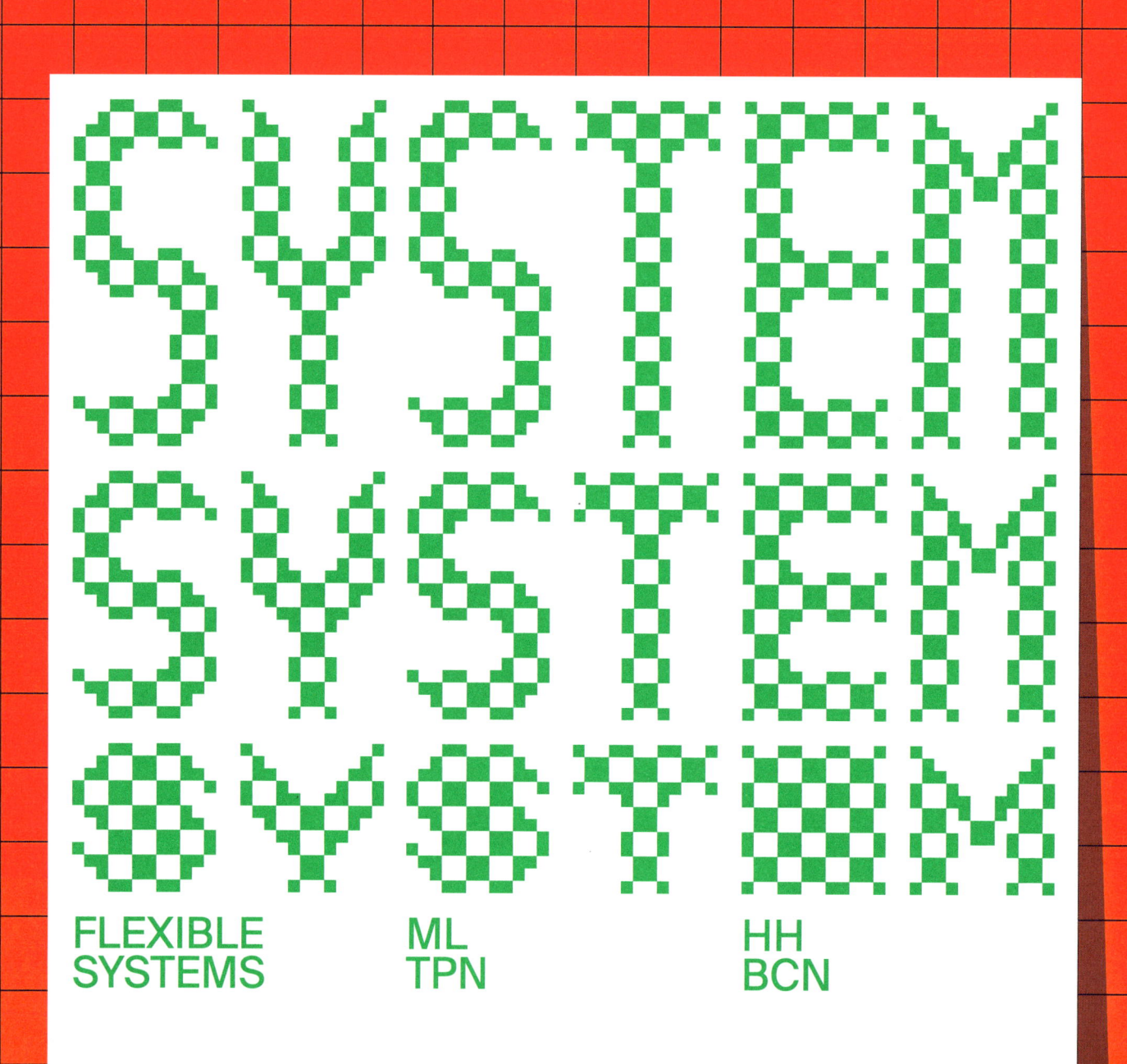

FLEXIBLE
SYSTEMS

ML
TPN

HH
BCN

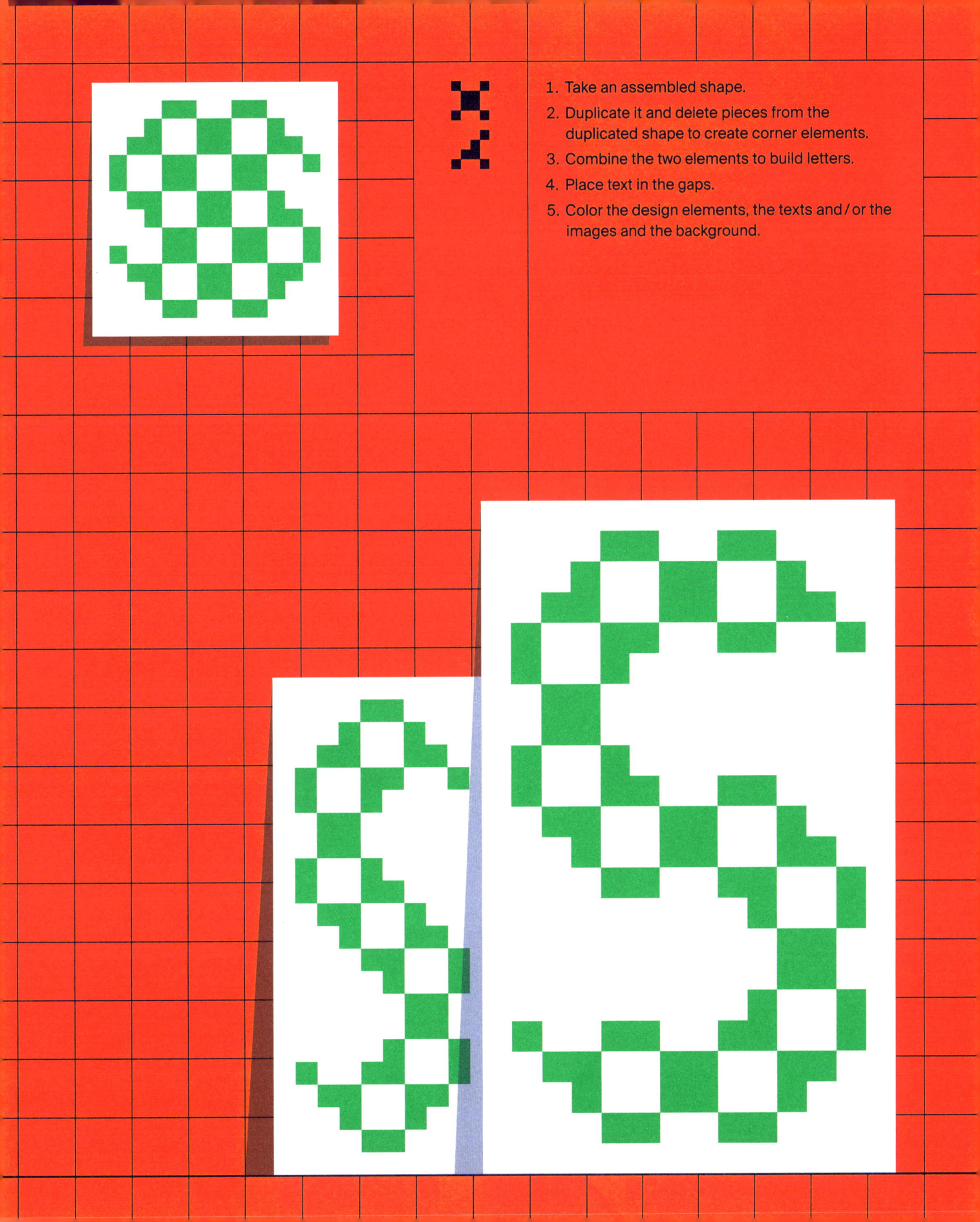

1. Take an assembled shape.
2. Duplicate it and delete pieces from the duplicated shape to create corner elements.
3. Combine the two elements to build letters.
4. Place text in the gaps.
5. Color the design elements, the texts and/or the images and the background.

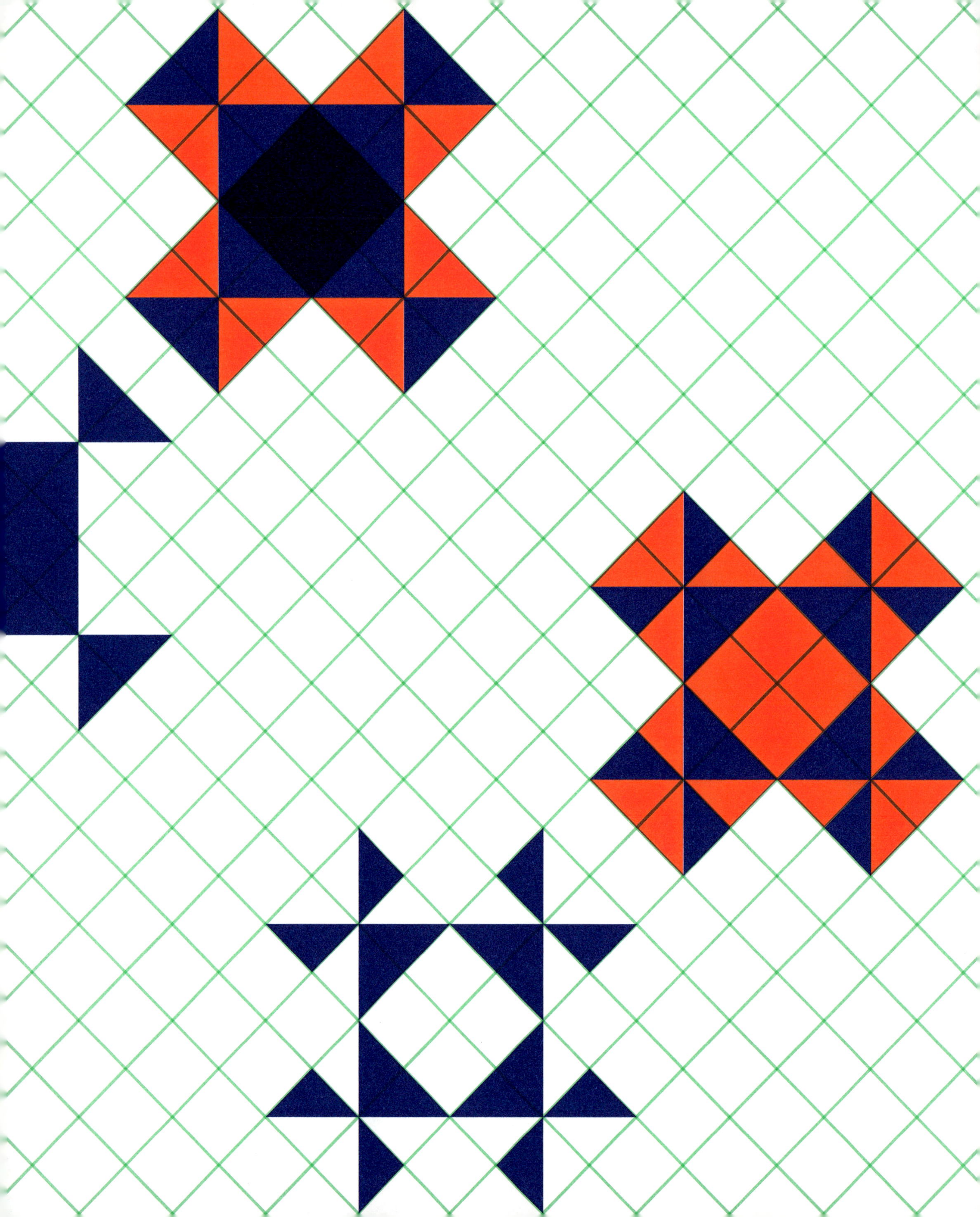

Form: Pentagon (made of acute triangles)

Part 1

Form:
Asset:

Form-based FVS

Pentagon
Symbol

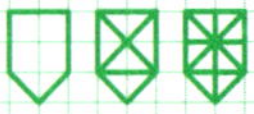

A pentagon made of triangles. 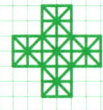   Rotated 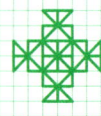   Deleted triangles

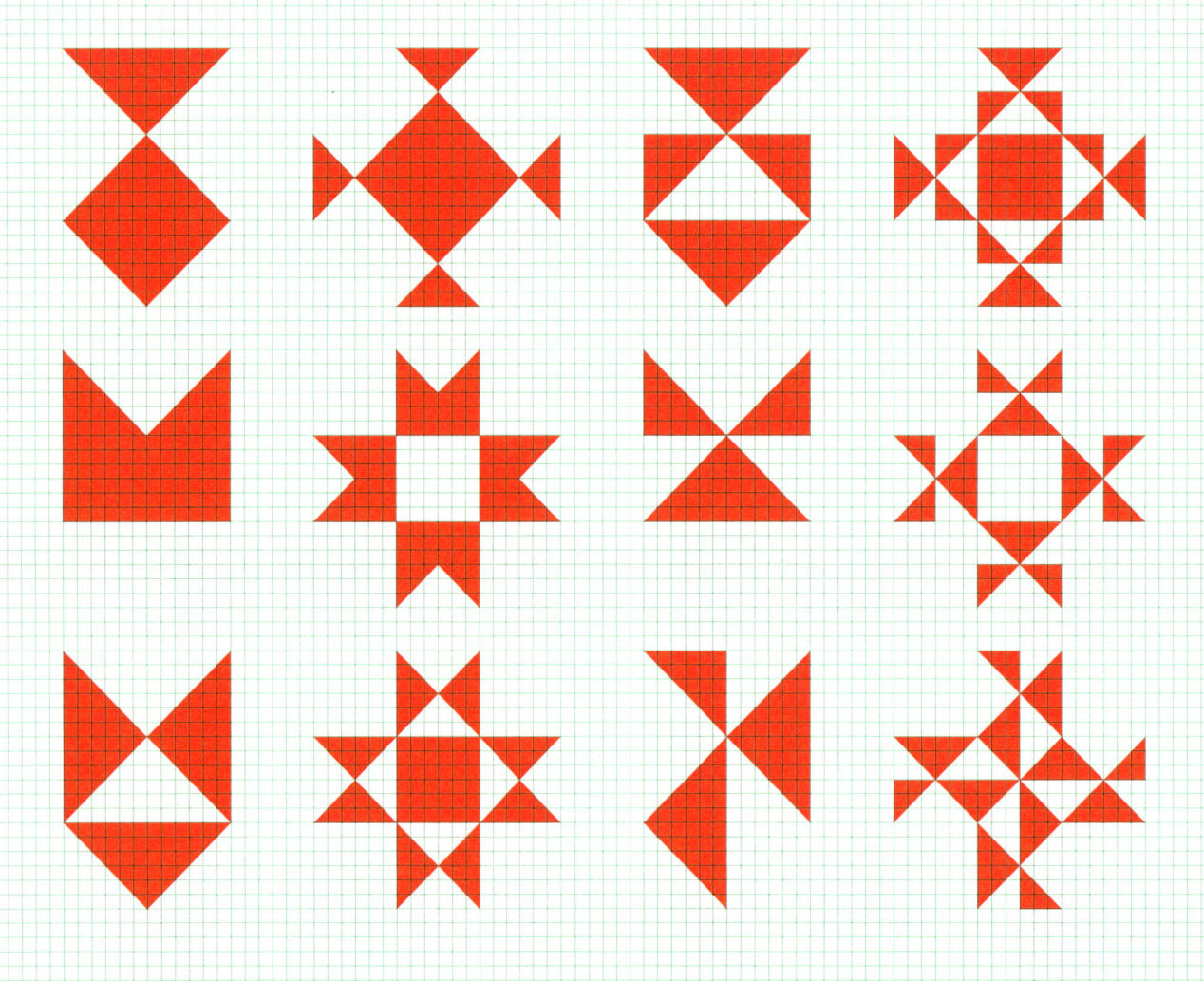

Part 1

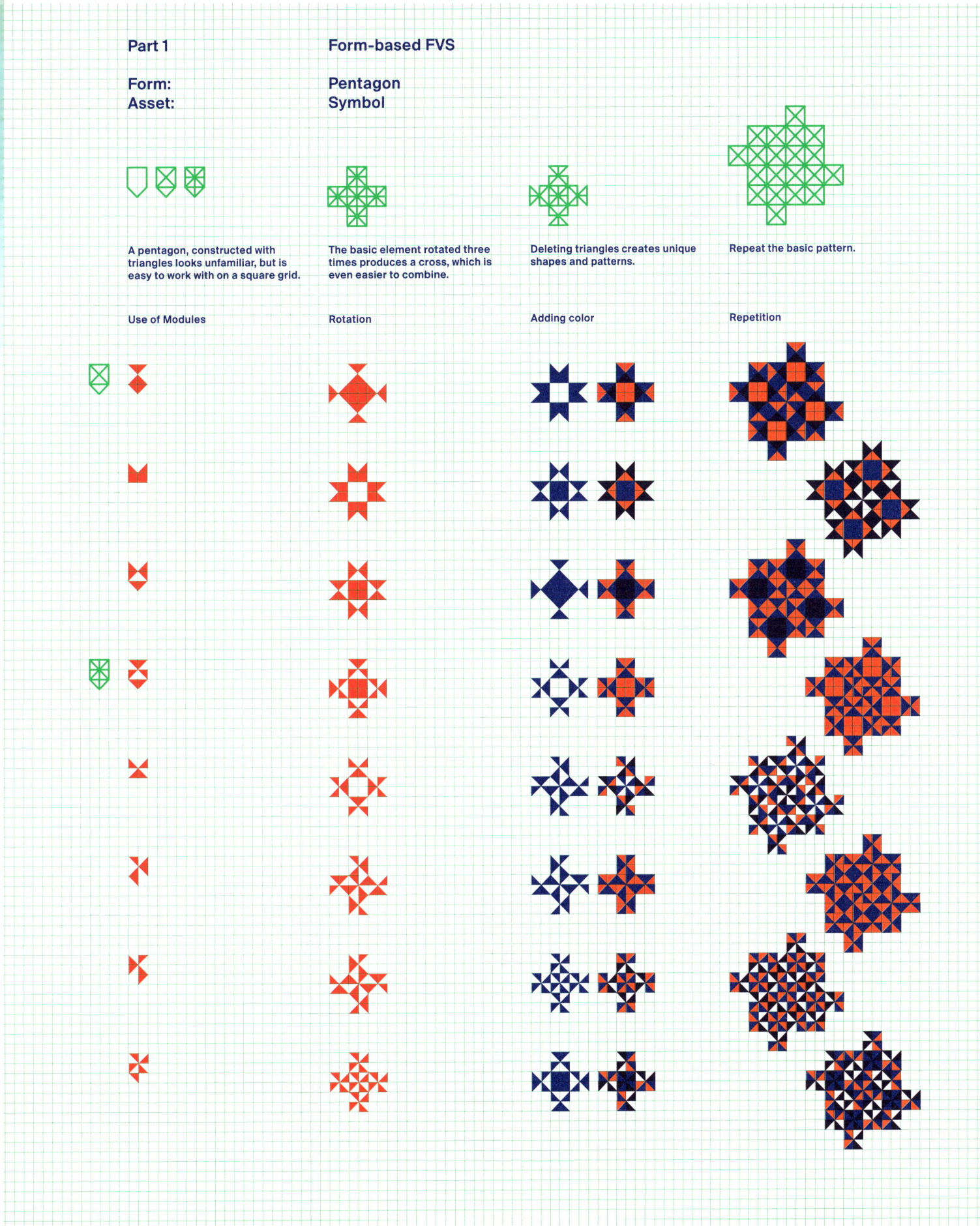

Form-based FVS

Form:
Asset:

Pentagon
Symbol

A pentagon, constructed with triangles looks unfamiliar, but is easy to work with on a square grid.

The basic element rotated three times produces a cross, which is even easier to combine.

Deleting triangles creates unique shapes and patterns.

Repeat the basic pattern.

Use of Modules

Rotation

Adding color

Repetition

Part 1

Form: **Pentagon**
Asset: **Line**

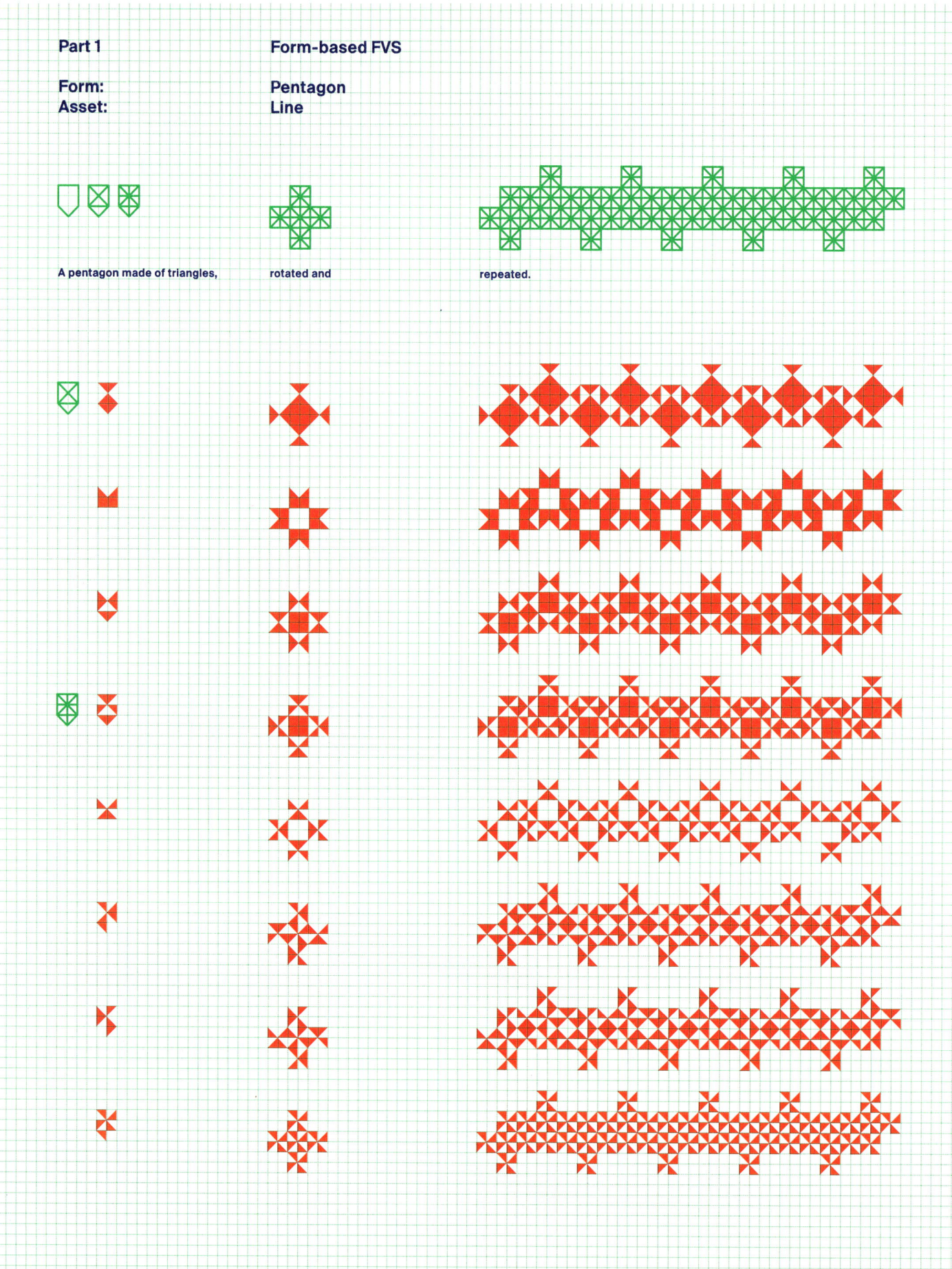

Form-based FVS

A pentagon made of triangles, rotated and repeated.

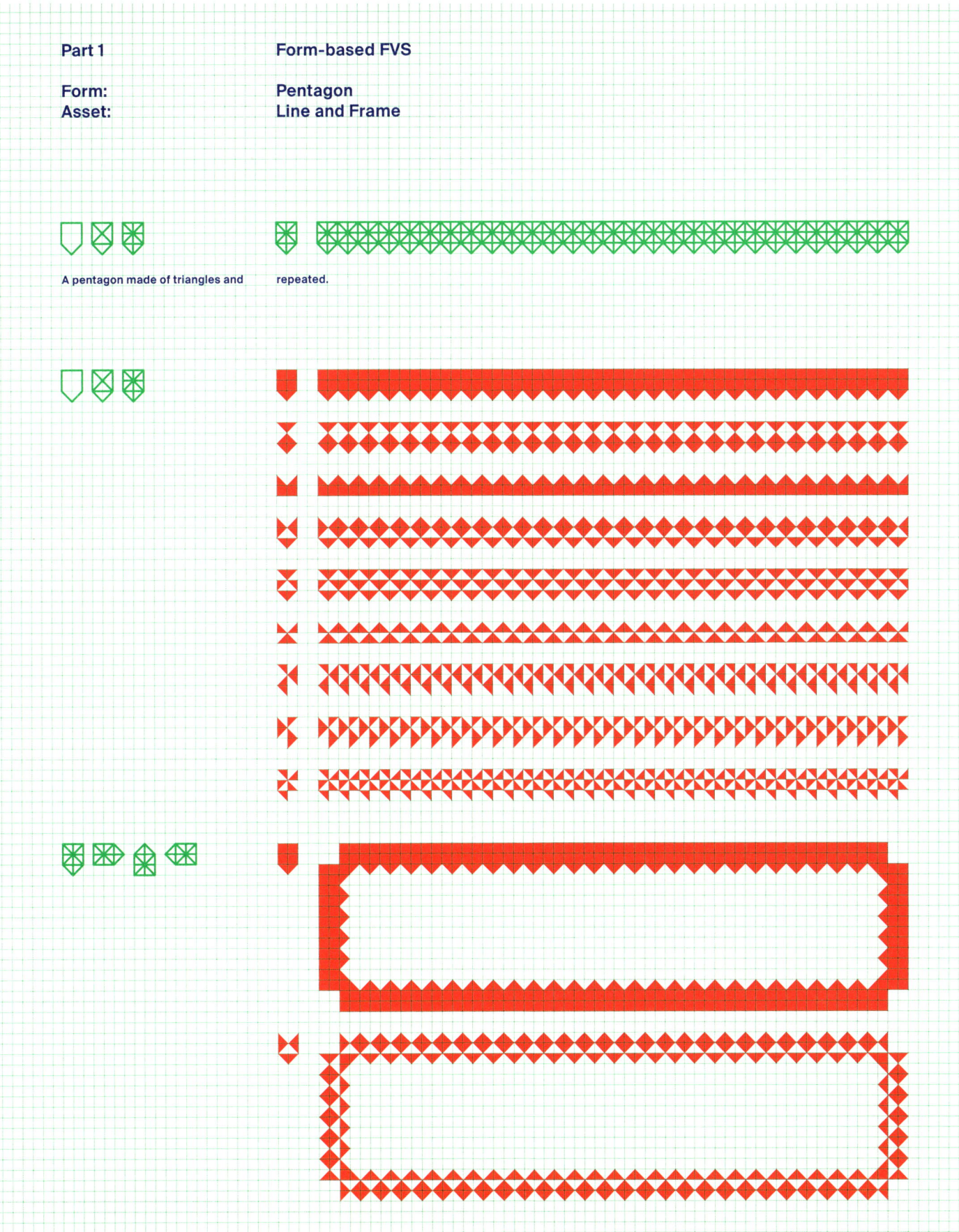

Part 1 Form-based FVS

Form: Pentagon
Asset: Line and Frame

A pentagon made of triangles and repeated.

Part 1

Form-based FVS

Form: Pentagon
Asset: Label

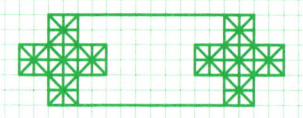

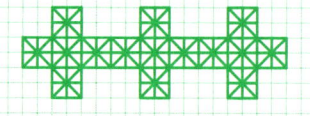

A pentagon made of triangles, rotated, interspace filled and gaps filled with components.

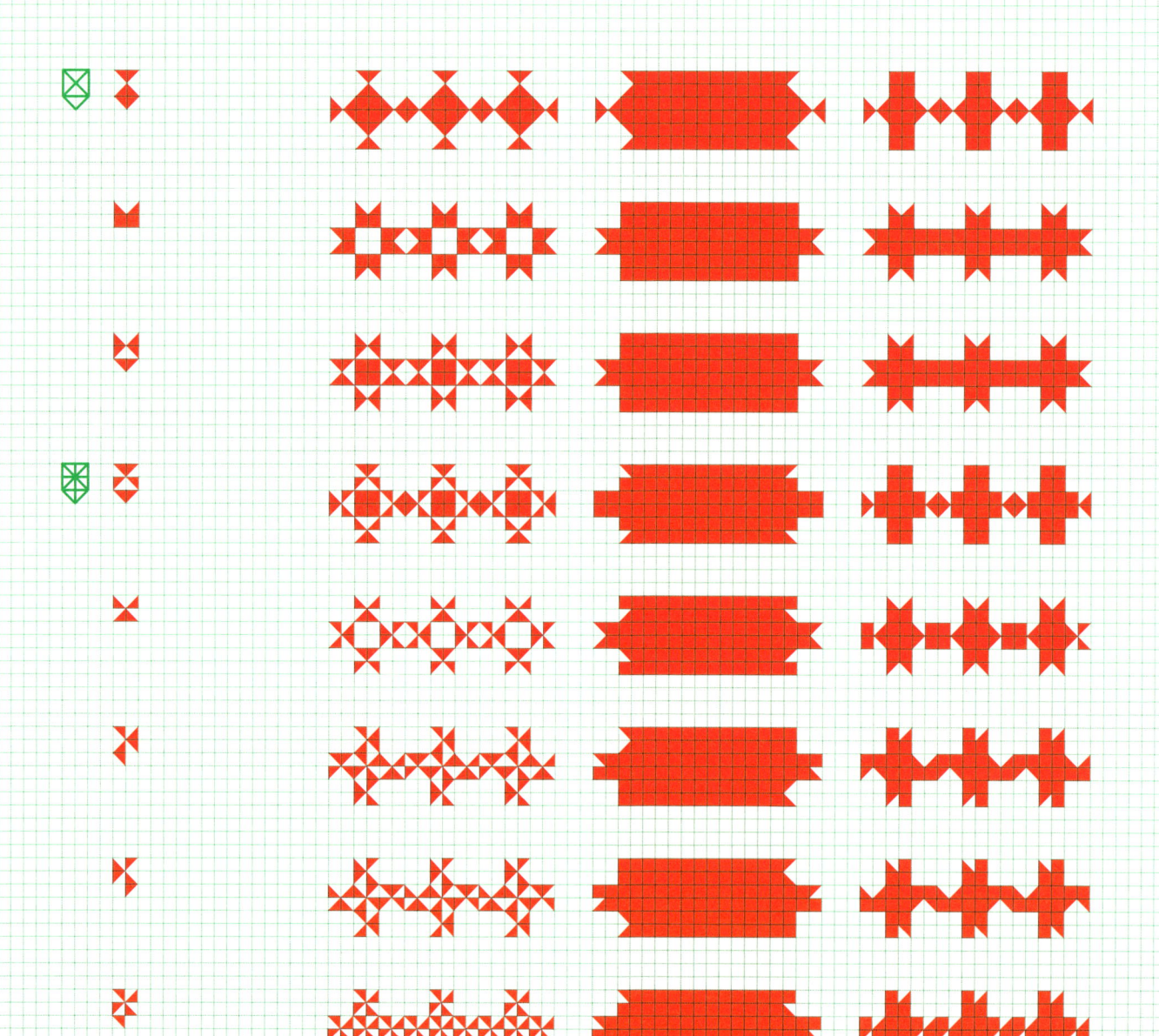

Part 1 　　　　**Form-based FVS**

Form: 　　　　Pentagon
Application: 　　on 12 Formats

Repetition of the assets　　　　　　　　　　　　*Vertical repetition and horizontal distortion of the assets*

Horizontal repetition and vertical distortion of the assets　　　*Horizontal and vertical distortion of the assets*

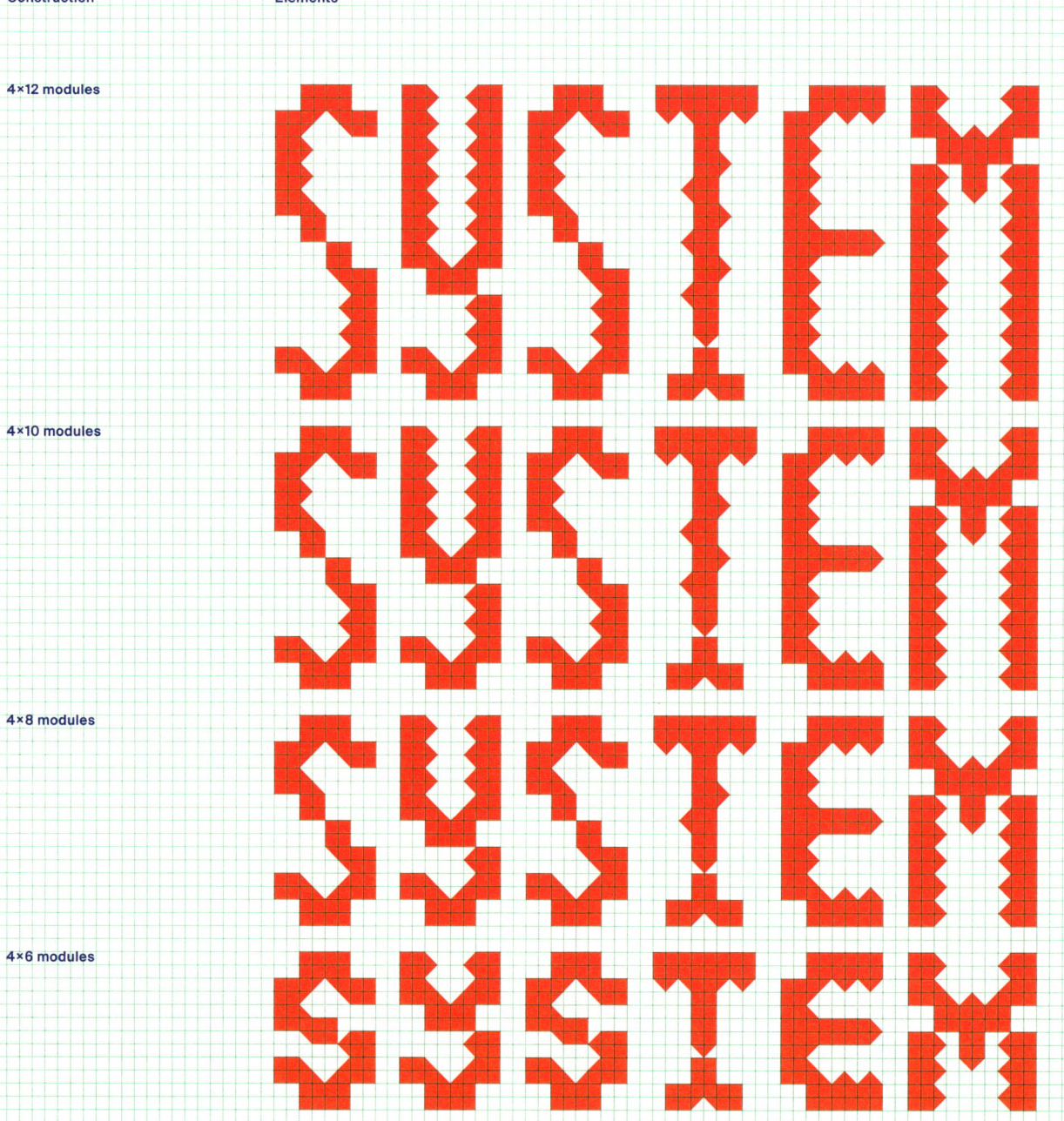

Part 1

Form:
Asset:

Form-based FVS

Pentagon
Letters

Construction

Elements

4×12 modules

4×10 modules

4×8 modules

4×6 modules

Part 1

Form:
Asset:

Form-based FVS

Pentagon
Letters

Construction

Elements

4×12 modules

4×10 modules

4×8 modules

4×6 modules

1. Take an assembled shape.
2. The shape may be rotated 90°, 180°, and 270°.
3. Fill the format with shapes.
4. Place text and/or images in the triangles.

FLEXIBLE

SYSTEMS

ML   TPN

FLEXIBLE SYSTEMS

FLEXIBLE   SYSTEMS

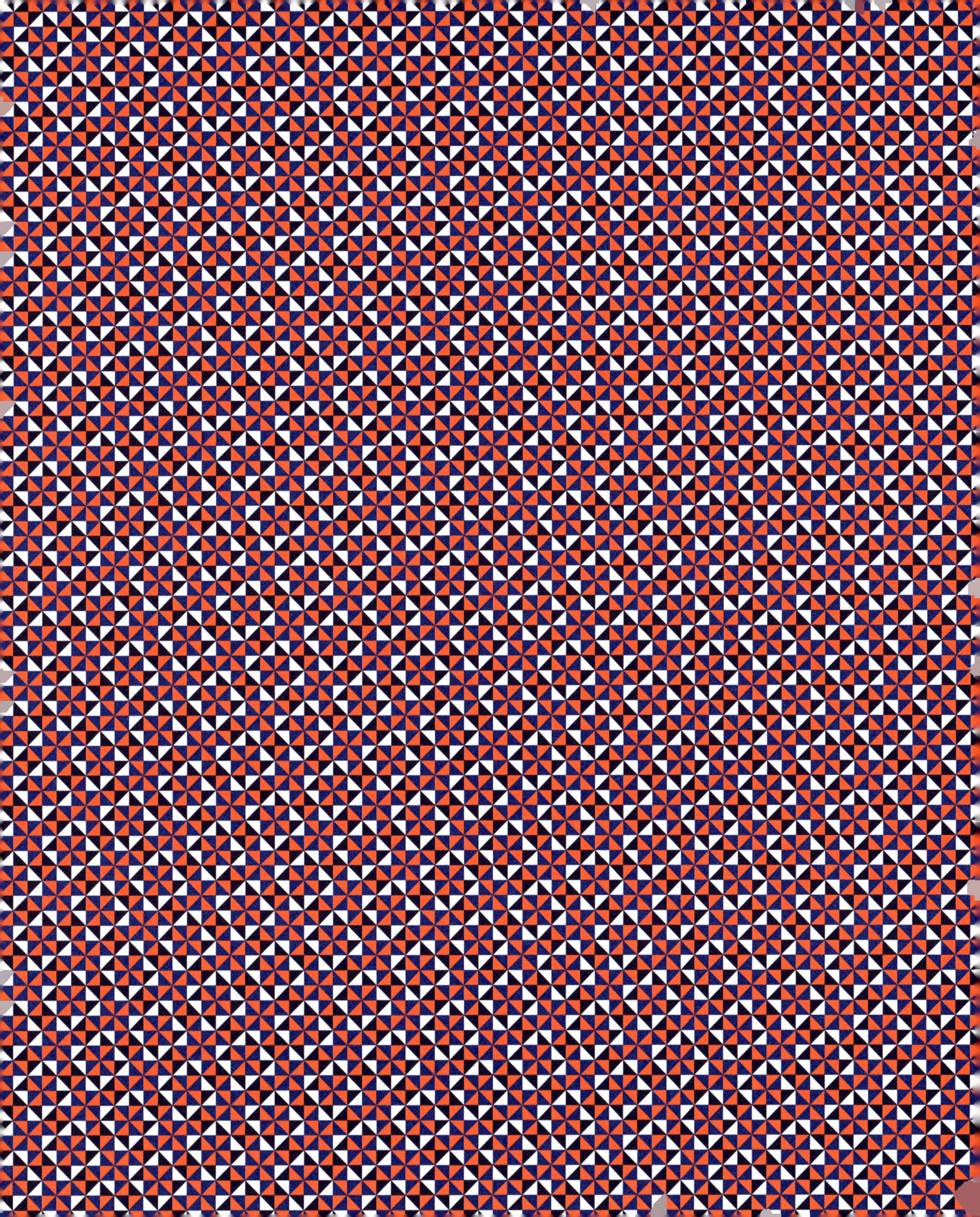

1. Take an assembled shape.
2. Rotate it 90°, 180°, and 270°.
3. Create patterns and frames.
4. Place texts and/or images in the empty areas.
5. Color the patterns, frames, images, texts, and background.

SYSTEMS

FLEXIBLE VISUAL
SYSTEMS

ML TPN
BCN HH

FLEXIBLEVISUALSYS

SYSTEM

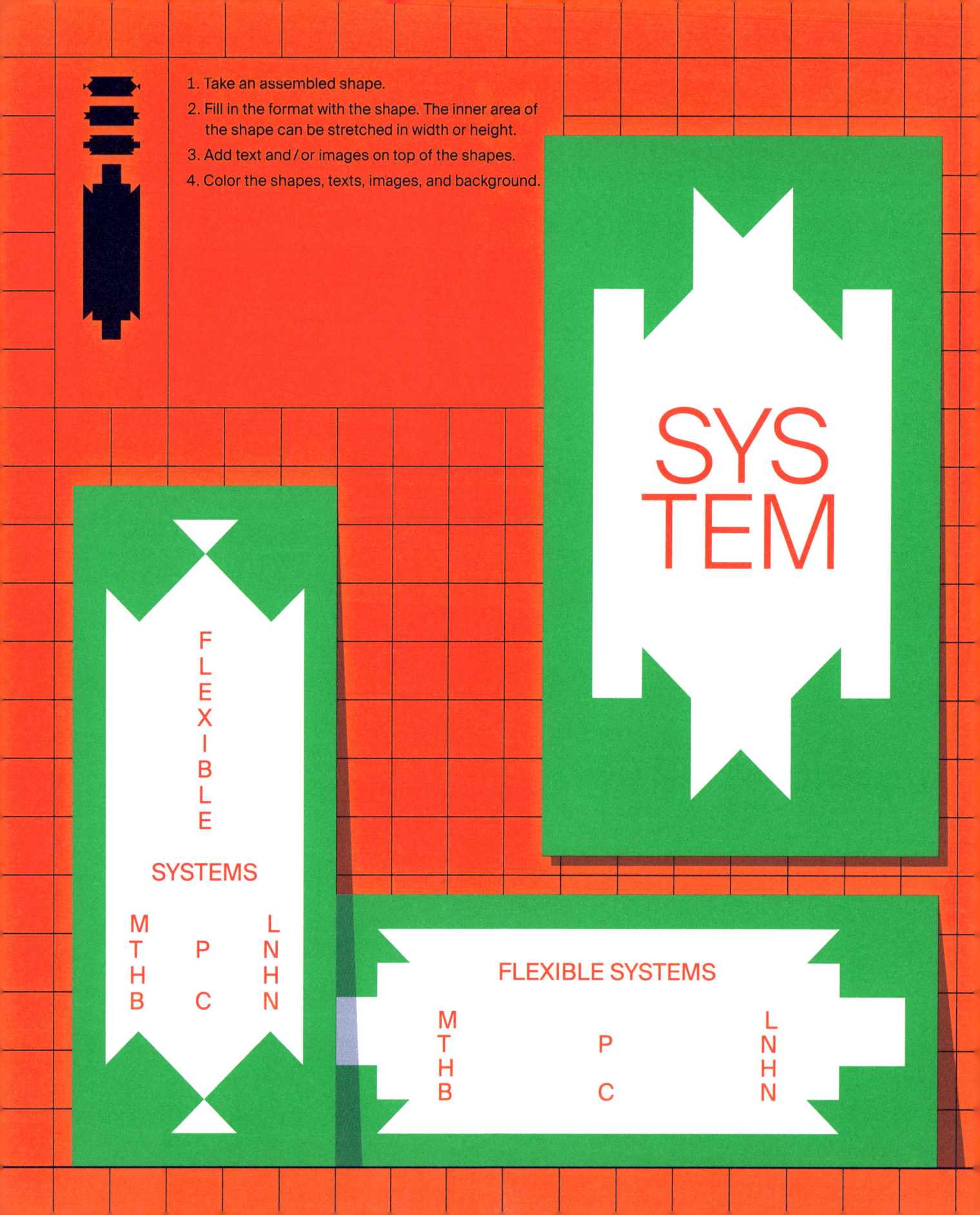

1. Take an assembled shape.
2. Fill in the format with the shape. The inner area of the shape can be stretched in width or height.
3. Add text and / or images on top of the shapes.
4. Color the shapes, texts, images, and background.

SYS TEM

FLEXIBLE

SYSTEMS

M T H B   P C   L N H N

FLEXIBLE SYSTEMS

M T H B   P C   L N H N

1. Take an assembled shape.
2. Duplicate and rotate it 90°, 180°, and 270°.
3. Put all the variations together.
4. Distort them to fill the format.
5. Color the pattern and background.
6. Place rectangles with a different color on top of the pattern and use them for texts and / or images.

SYSTEMS

FVS

FLEXIBLE SYSTEMS

ML TPN
HH BCN

FLEXIBLE SYSTEMS

1. Take an assembled shape.
2. Duplicate and rotate it 90°, 180°, and 270°.
3. Design letters with the shapes.
4. Fill in the format with letters.
5. Add texts and/or images to the empty areas.
6. Color the letters, texts, images and/or background.

FLEXIBLE SYSTEMS
ML TPN HH BCN
FLEXIBLEVISUALSYSTEMS.INFO

This is a variation of the system on the left page, but almost a new visual identity.

FLEXIBLE
VISUAL
SYSTEMS
.INFO

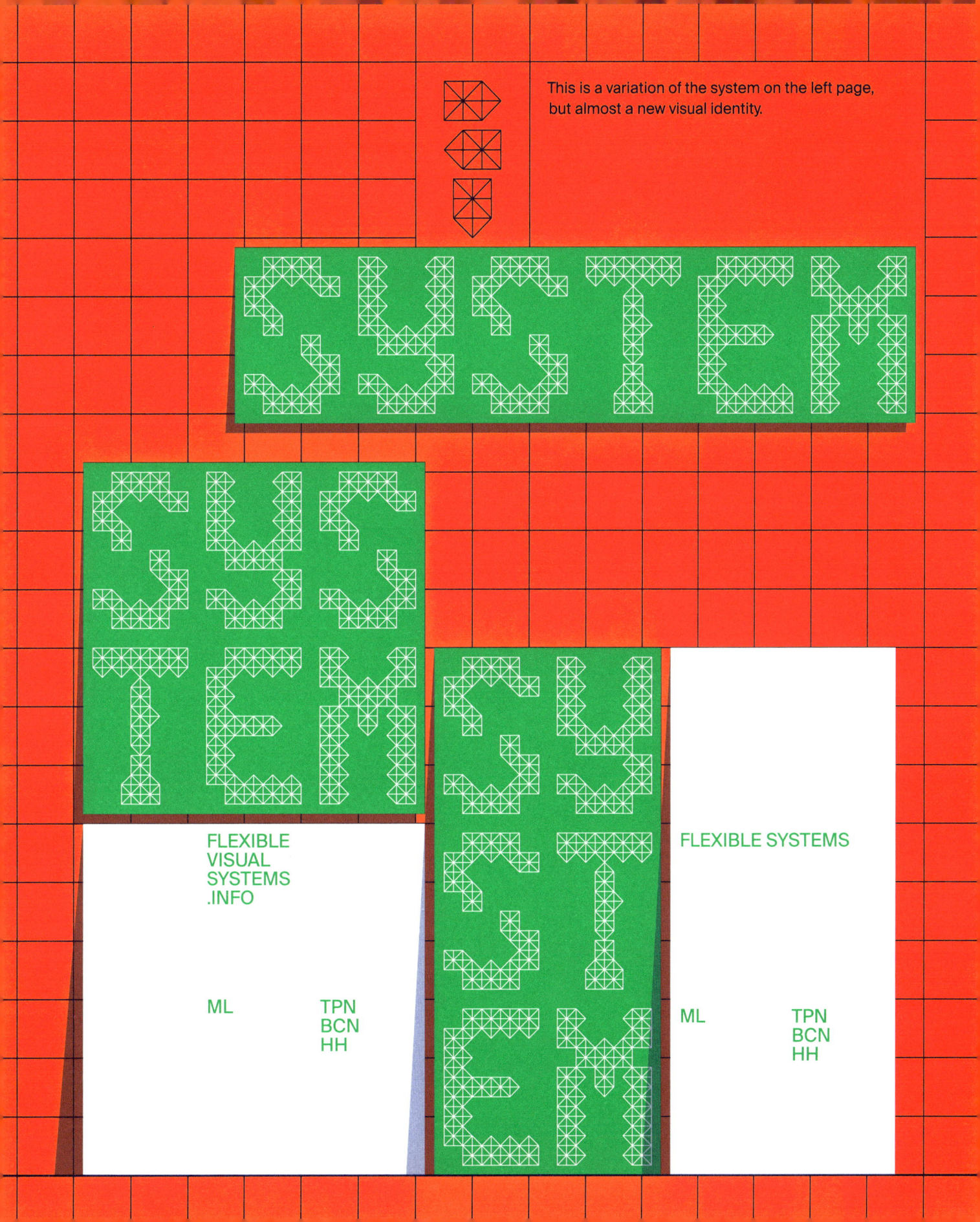

ML   TPN
      BCN
      HH

FLEXIBLE SYSTEMS

ML   TPN
      BCN
      HH

Form: Hexagon (made with right triangles)

Part 1

Form:
Asset:

Form-based FVS

Hexagon
Symbol

A hexagon constructed with eight triangles is the starting point. Removing triangles allows me create unique basic elements,

which can be duplicated or

mirrored over one axis or

two axes.

The examples on this page were drawn with a hexagon made of triangles.

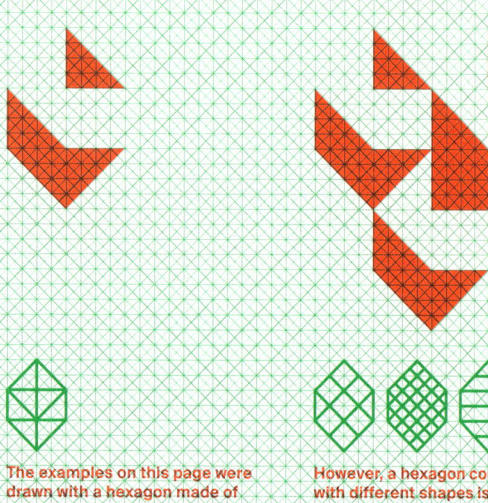

However, a hexagon constructed with different shapes is possible too and would obtain other results.

Part 1

Form:
Asset:

Form-based FVS

Hexagon
Symbol

Fragmented components, rearranged and rotated to obtain more variations.

Duplicated over one axis and rotated.

Duplicated, mirrored over one axis and rotated.

Duplicated, mirrored over two axes and rotated.

Rearrangement

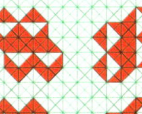

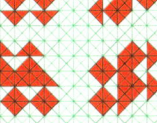

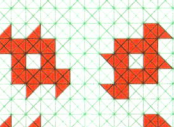

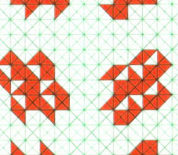

Repetition / Rotation

Mirroring over one axis

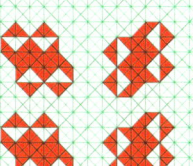

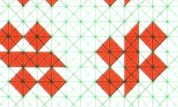

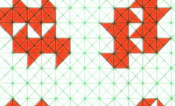

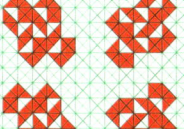

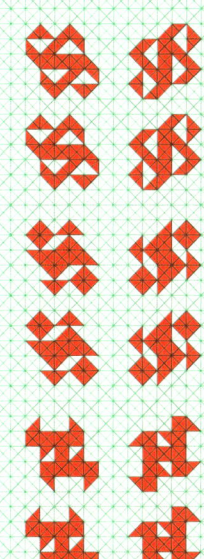

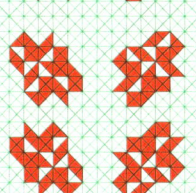

Mirroring over two axes

Elements have been deleted from the pattern in the first row to create new, lighter patterns

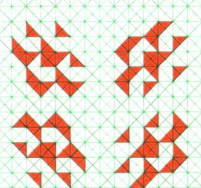

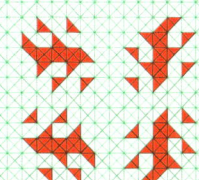

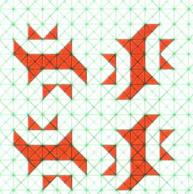

● Lighter patterns can be used in infographics or cartographies to show lower values.

Part 1

Form:
Asset:

Form-based FVS

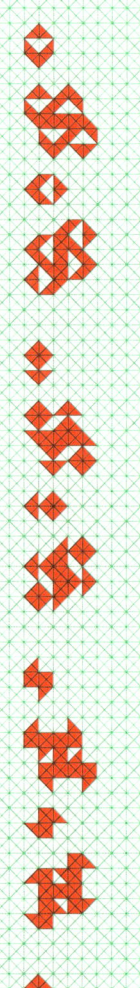

Hexagon
Line

Component

Repetition / Rotation

Part 1

Form:
Asset:

Form-based FVS

Hexagon
Frame

A hexagon constructed with eight triangles is the starting point. Removing triangles to create different patterns.

Duplicating the hexagon twice and then rotating it ...

... to fill gaps in lines.

It is easier for hexagonal shapes to draw diagonal lines than it is for square shapes.

Frame made with one element

Line made with two elements

Line made with one element

Colored elements

Corner and connecting elements

Frame made with one element

Line made with two elements

Line made with one element

Part 1

Form:
Asset:

Form-based FVS

Hexagon
Label

Hexagon as component

Mirrored over two axes

Part 1 **Form-based FVS**

Form: Hexagon
Application: on 12 Formats

Repetition of the assets

Vertical repetition and horizontal distortion of the assets

Horizontal repetition and vertical distortion of the assets

Horizontal and vertical distortion of the assets

Part 1   **Form-based FVS**

Form: **Hexagon**
Asset: **Letters**

Construction

Corner, connection, and center elements

Monospaced 3×5 modules

Construction

Corner, connection, and center elements

Construction

Corner, connection, and center elements

Part 1

Form: Hexagon
Asset: Letters

Form-based FVS

Corner, connection and center elements

2×5 modules   3×5 modules   4×5 modules   8×5 modules

TPN	FLEXIBLE VISUAL SYSTEMS .INFO	TPN	FLEXIBLE VISUAL SYSTEMS .INFO
HH BCN	ML	HH BCN	ML

1. Take an assembled shape.
2. Color each element of the assembled shape differently.
3. Position the shape in the middle, left, or right of the format.
4. Add texts and/or images below or besides to the shapes.

TPN   HH BCN

FLEXIBLE
VISUAL
SYSTEMS
.INFO

TPN   HH BCN

FLEXIBLE
VISUAL
SYSTEMS
.INFO

HH BCN   ML

FLEXIBLE VISUAL SYSTEMS

FLEXIBLE VISUALSYSTEMS .INFO

ML
TPN
HH BCN

FLEXIBLE VISUAL SYSTEMSS

1. Take an assembled shape.
2. Duplicate it to create lines.
3. Insert text and / or images in the spaces between the lines.
4. Color the lines, texts, images and / or backgrounds.

TEXT

SYSTEM

F
S

FLEXIBLE VISUAL SYSTEMS

FLEXIBLEVISUAL SYSTEMS .INFO

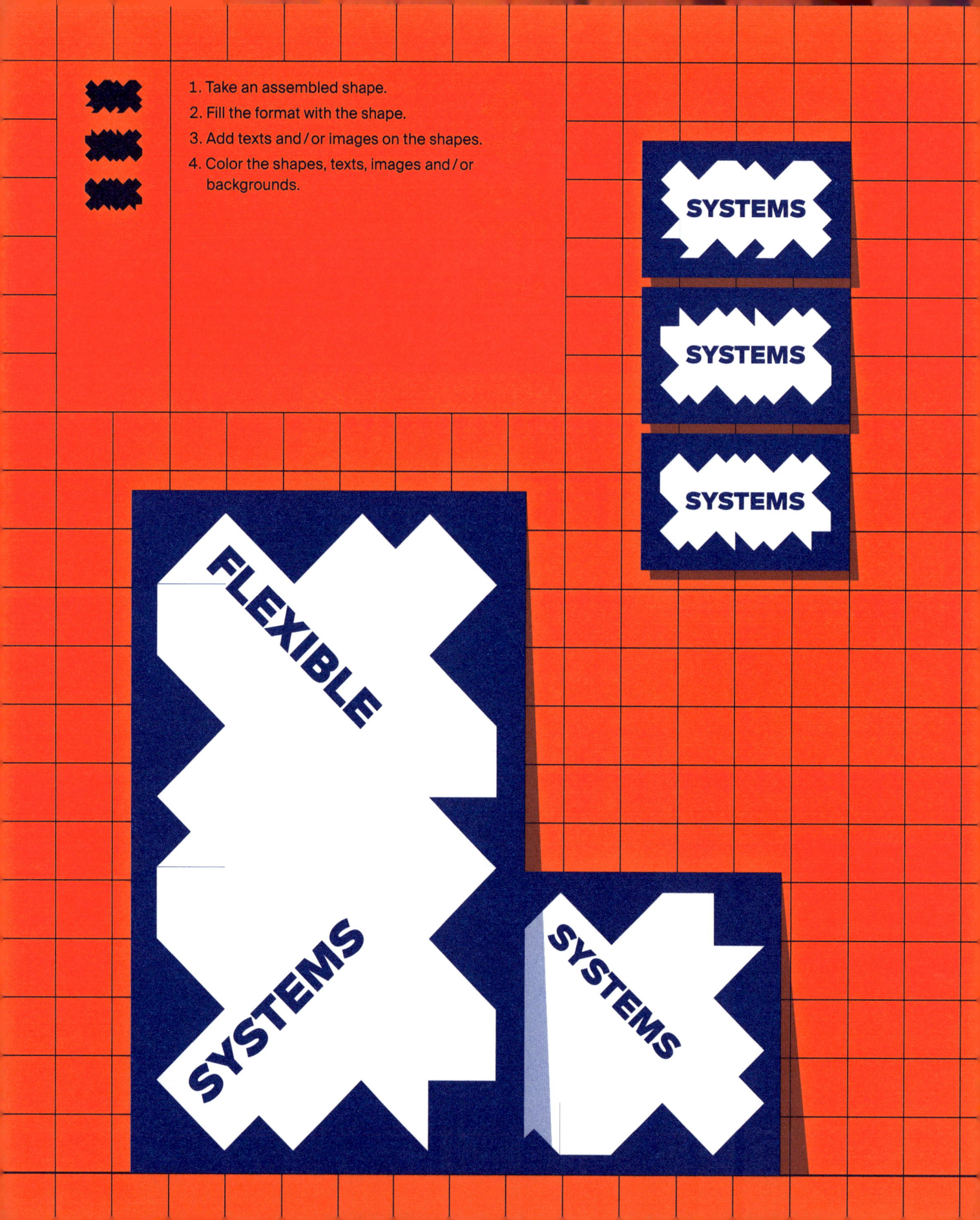

1. Take an assembled shape.
2. Fill the format with the shape.
3. Add texts and/or images on the shapes.
4. Color the shapes, texts, images and/or backgrounds.

SYSTEMS

SYSTEMS

SYSTEMS

FLEXIBLE SYSTEMS

SYSTEMS

1. Take an assembled shape.
2. Duplicate it.
3. Stretch it.
4. Put all the variations together.
5. Color the pattern.
6. Add texts and/or images to the empty areas.

FLEXIBLE
VISUAL
SYSTEMS

.INFO

FLEXIBLE
VISUAL
SYSTEMS

TPN
HH BCN

.INFO   ML

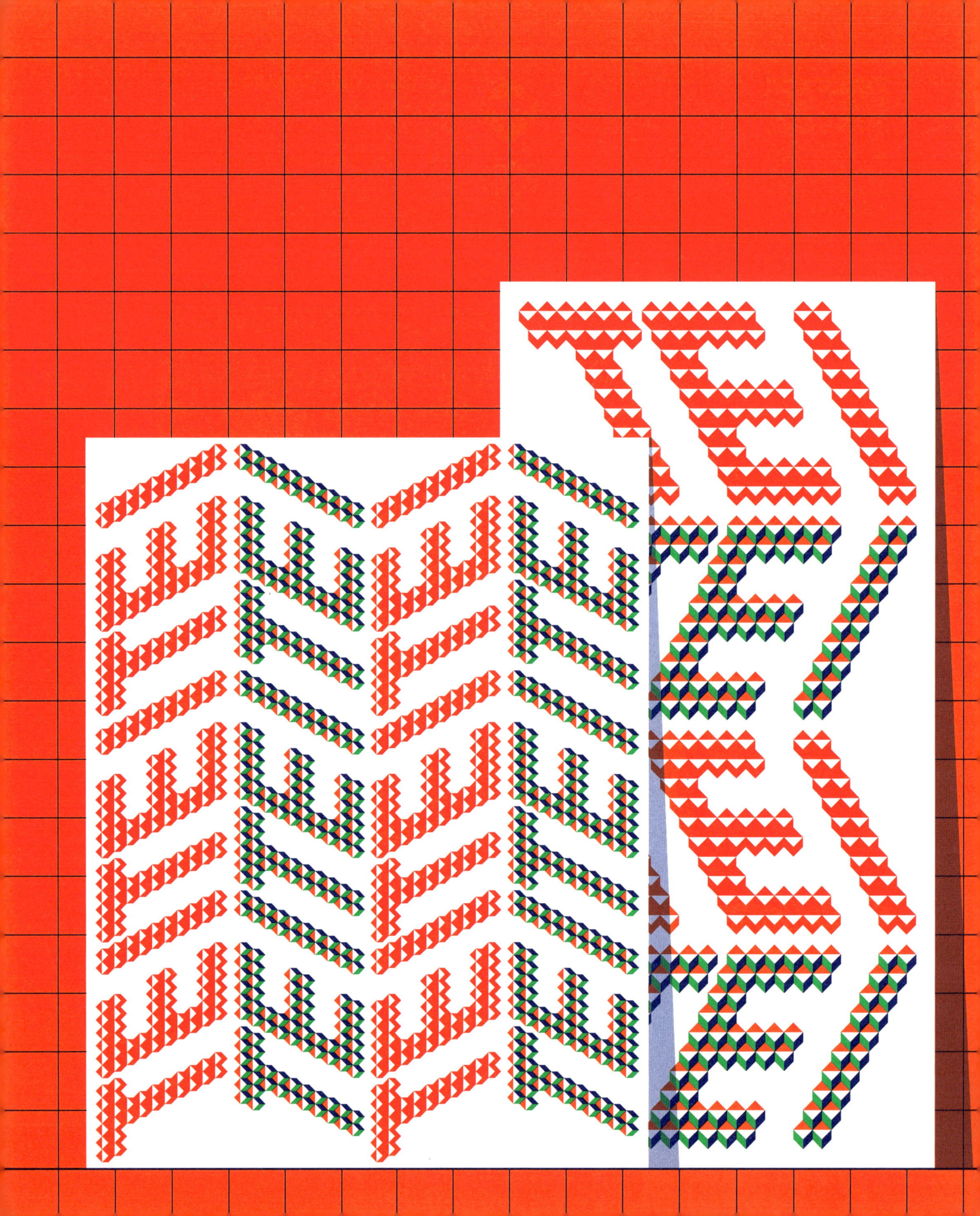

1. Take an assembled shape.
2. Design letters with the shape.
3. Fill the format with letters.
4. Add texts and / or images in the empty areas.
5. Color the letters, texts, images and / or backgrounds.

Form: Hexagon (made with acute triangles)

Part 1

Form:
Asset:

Form-based FVS

Hexagon
Symbol

A hexagon that was constructed from six triangles is the initial shape. Triangles are deleted in order to obtain new shapes.

The hexagon is duplicated over two axes,

mirrored over one axis and

mirrored over two axes.

Part 1

Form: Hexagon
Asset: Symbol

Form-based FVS

A hexagon with four from six triangles.

The hexagon is duplicated over two axes,

mirrored over one axis and

mirrored over two axes.

Rearrangement

Repetition, mirroring, rotation

Mirroring over one axis

Mirroring over 2 axes

Elements have been deleted from the pattern in the first row to create new, lighter patterns.

Part 1

Form:
Asset:

Form-based FVS

Hexagon
Line

A hexagon that was constructed from six triangles is the initial shape. Triangles are deleted in order to obtain new shapes.

The hexagon is duplicated over two axes,

mirrored over one axis and

mirrored over two axes.

Part 1

Form:
Asset:

Form-based FVS

Hexagon
Frame and Line

A hexagon that was constructed from six triangles is the initial shape. Triangles are deleted in order to obtain new shapes.

The hexagon is duplicated twice.

Corner and connecting parts.

It is easier for hexagonal shapes than square shapes to create diagonals, but they have the disadvantage that horizontal and vertical lines have different thicknesses.

Frame made from corner and connecting parts.

Line from two parts

Line from one part

Colored parts

Corner and connecting parts

Frame made from corner and connecting parts.

Line of connecting parts

Line made of corner parts

Part 1　　　　　　　　Form-based FVS

Form:　　　　　　　　Hexagon
Asset:　　　　　　　　 Label

A hexagon made of triangles.　　duplicated over two axes,　　mirrored over one axis and　　mirrored over two axes.

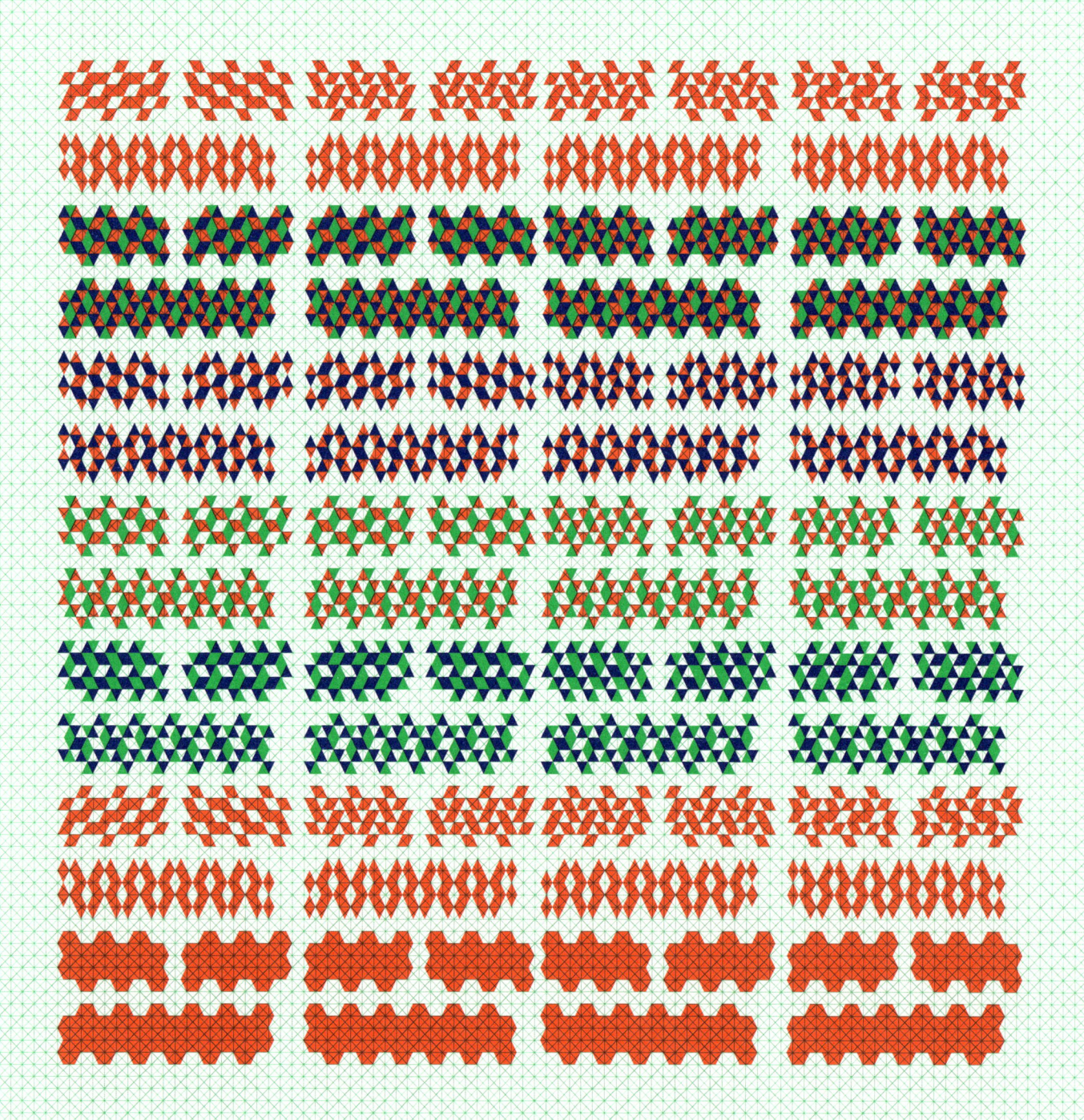

Part 1　　　　　　　　**Form-based FVS**

Form:　　　　　　　　**Hexagon**
Application:　　　　　**on 12 Formats**

Repetition of the assets　　　　　　　　　**Vertical repetition and horizontal distortion of the assets**

Horizontal repetition and vertical distortion of the assets　　**Horizontal and vertical distortion of the assets**

Part 1

Form:
Asset:

Form-based FVS

Hexagon
Letters

Construction scheme

• It is easier to compose diagonals with hexagonal shapes than horizontal or vertical lines.

Construction scheme

Construction scheme

Construction scheme

Construction scheme

Construction scheme

Part 1

Form: Hexagon
Asset: Letters

Form-based FVS

Construction scheme

Construction scheme

Construction scheme

Construction scheme

Construction scheme

Construction scheme

1. Take an assembled shape.
2. Fill in the format with the shape.
3. Add text and / or images in the shapes or in the empty spaces around the shapes.
4. Color the shapes, texts, images and / or backgrounds.

S

SYSTEM

FLEXIBLE
SYSTEMS

ML TPN HH BCN
FLEXIBLEVISUALSYSTEMS.INFO

FLEXIBLE VISUAL SYSTEMS

ML TPN
HH BCN

FLEXIBLEVISUAL
SYSTEMS.INFO

SYSTEM

FLEXIBLE SYSTEMS

ML TPN HH BCN
FLEXIBLEVISUALSYSTEMS.IN

FLEXIBLE VISUAL SYSTEMS   ML TPN HH BCN   FLEXIBLEVISUAL SYSTEMS.INFO

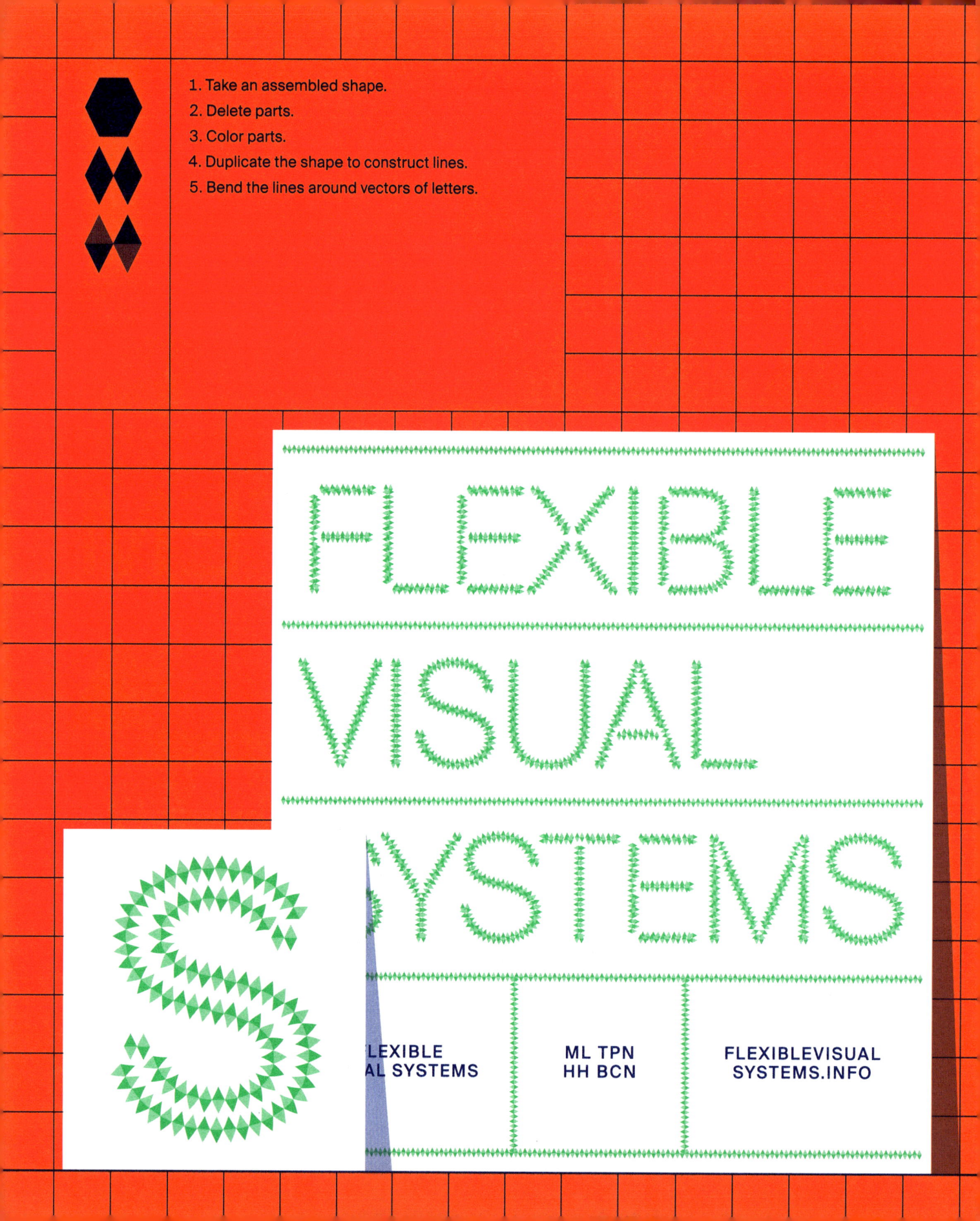

1. Take an assembled shape.
2. Delete parts.
3. Color parts.
4. Duplicate the shape to construct lines.
5. Bend the lines around vectors of letters.

FLEXIBLE VISUAL SYSTEMS

FLEXIBLE ML TPN FLEXIBLEVISUAL
VISUAL SYSTEMS HH BCN SYSTEMS.INFO

FLEXIBLE VISUAL SYSTEMS

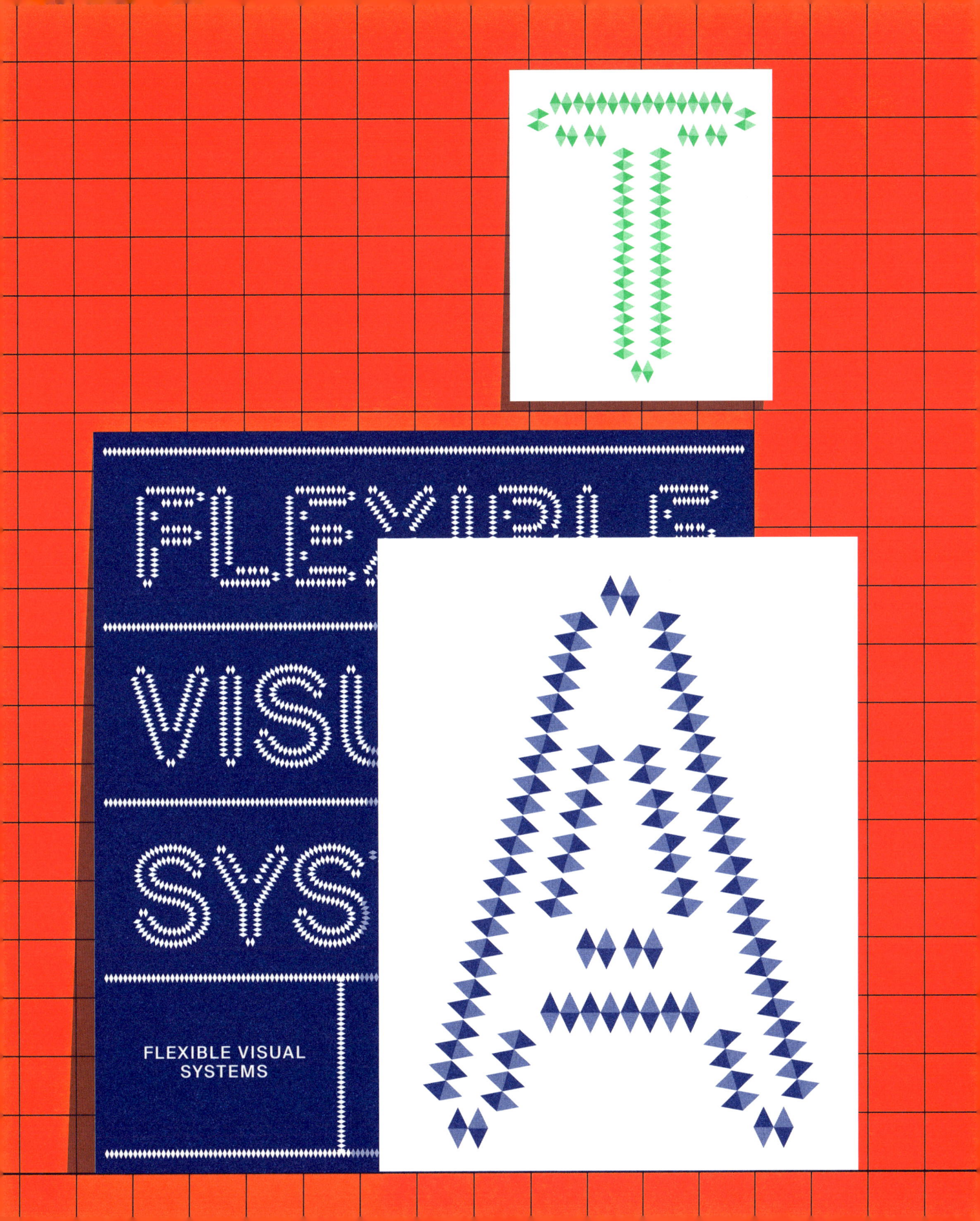

1. Take an assembled shape.
2. Duplicate and mirror it.
3. Combine the variations as you like.
4. Add texts and / or images. Skew them so they appear to be three-dimensional.

FLEXIBLE VISUAL SYSTEMS

ML TPN HH BCN

FLEXIBLE VISUAL SYSTEMS .INFO

ML TPN HH BCN

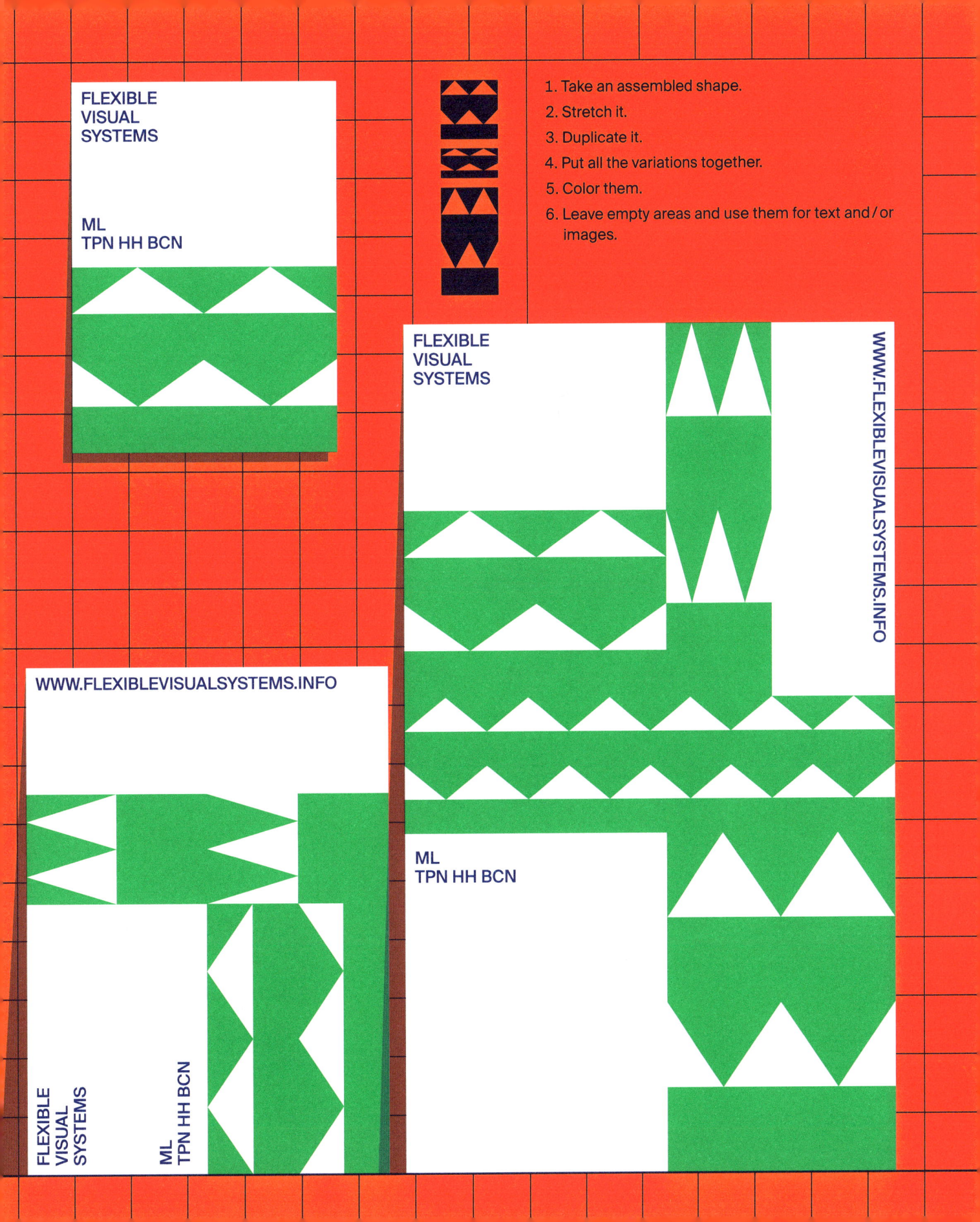

FLEXIBLE
VISUAL
SYSTEMS

ML
TPN HH BCN

1. Take an assembled shape.
2. Stretch it.
3. Duplicate it.
4. Put all the variations together.
5. Color them.
6. Leave empty areas and use them for text and / or images.

FLEXIBLE
VISUAL
SYSTEMS

WWW.FLEXIBLEVISUALSYSTEMS.INFO

ML
TPN HH BCN

WWW.FLEXIBLEVISUALSYSTEMS.INFO

FLEXIBLE
VISUAL
SYSTEMS

ML
TPN HH BCN

1. Take an assembled shape.
2. Change the brightness of the fragments.
3. Construct letters.
4. Fill in the format with the letters.
5. Use the empty spaces to add texts and / or images.
6. Color the letters, texts, images and / or backgrounds.

FLEXIBLE
SYSTEMS

ML
TPN HH BCN

WWW.FLEXIBLEVISUALSYSTEMS.INFO

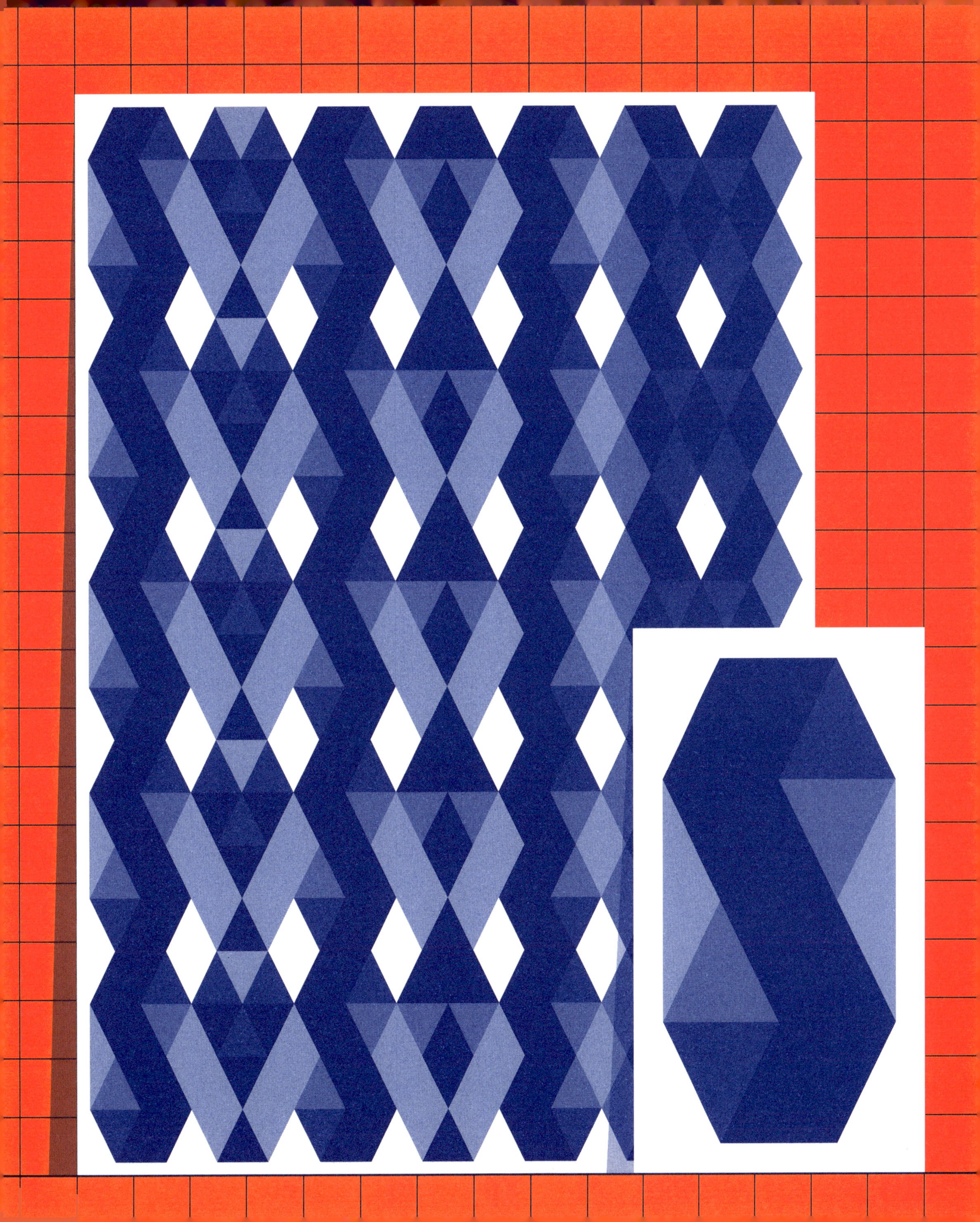

FVS:
OBJECT-BASED

FVS:
INTERACTION-BASED

Part 1   **Platonic solids**

	Tetrahedron	Hexahedron	Octahedron	Dodecahedron	Icosahedron
Body mesh	Equilateral triangles	Squares	Equilateral triangles	Regular pentagons	Equilateral triangles
Frontal view on corner					
Frontal view on edge					
Frontal view on side					

OBJECT-BASED
FLEXIBLE VISUAL SYSTEMS

The examples on these spreads show how applications can arise from three-dimensional objects, for example a three-dimensional logo, sculpture, product, building, or structure for small or big surfaces.

With a few exceptions, like packaging, three-dimensional design hasn't been the typical task for a communication designer of the last decades. But that has changed recently for two main reasons. The demand for (3D) animations in social media has increased as they attract more attention and because the difficulty to use professional (3D) motion design software has decreased. Apart from that the hardware, able to manage 3D software has become affordable. New opportunities create new needs.

New opportunities not only create new needs, new needs can also create new opportunities. It is quite conceivable that three-dimensional design by communication designers will not remain in social networks and thus in the virtual world, but will penetrate into physical space. The new applications do not have to be physical per se. Augmented Reality could, for example, take over many applications of communication design in space. Target group-specific information or advertising, temporary lettering in space or three-dimensional narration for publications are just a few examples. Just as moving design is natural in moving media, three-dimensional design will be natural in three-dimensional space.

Another interesting new field for communication designers might become three-dimensional transformative systems. We can see today the beginnings of it in the form of face-filters on social media. While today it might look like a game or an attempt to trick the audience, it is an attempt to construct an alternative identity, which could benefit the communication. This identity is built on a distortion of reality, which might sound wrong, but in my opinion, offers a lot of opportunities. How often communication does not happen because of the prejudices of the persons communicating. Superficial characteristics, such as skin color, might taint the information that should be communicated. Choosing a custom identity that minimizes the noise would help to improve communication. Also, the built identity becomes the identity for more than one individual. It can become the identity for a group of persons or even no person at all, it can become the representation of an idea.

Part 1 3D Symbols, Objects and Structures

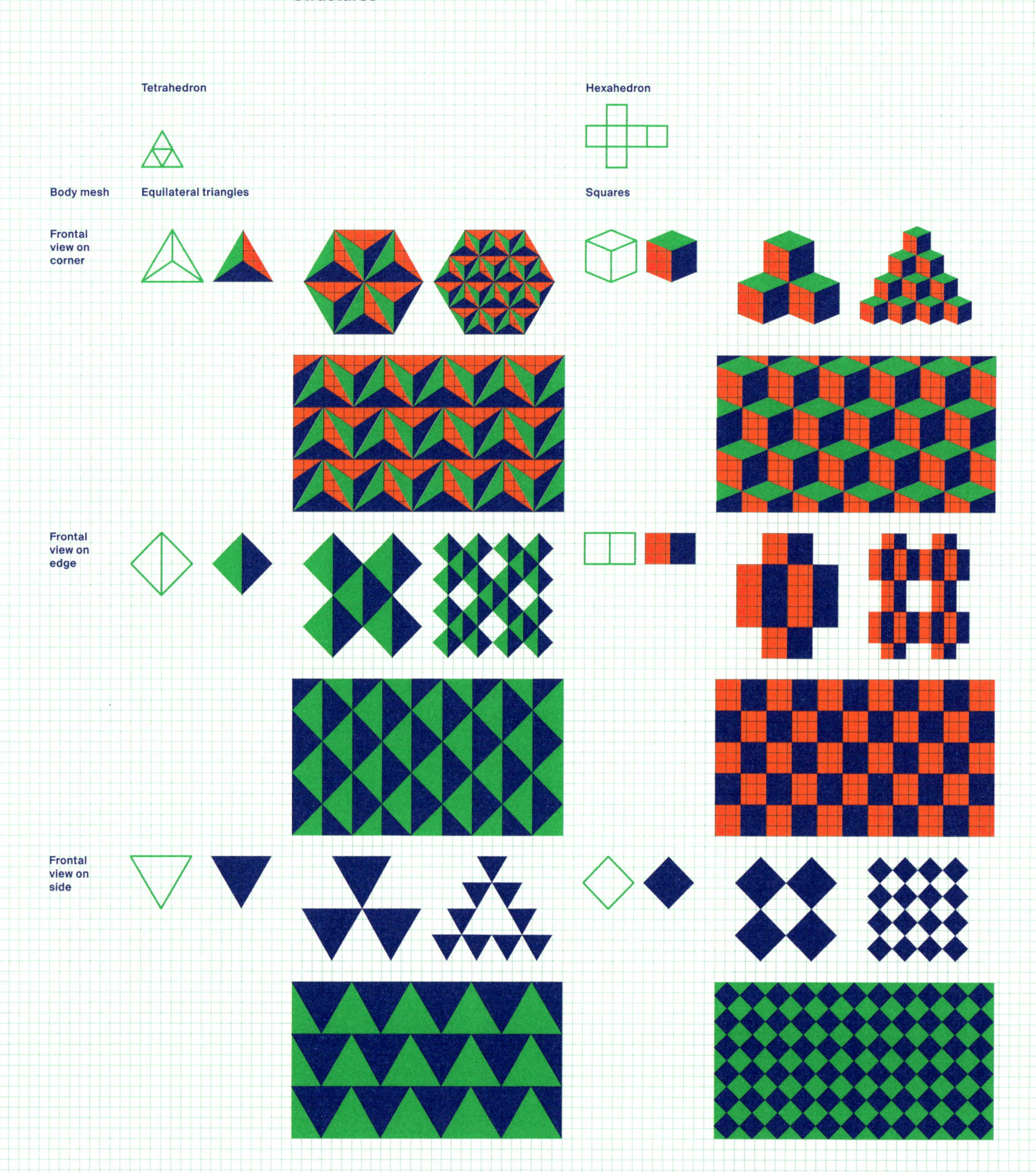

Tetrahedron

Hexahedron

Body mesh Equilateral triangles

Squares

Frontal view on corner

Frontal view on edge

Frontal view on side

Part 1

3D Symbols, Objects and Structures

Octahedron

Dodecahedron

Body mesh — Equilateral triangles / Regular pentagons

Frontal view on corner

Frontal view on edge

Frontal view on side

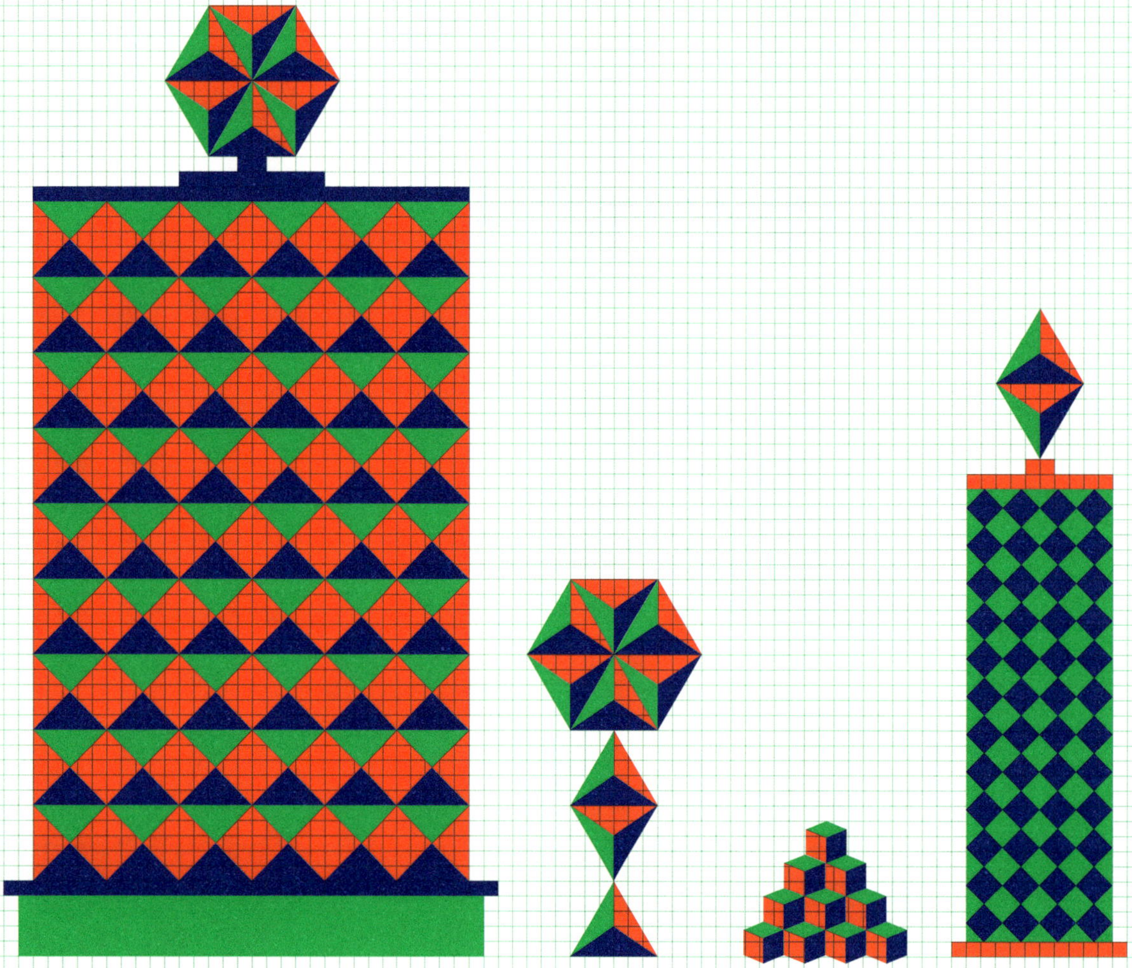

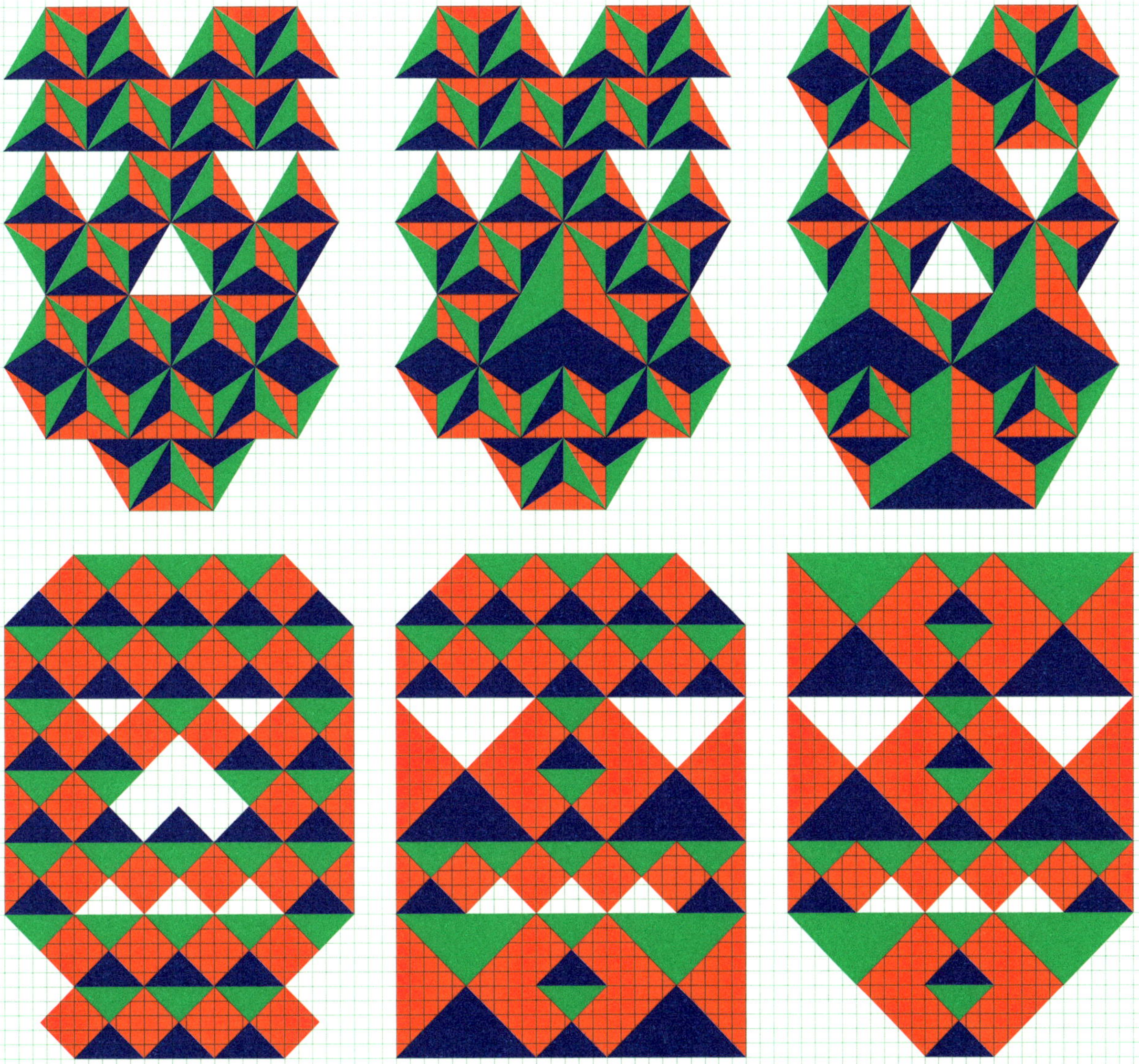

INTERACTION-BASED FLEXIBLE VISUAL SYSTEMS

All of the visual systems on the previous pages work with geometric shapes as identification elements. Combining different shapes gives you even more opportunities. Not just the mere mix of shapes is interesting, but also how they are combined and how they interact with each other.

     A system based on the interaction of shapes is a transitional type between form-based and transformative visual systems. It is often based on specific shapes, but the identification happens through the way they interact. How can shapes interact with each other? Materials can be transparent, translucent, or opaque. They can have a color which, when translucent, mixes with the color below. Depending on the design program, the range of interactive properties can be even augmented. Shapes can be united, intersected, excluded, multiplied, subtracted, they can darken or lighten the shape they are interacting with. Any mathematical transformation imaginable between two or more sets of data is possible. On the following spreads I am just illustrating one of the many possibilities. The illustrated solution is one of the most frequently used in flexible visual identities.

Mixed Type

Transformation:
Asset:

Transformed Form

Subtract
Symbol

I demonstrate here the interaction between two-dimensional shapes with circles and squares.

The circle is arranged in a 2×2, 3×3 and 4×4 grid. It is assigned a color.

The square is arranged in a 2×2, 3×3 and 4×4 grid.

The square elements are substracted from the circle elements.

Basic elements

Subtracted elements

Mixed Type   **Transformed Form**

Transformation: Multiply
Asset: Symbol

I demonstrate here the interaction between two-dimensional shapes with circles and squares.

The circle is arranged in a 2×2, 3×3 and 4×4 grid. It is assigned a color.

The square is arranged in a 2×2, 3×3 and 4×4 grid.

The square elements are added to the circle elements.

Basic elements

Multiplied elements

Mixed Type

Transformation: Asset:

Transformed Form

Interaction Line

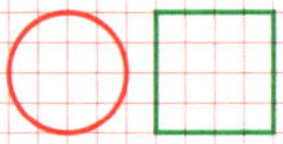

Components

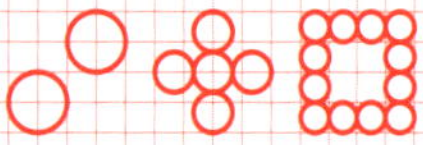

Circle elements

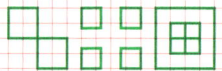

Square elements

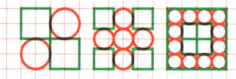

Combination

Subtract

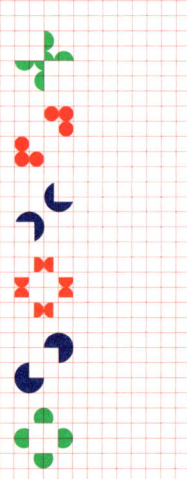

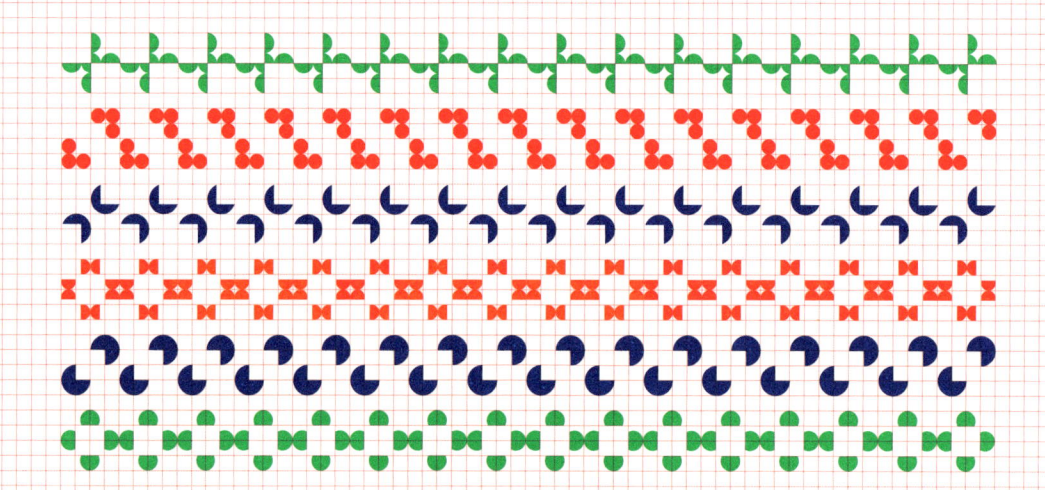

Multiply

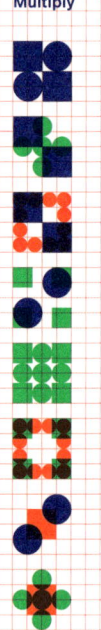

Mixed Type

Transformation: **Interaction**
Asset: **Frame**

Transformed Form

Components

Circle elements

Square elements

Combination

Basic element

Frame

Basic element

Frame

Basic element

Frame

Subtract

Multiply

Mixed Type **Transformed Form**

Transformation: Interaction
Asset: Letters

Basic elements

3×9 modules

3×7 modules

3×7 modules

3×… modules

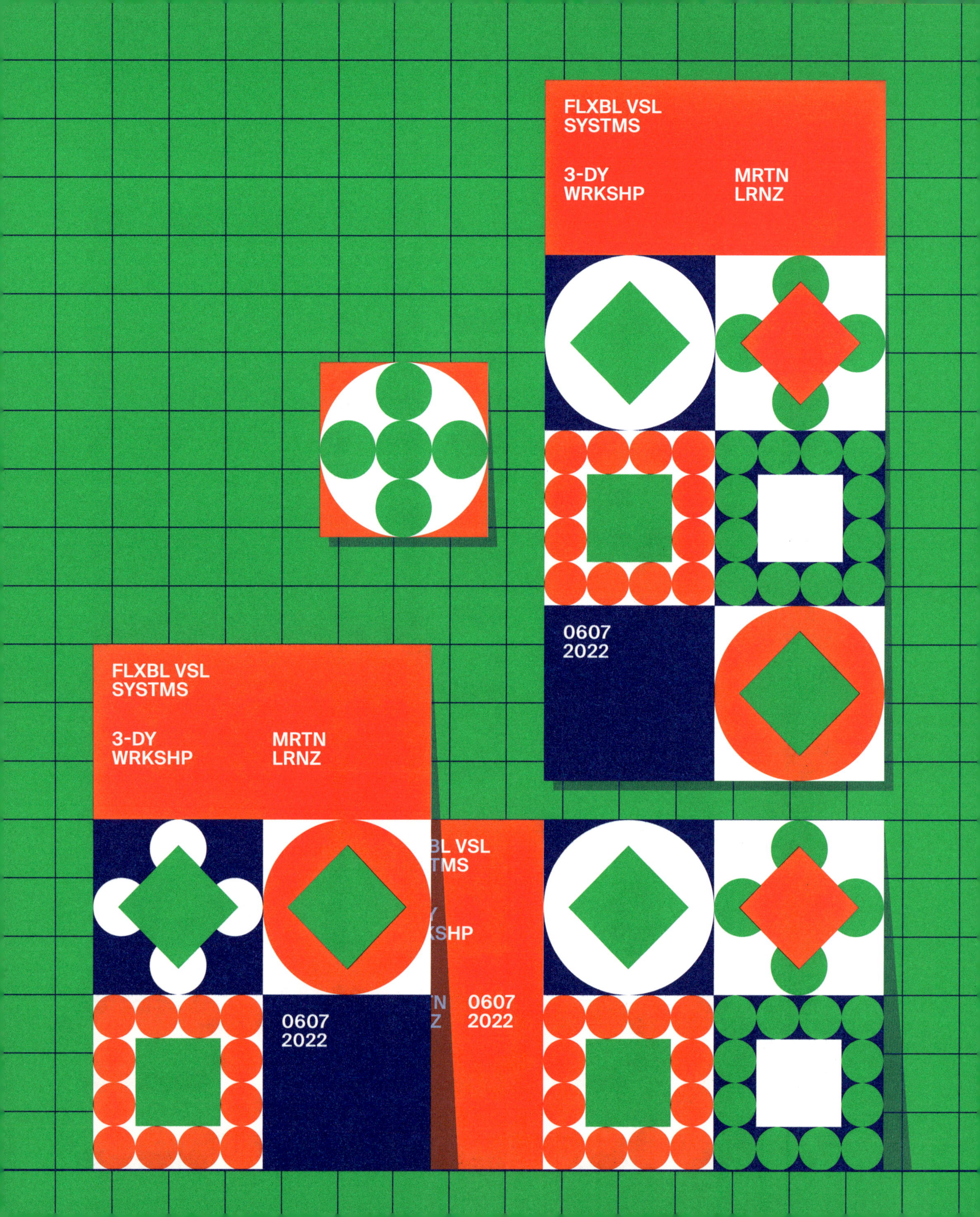

FLXBL VSL
SYSTMS
3-DY
WRKSHP
MRTN
LRNZ
0607
2022
FLXBL VSL
SYSTMS
3-DY
WRKSHP
MRTN
LRNZ
0607
2022
0607
2022

FLXBL VSL
SYSTMS

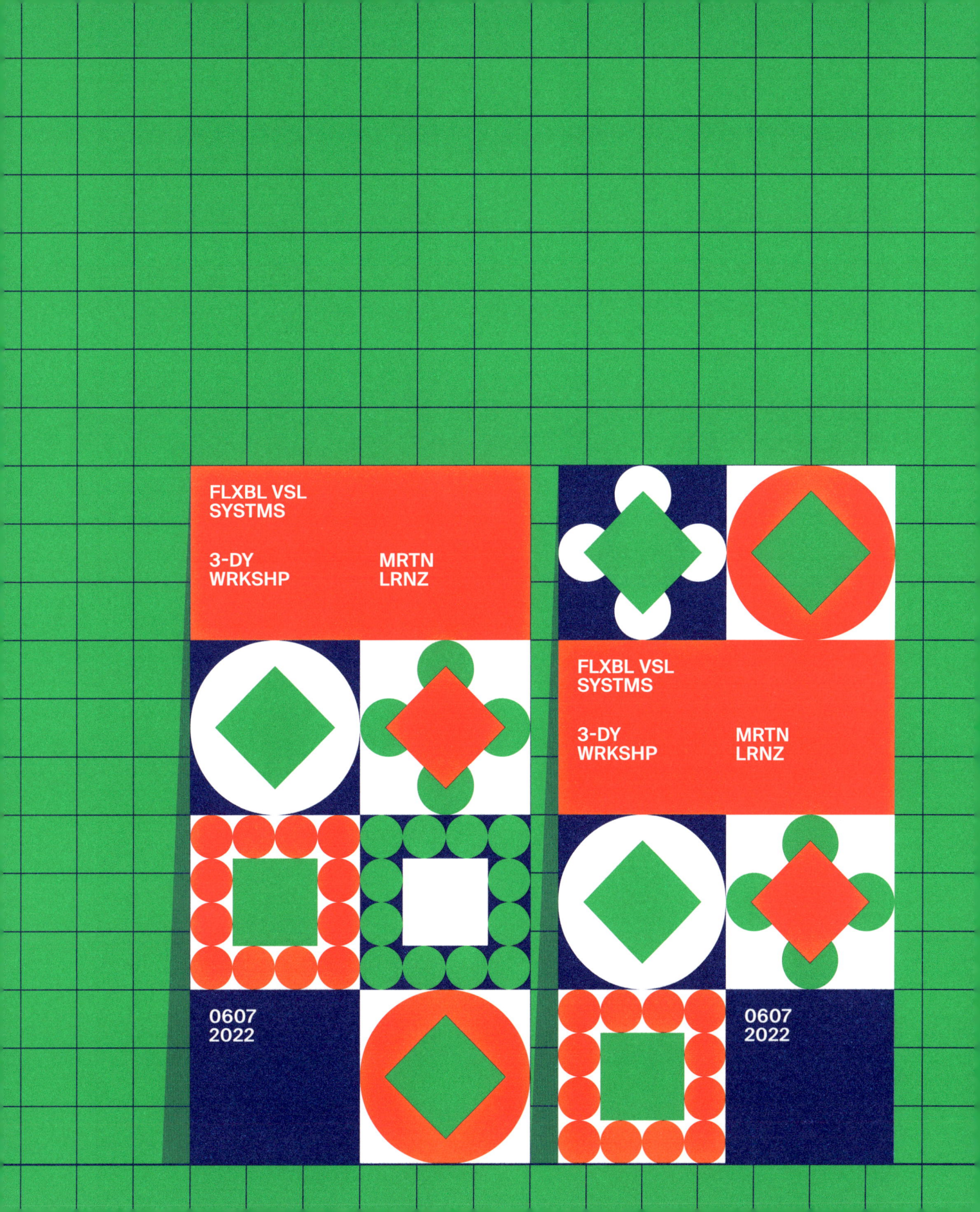

3-DY   MRTN
WRKSHP   LRNZ

FLXBL VSL
SYSTMS

3-DY   MRTN
WRKSHP   LRNZ

0607
2022

0607
2022

FVS:
TRANSFORMATION-BASED

TRANSFORMATION-BASED FVS

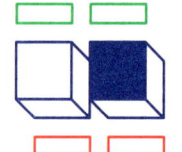

*In reference to format or grid.

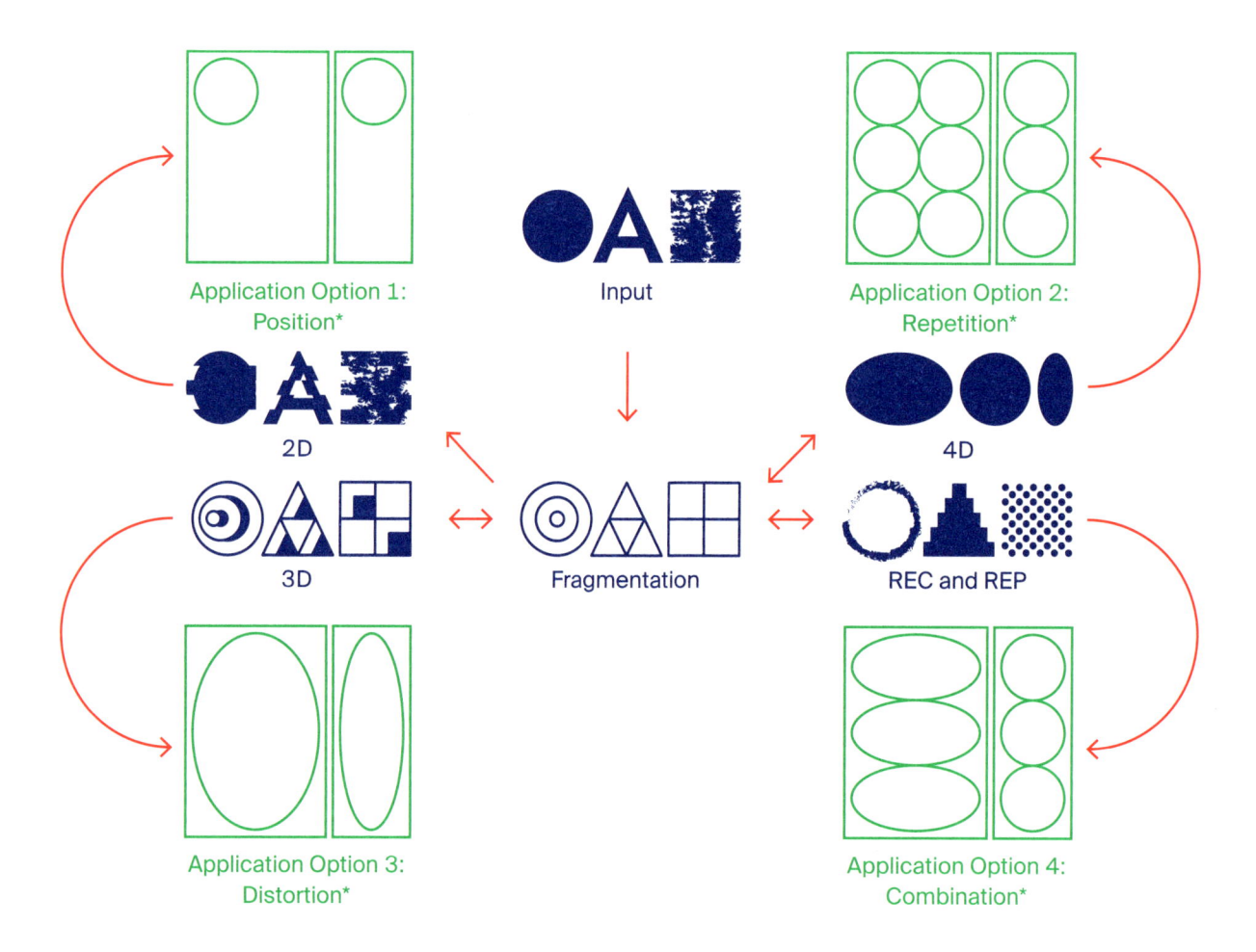

Input

Application Option 1: Position*

2D

3D

Application Option 3: Distortion*

Fragmentation

Application Option 2: Repetition*

4D

REC and REP

Application Option 4: Combination*

TRANSFORMATION-BASED FLEXIBLE VISUAL SYSTEMS

Systems based on transformation can start with a shape too, but they don't need to. A specific production tool can provoke an identifiable transformation. The main idea of a transformation based system is the design of processing too. This example starts with a basic pattern instead of a shape, as in the form-based approach. I use the pattern to cut text, photo, or other material into pieces and then transform by two-, three-, or four-dimensional distortion. A distinguishable recording or reproduction technique can be a transformation process too. At last an application system defines how the produced images are applied to the deliverables.

On the following pages I present approaches to developing flexible visual systems based on transformative processes.

As you have read in the introduction to this book I distinguish between visual systems based on form and visual systems based on transformation. While a system based on form achieves identification through a distinctive form, the system based on transformation becomes recognizable through a distinctive design process.

Where to Start?

Fragmentation: On the following pages I start with a geometric shape like circle, triangle, and square to fragment images. Choosing a shape is not necessary, transformations can be completely seamless, but it helps to make the visual system even more distinctive.

2D: Fragmentation especially helps you with two-dimensional distortion of source material. It is frequently used in graphic design today. The fragmentation is particularly helpful for this type of system. It supports the visibility of the transformation. In addition, the patterns can be used as grids for texts and images.

3D: The three-dimensional transformation contains all possible distortions by objects and space. The source material could be projected onto an object or viewed through a transparent object and thus be distorted, or the source material is an object and generates a large number of different images by recording it from different perspectives. Today there are few examples of three-dimensional transformations in visual identities, but since 3D programs have become standard tools for graphic designers more three-dimensional solutions can be expected in the near future.

4D: For the same reason, more solutions based on the fourth dimension, time, or movement, can be expected soon. Of course, everything can be animated, but in this model 4D stands for a type of transformation that can only arise through time, such as motion blur, aging, or AR filters that create environments that are responsive to time, place, and users and therefore never the same. In this context communication design can learn a lot from game design.

REC and REP, stands for recording and reproduction. The type of recording or reproduction can leave visual traces that change an image, shape, text, or any other input in such a way that it can create recognizability. Think of a photo that you take with the flash or a scan in which you move the item while scanning. The type of recording changes the aesthetics of the source material. Reproduction can also generate recognition. The printing process, the coarse rasterization, the limited choice of colors and the slight misalignment of the colors due to the inaccuracy of the printer can create a recognizable identity. Even drawing is a reproduction of source material. If you always use the same pencil in a certain way, the tool and how you use it will become recognizable.

FVS:
TRANSFORMATION-BASED

The following pages show graphics,
letters, and photos transformed
by gradation, skew, shift, rotation,
repetition, and mirroring.

TRANSFORMATION: GRADATION

236

DIVISION: CIRCLE

237 | Original | Gradation 1 | Gradation 2 | Original | Gradation 1 | Gradation 2

A

B

C

D

A + D

B + C

A + C

B + D

Original	Gradation 1	Gradation 2	Gradation 3	Gradation 4	Gradation 5	
A						A
B						B
C						C
D						D
FLEX IBLE SYS TEME						E
VISU ELLE IDEN TITAT						F
TRANS FOR MATI VE						G
TEXT TEXT TEXT TEXT						H

239

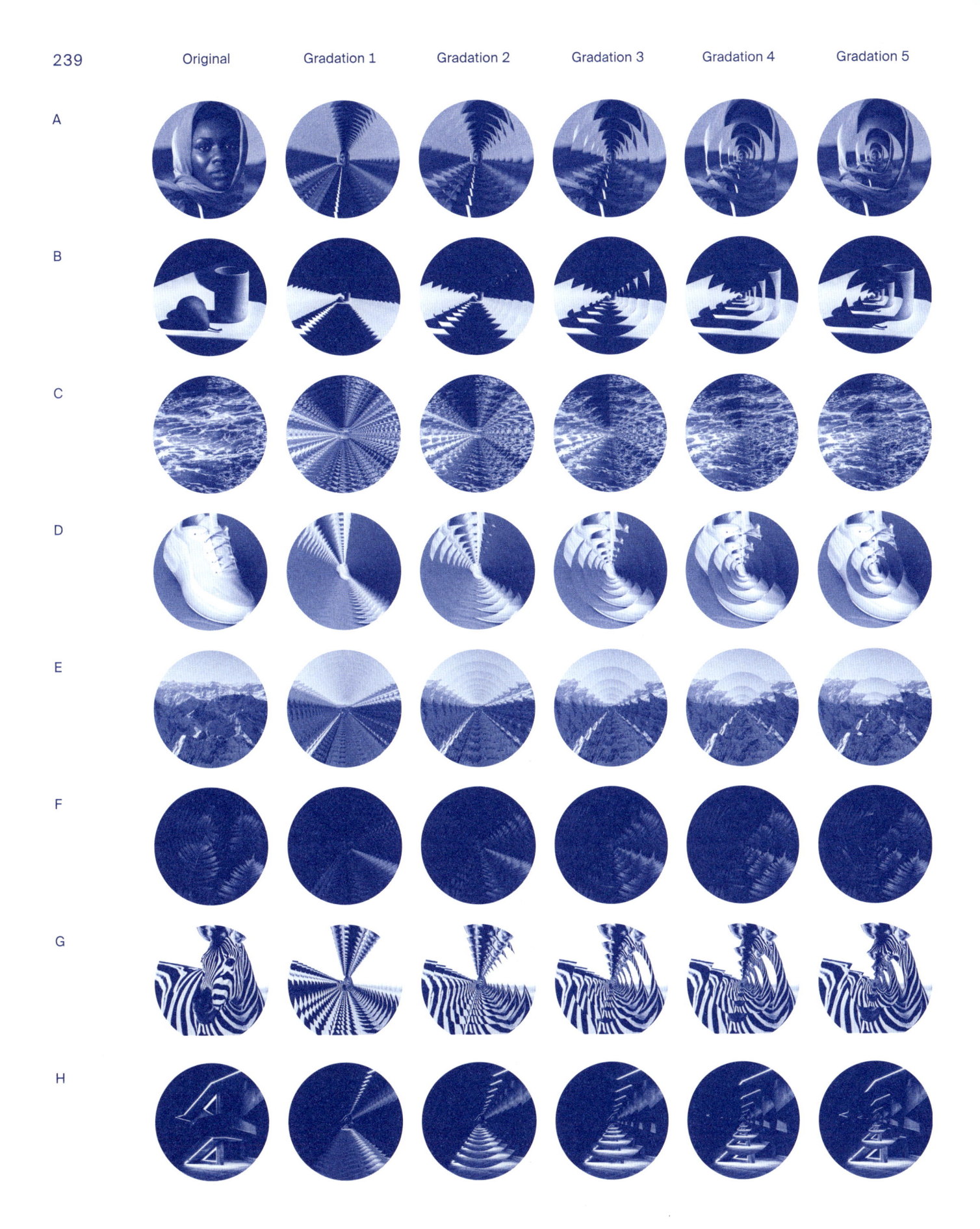

	Original	Gradation 1	Gradation 2	Gradation 3	Gradation 4	Gradation 5
A						
B						
C						
D						
E						
F						
G						
H						

FLEXIBLE
VISUAL
SYSTEMS
.INFO

ML
TPN
HH
BCN

ML
TPN
HH
BCN

FLEXIBLE
VISUAL
SYSTEMS
.INFO

FLEXIBLEVISUALSYSTEMS.INFO

ML
TPN
HH
BCN

FLEXIBLE
VISUAL
SYSTEMS
.INFO

FLEXIBLEVISUALSYSTEMS.INFO

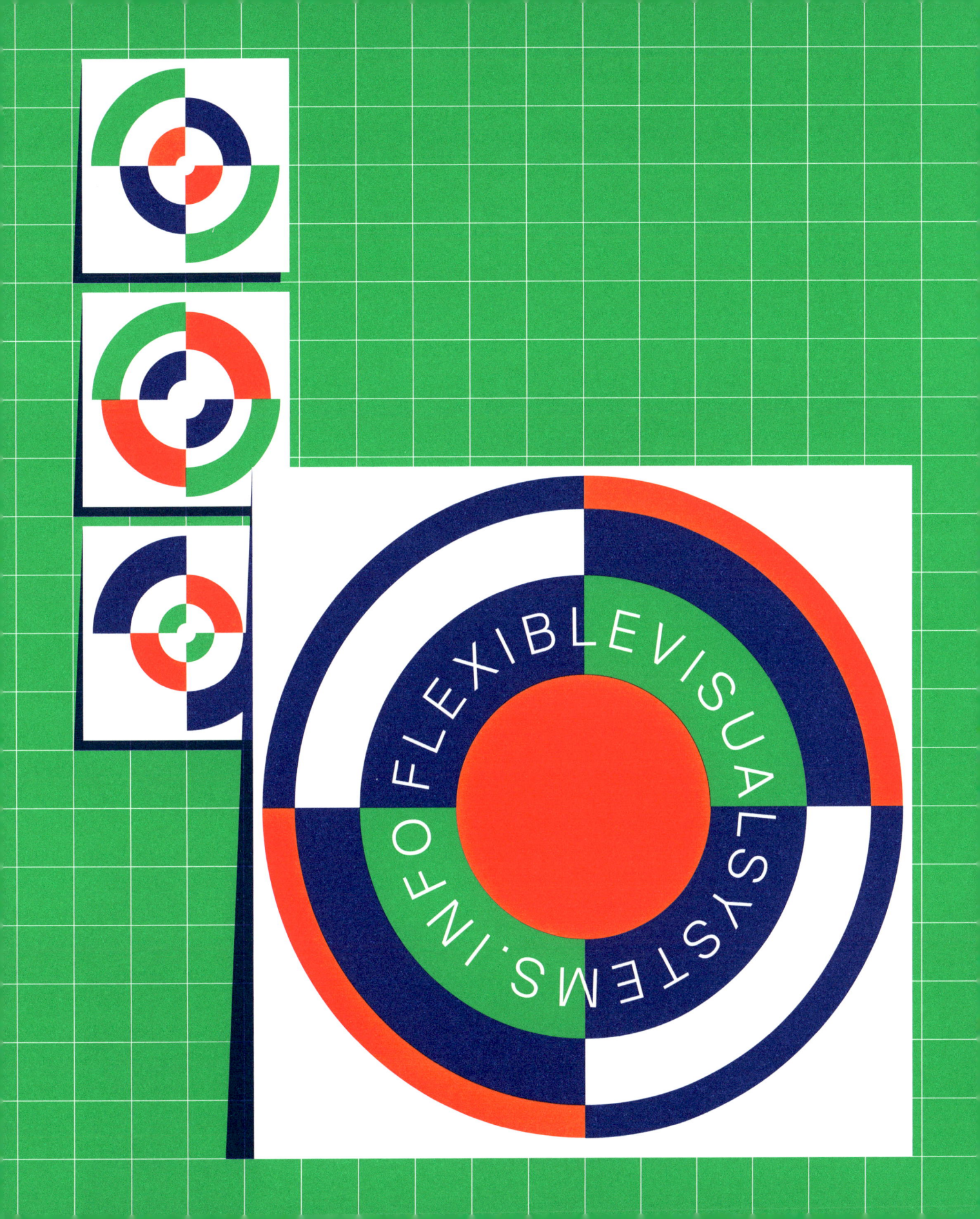

TRANSFORMATION:
ROTATION

242

DIVISION:
CIRCLE

243

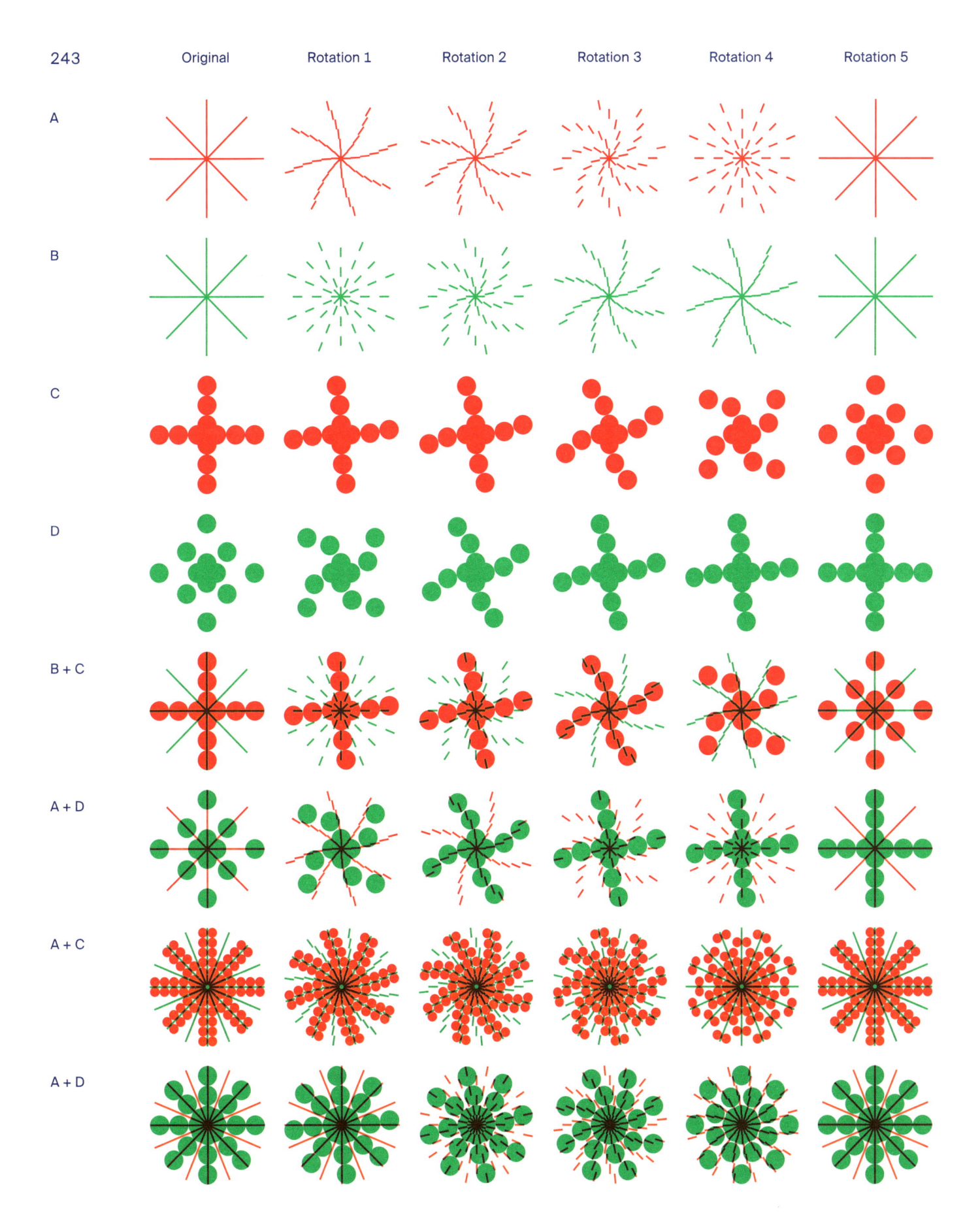

	Original	Rotation 1	Rotation 2	Rotation 3	Rotation 4	Rotation 5
A						
B						
C						
D						
B + C						
A + D						
A + C						
A + D						

	Original	Rotation 1	Rotation 2	Rotation 3	Rotation 4	Rotation 5
A						
B						
C						
D						
E	FLEXIBLE SYSTEME					
F	VISUELLE IDENTITAT					
G	TRANSFORMATIVE					
H	TEXT TEXT TEXT TEXT					

245

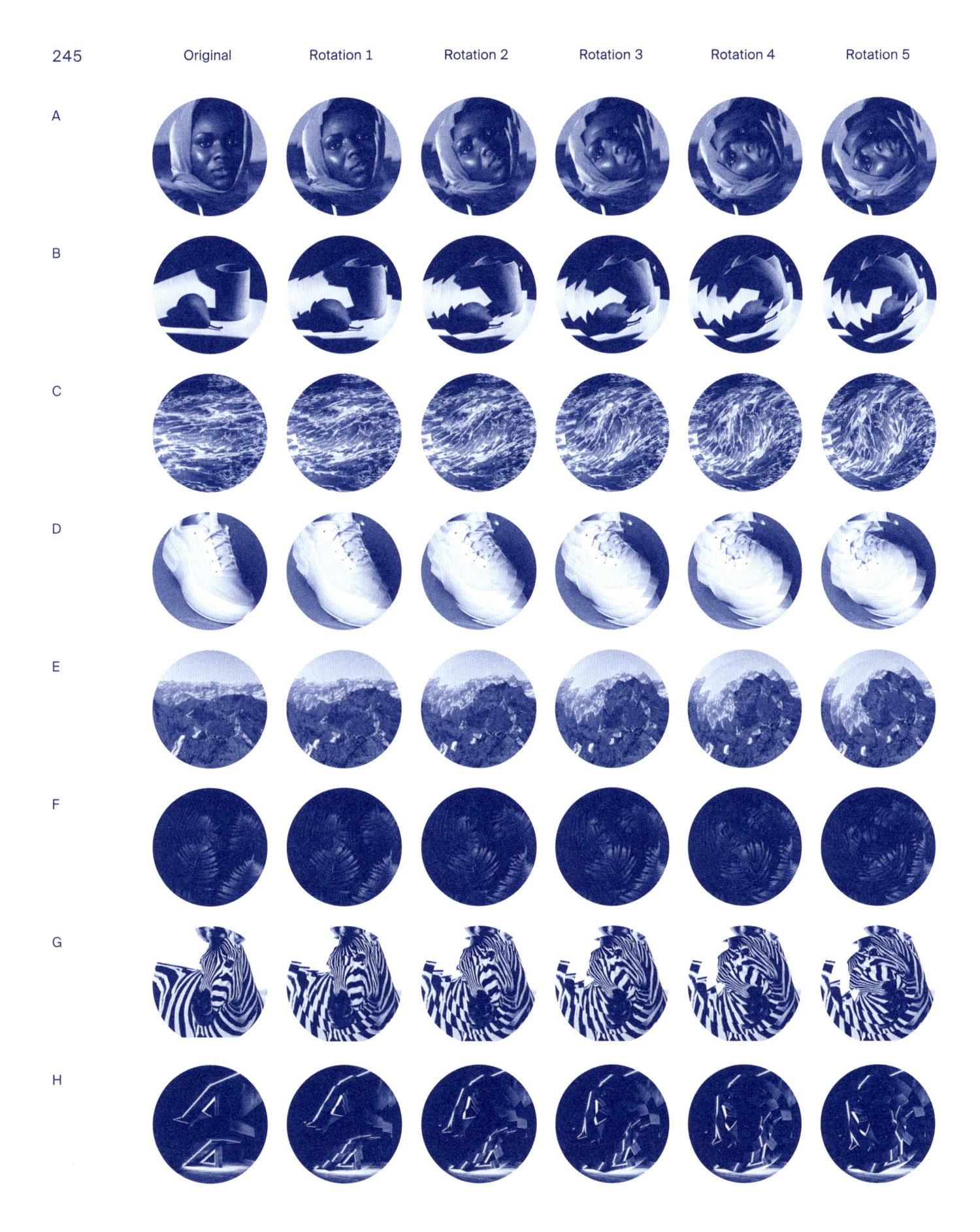

	Original	Rotation 1	Rotation 2	Rotation 3	Rotation 4	Rotation 5
A						
B						
C						
D						
E						
F						
G						
H						

FLEXIBLE
VISUAL
SYSTEMS
.INFO

ML
TPN
HH
BCN

FLEXIBLE
VISUAL
SYSTEMS
.INFO

ML
TPN
HH
BCN

FLEXIBLE
VISUAL
SYSTEMS
.INFO

FLEXIBLE
VISUAL
SYSTEMS
.INFO

FLEXIBLEVISUALSYSTEMS.INFO ML TPN HH BCN

TRANSFORMATION: REPETITION

DIVISION: CIRCLE

249

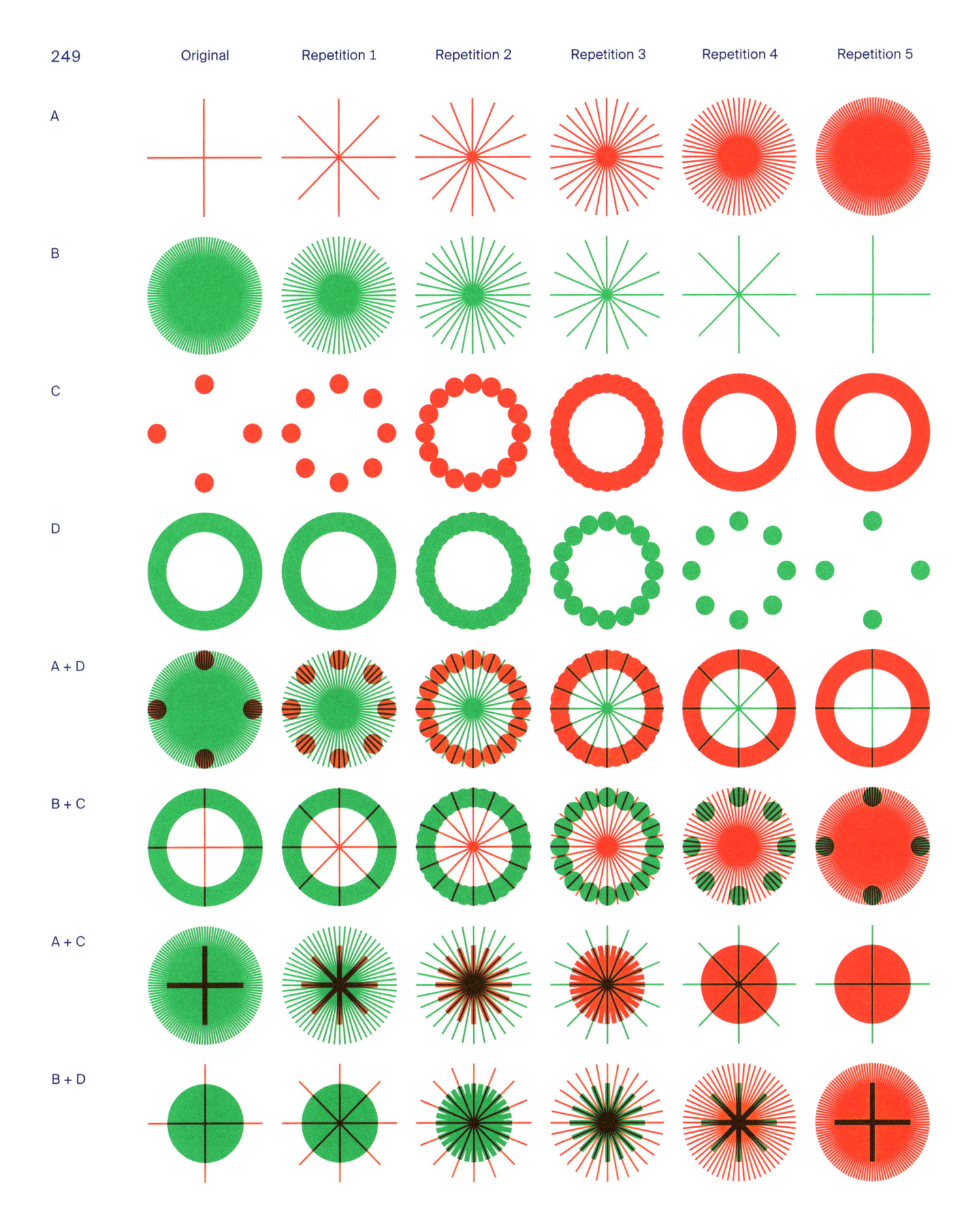

	Original	Repetition 1	Repetition 2	Repetition 3	Repetition 4	Repetition 5
A						
B						
C						
D						
A + D						
B + C						
A + C						
B + D						

Original
Repetition 1
Repetition 2
Repetition 3
Repetition 4
Repetition 5
A
B
C
D
E
F
G
H
FLEX IBLE SYS TEME
VISU ELLE IDEN TITAT
TRAN SFOR MATI VE
TEXT TEXT TEXT TEXT

	Original	Repetition 1	Repetition 2	Repetition 3	Repetition 4	Repetition 5
A						
B						
C						
D						
E						
F						
G						
H						

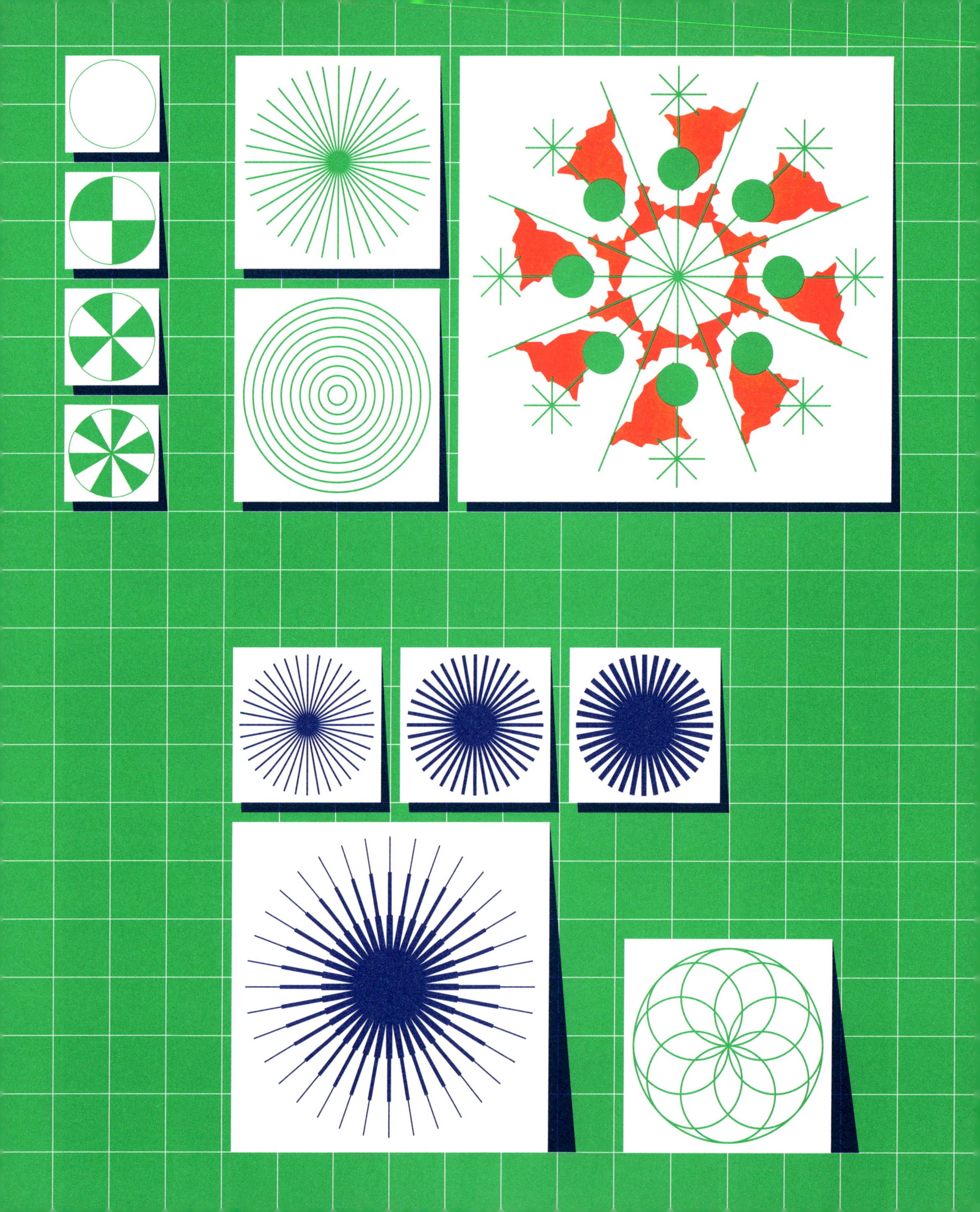

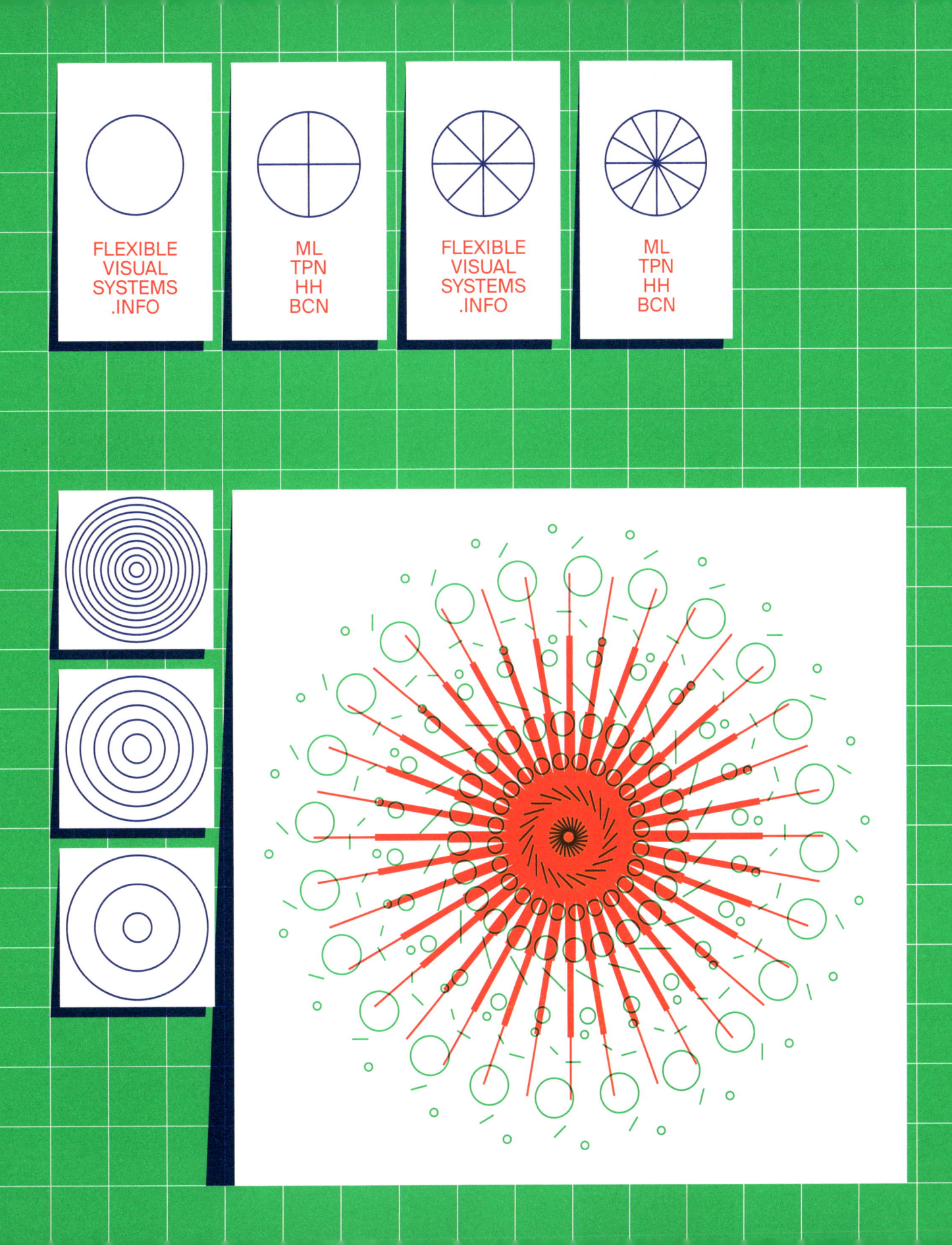

FLEXIBLE
VISUAL
SYSTEMS
.INFO

ML
TPN
HH
BCN

FLEXIBLE
VISUAL
SYSTEMS
.INFO

ML
TPN
HH
BCN

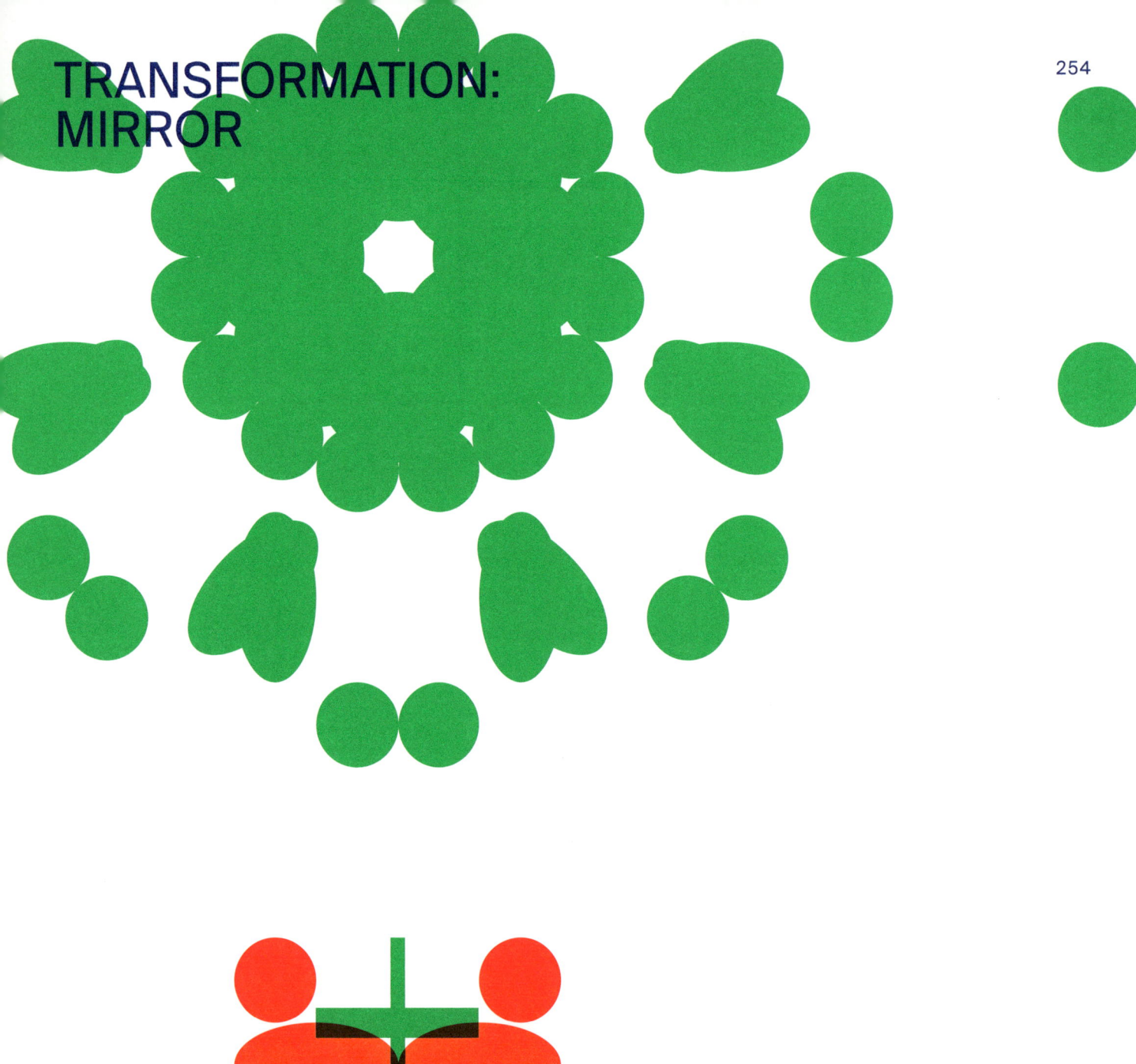

TRANSFORMATION: MIRROR

DIVISION: CIRCLE

254

255

Original
Mirror 1
Mirror 2
Mirror 3
Mirror 4
Mirror 5
A
B
C
D
E
F
G
H
FLEX IBLE SYS TEME
VISU ELLE IDEN TITAT
TRAN SFOR MATI VE
TEXT TEXT TEXT TEXT

257

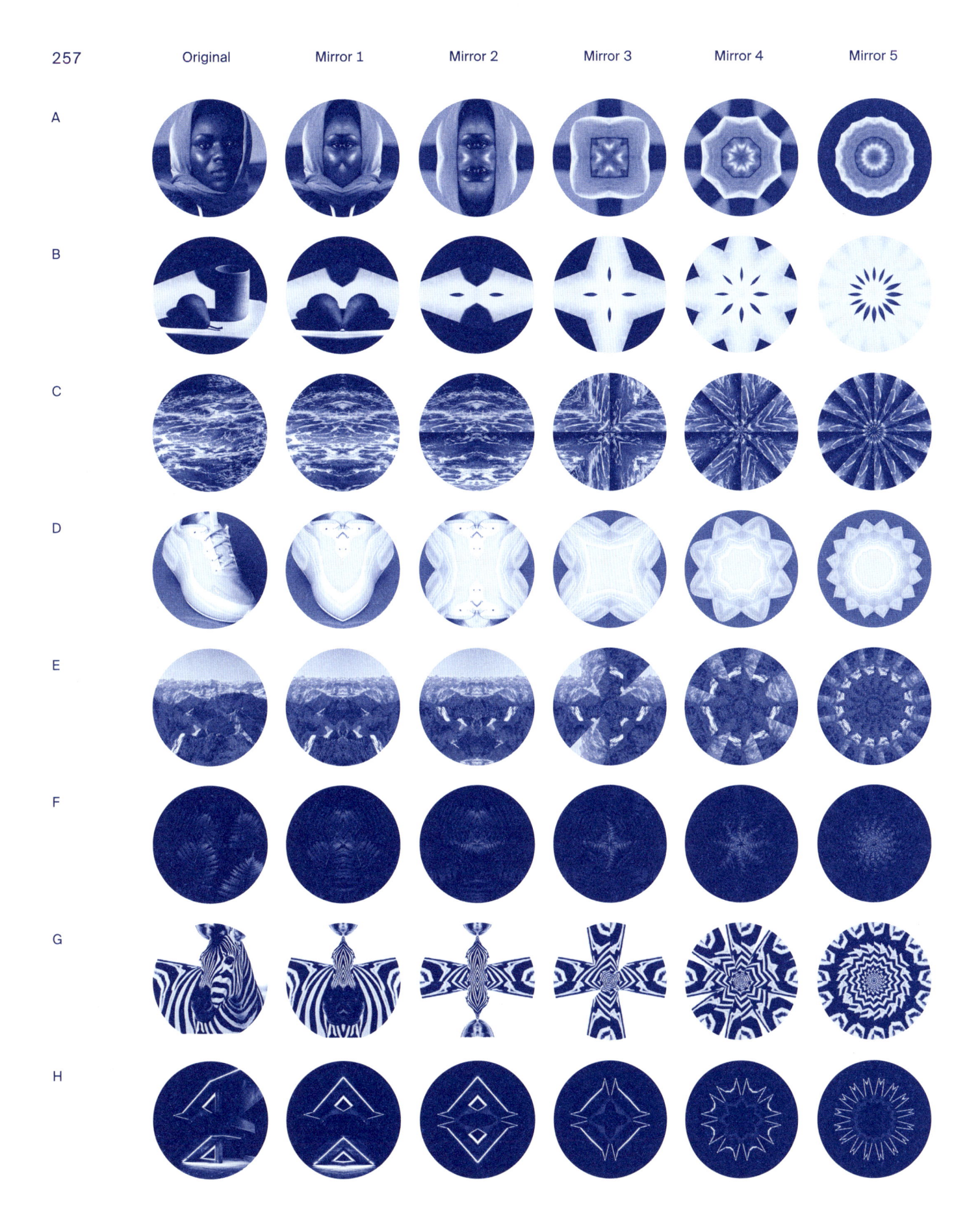

	Original	Mirror 1	Mirror 2	Mirror 3	Mirror 4	Mirror 5
A						
B						
C						
D						
E						
F						
G						
H						

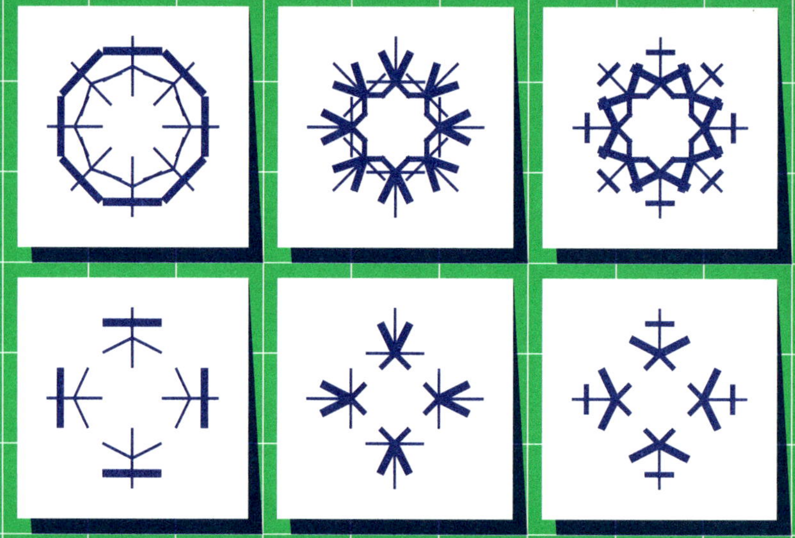

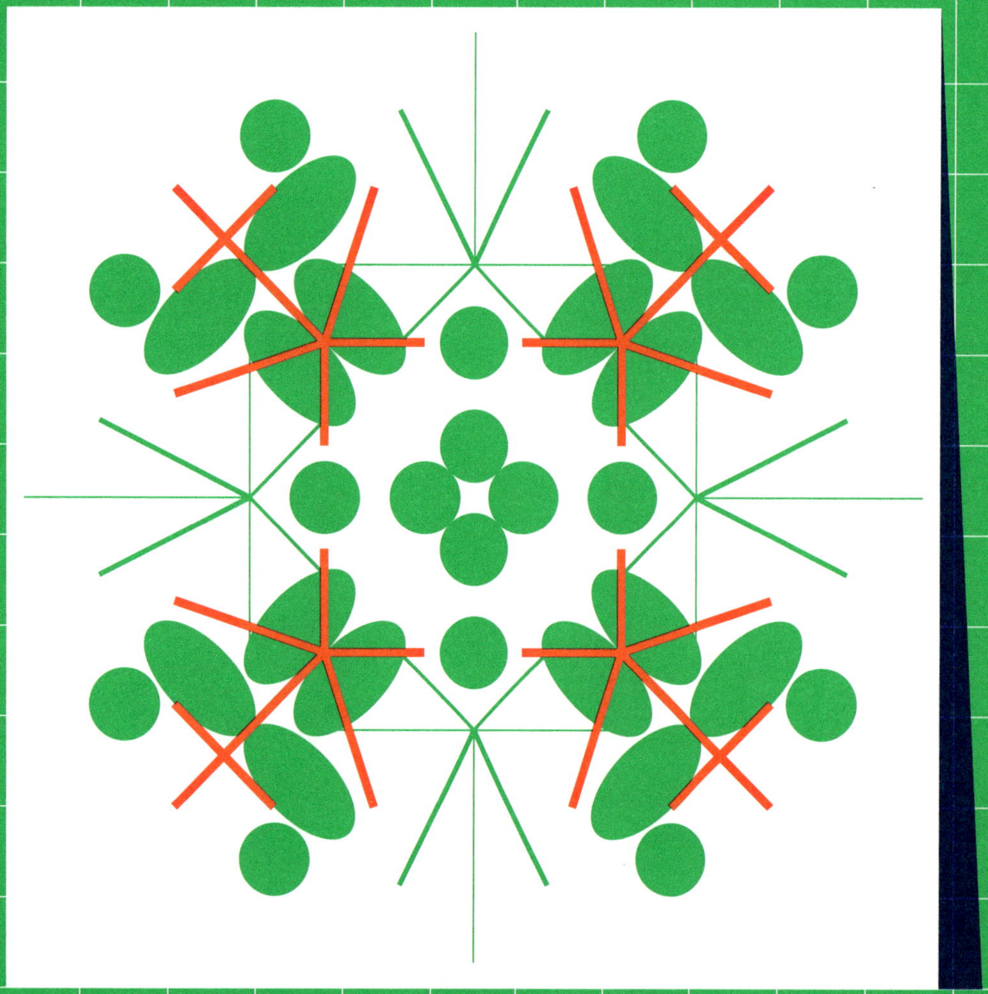

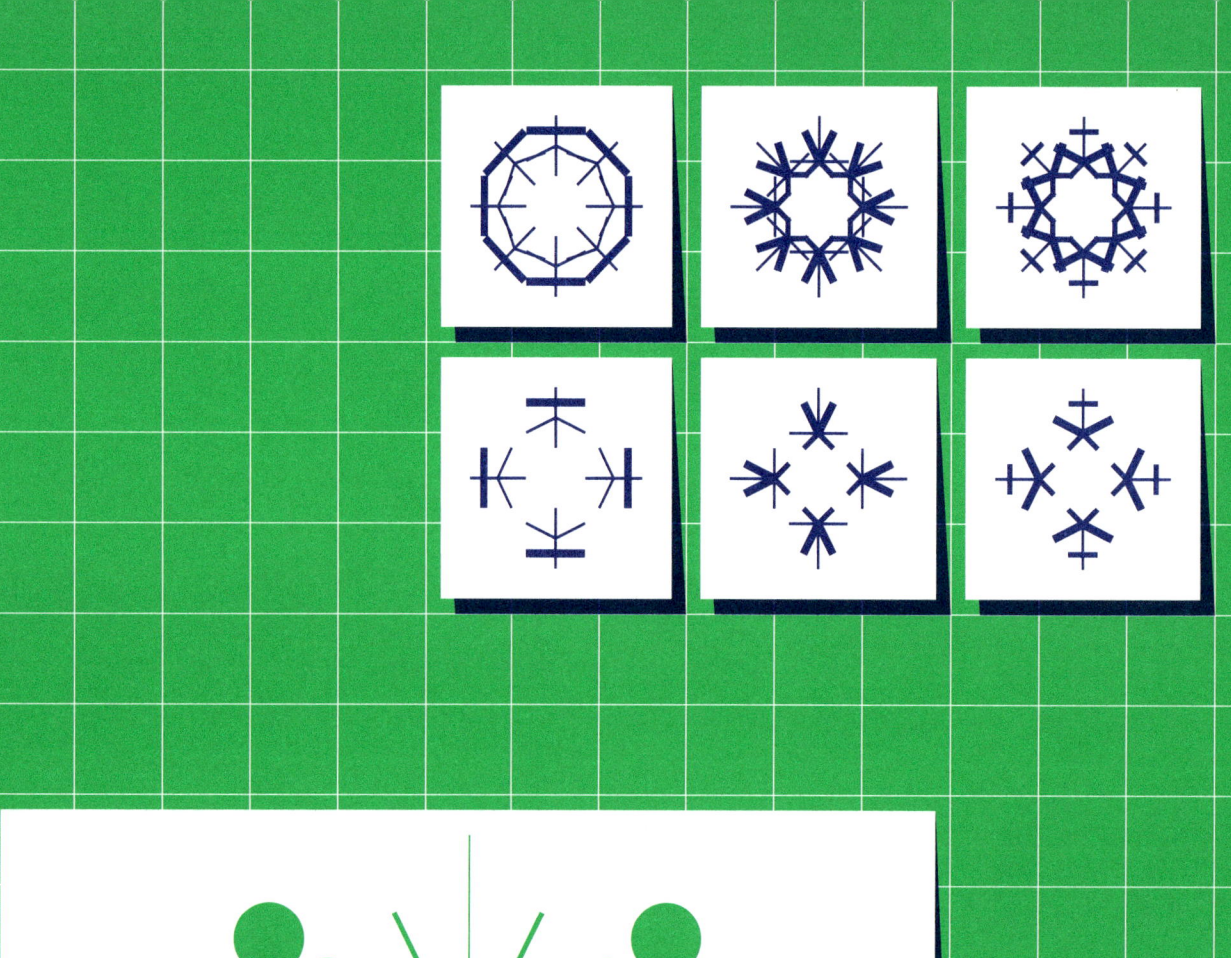

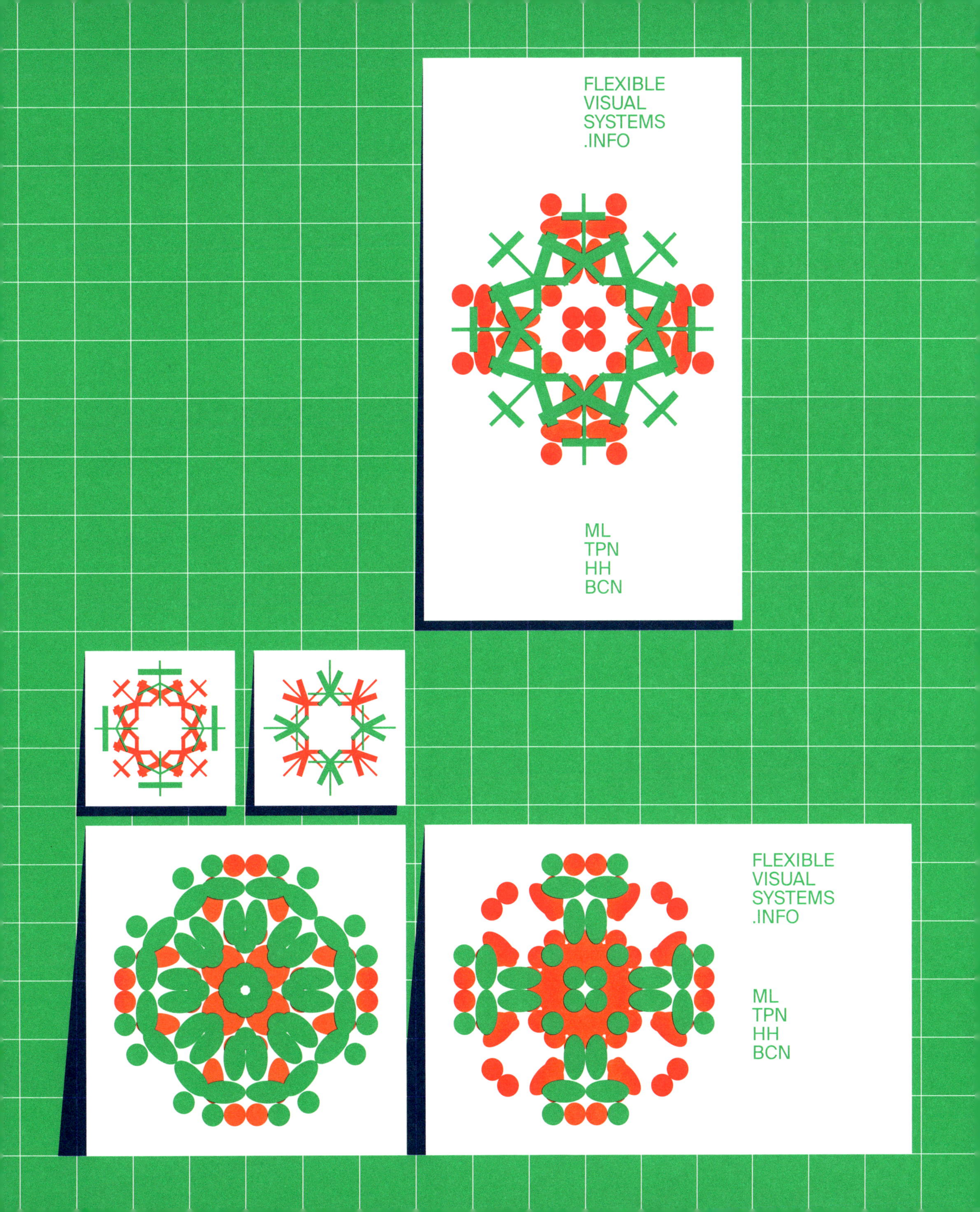

FLEXIBLE
VISUAL
SYSTEMS
.INFO

ML
TPN
HH
BCN

FLEXIBLE
VISUAL
SYSTEMS
.INFO

ML
TPN
HH
BCN

TRANSFORMATION: GRADATION

260

DIVISION: TRIANGLE

261 Vert. Gradation 1 Vert. Gradation 2 Vert. Gradation 3 Hor. Gradation 1 Hor. Gradation 2 Hor. Gradation 3

A

B

C

D

A2

B2

C2

D2

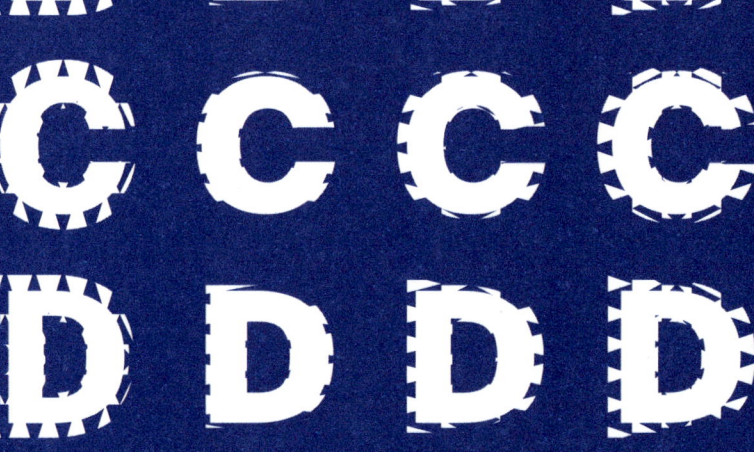

	Gradation 1	Gradation 2	Gradation 3	Gradation 4	Gradation 5	Gradation 6
A	A	A	A	A	A	A
B	B	B	B	B	B	B
C	C	C	C	C	C	C
D	D	D	D	D	D	D
E	FLEX IBLE SYS TEME	FLEX IBLE SYS TEME	FLEX IBLE SYS TEME	FLEX IBLE SYS TEME	FLEX IBLE SYS TEME	FLEX IBLE SYS TEME
F	VISU ELLE IDEN TITAT	VISU ELLE IDEN TITAT	VISU ELLE IDEN TITAT	VISU ELLE IDEN TITAT	VISU ELLE IDEN TITAT	VISU ELLE IDEN TITAT
G	TRAN SFOR MATI VE	TRAN SFOR MATI VE	TRAN SFOR MATI VE	TRAN SFOR MATI VE	TRAN SFOR MATI VE	TRAN SFOR MATI VE
H	TEXT TEXT TEXT TEXT	TEXT TEXT TEXT TEXT	TEXT TEXT TEXT TEXT	TEXT TEXT TEXT TEXT	TEXT TEXT TEXT TEXT	TEXT TEXT TEXT TEXT

263

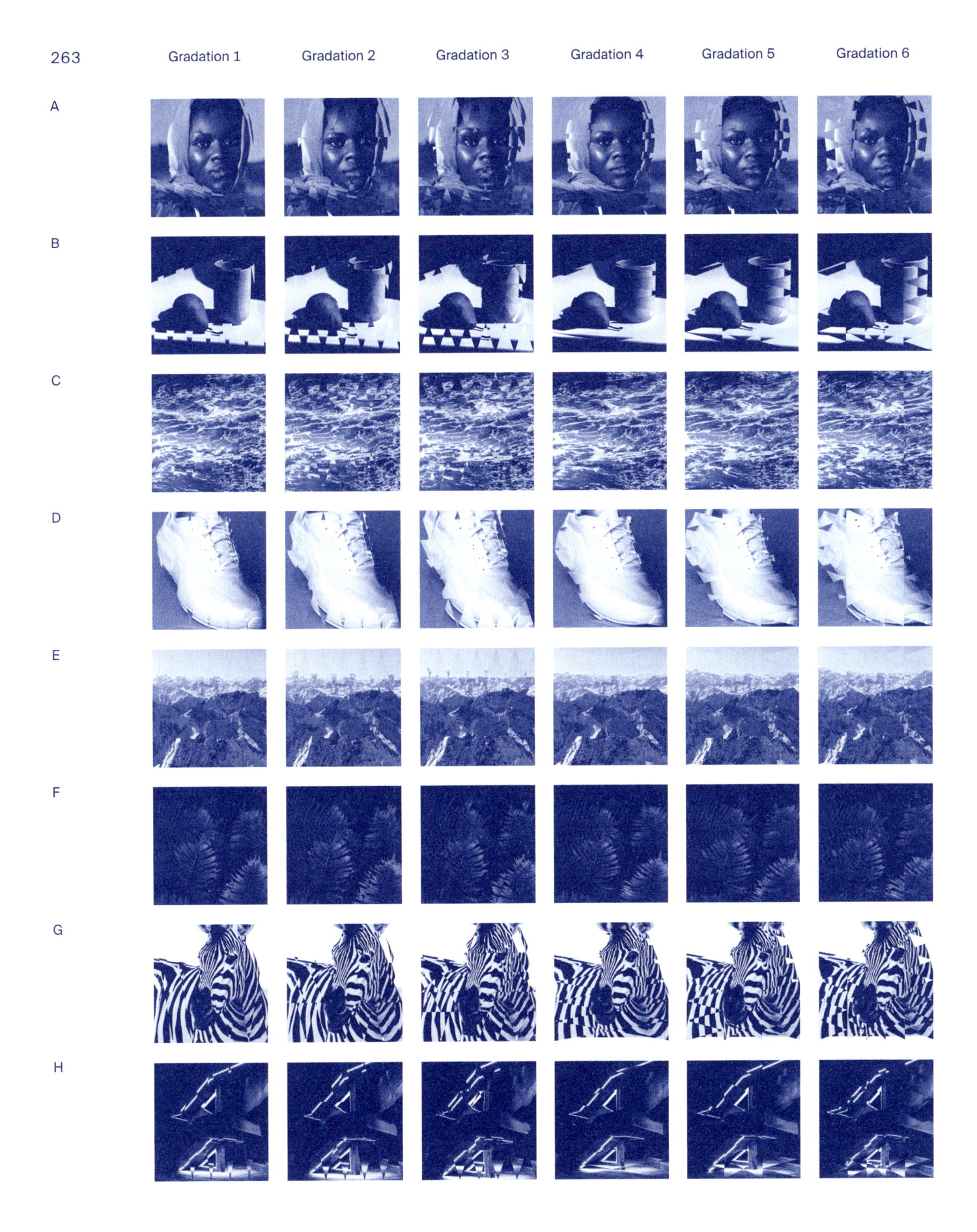

	Gradation 1	Gradation 2	Gradation 3	Gradation 4	Gradation 5	Gradation 6
A						
B						
C						
D						
E						
F						
G						
H						

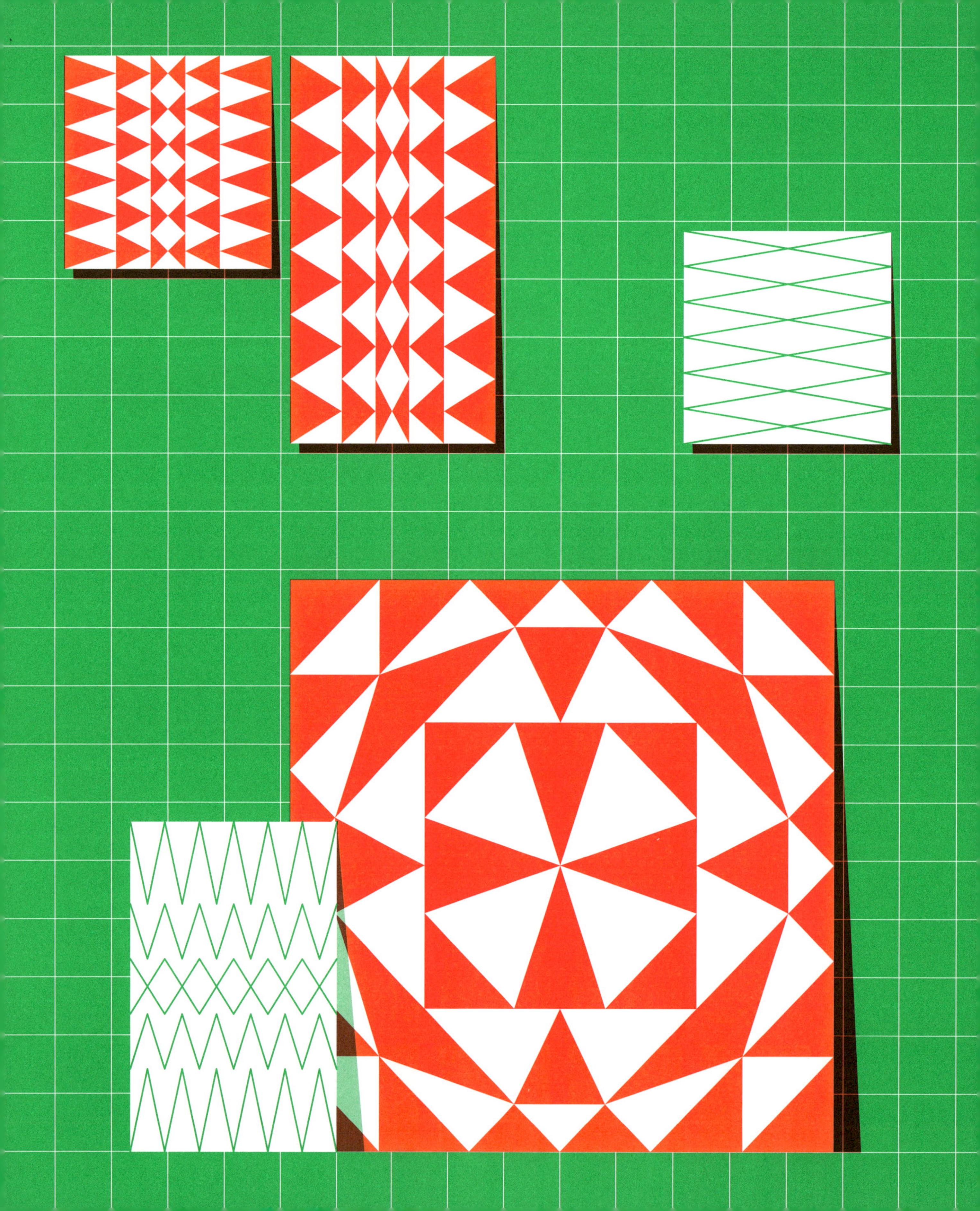

**FLEXIBLE
VISUAL
SYSTEMS**

TPN
HH BCN

ML

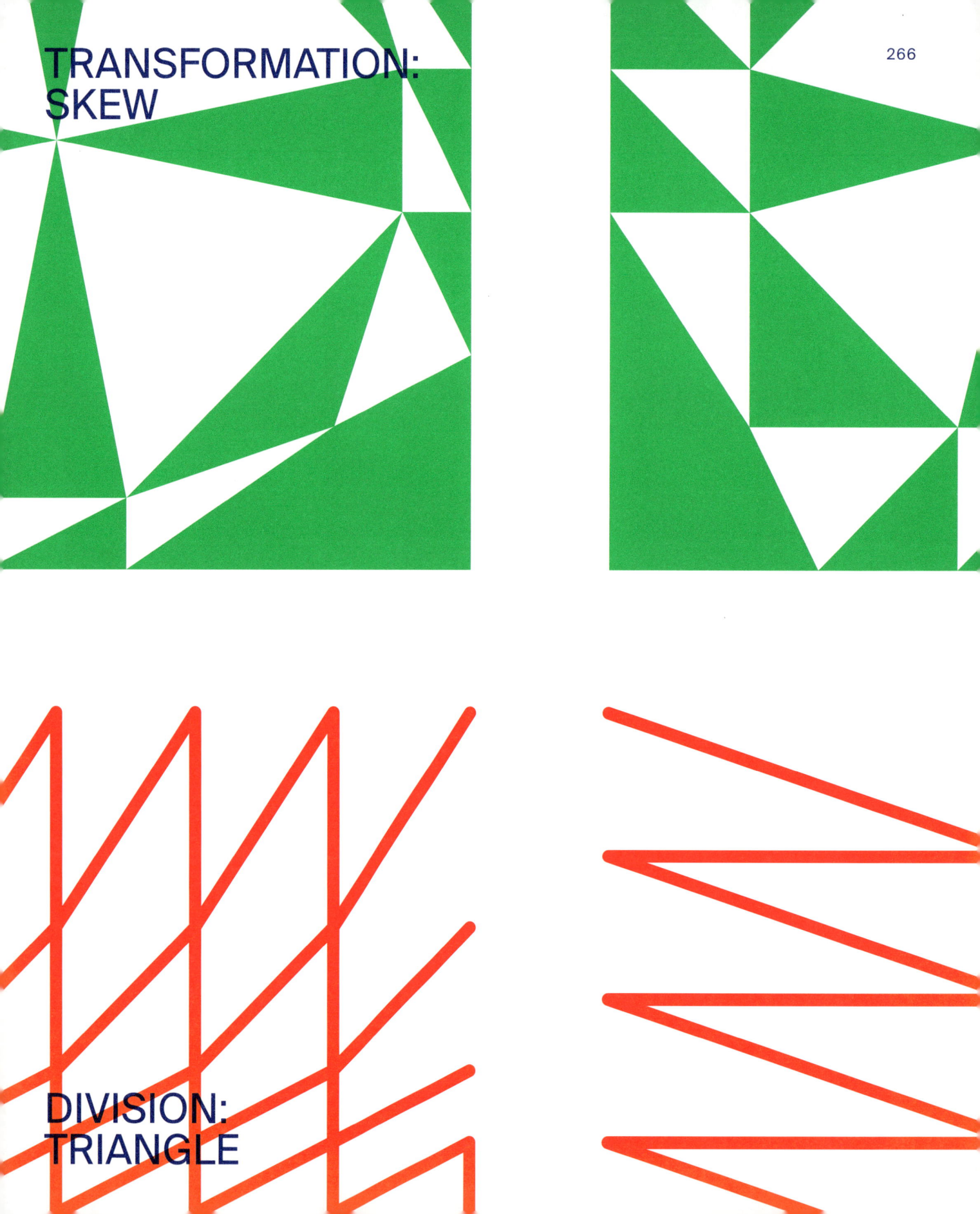

TRANSFORMATION: SKEW

DIVISION: TRIANGLE

267 | Skew 1 | Skew 2 | Skew 3 | Skew 4 | Skew 5 | Skew 6

A

B

C

D

A2

B2

C2

D2

Gradation 1   Gradation 2   Gradation 3   Gradation 4   Gradation 5   Gradation 6

269

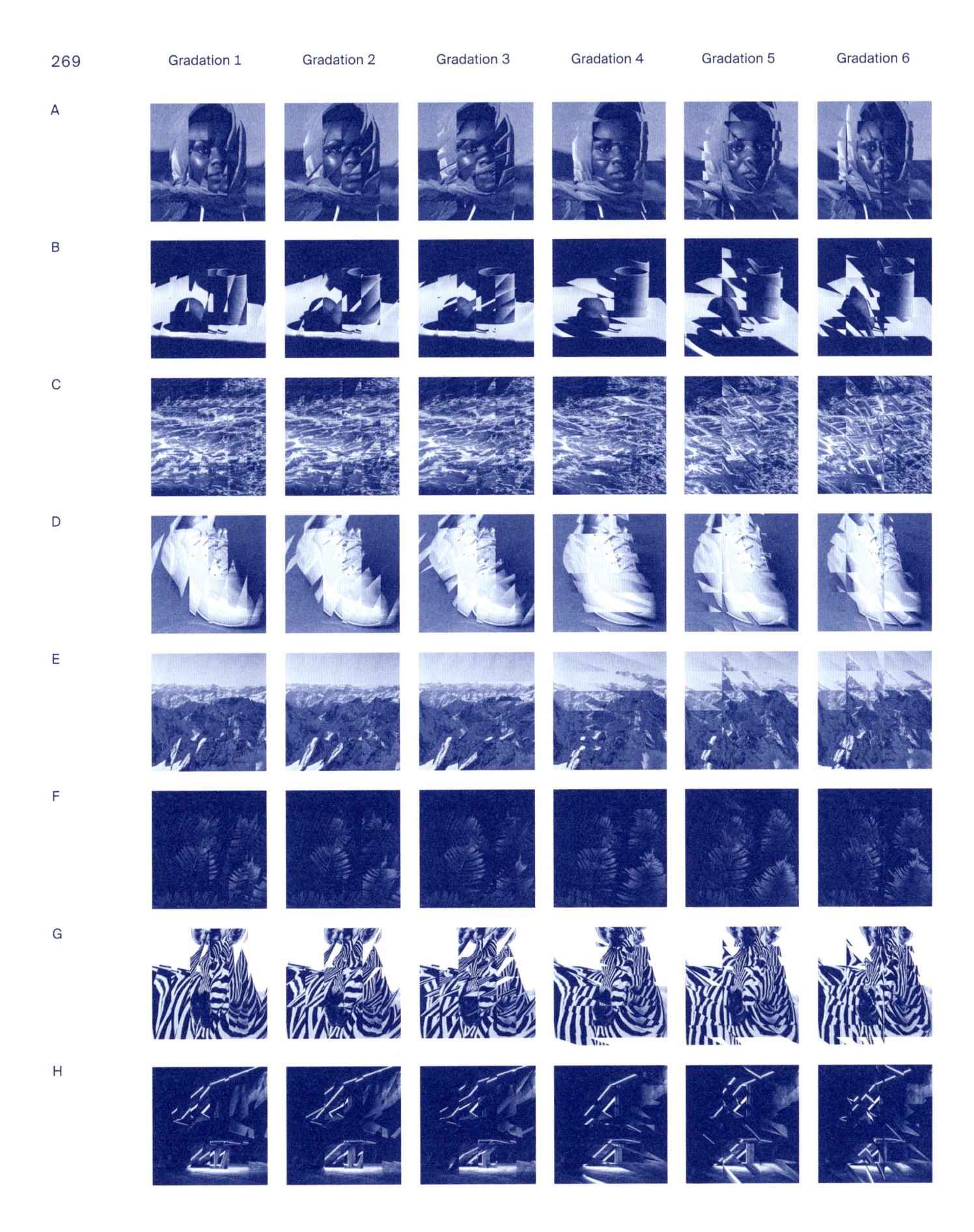

	Gradation 1	Gradation 2	Gradation 3	Gradation 4	Gradation 5	Gradation 6
A						
B						
C						
D						
E						
F						
G						
H						

FLEXIBLE
VISUAL
SYSTEMS

ML

TPN
HH BCN

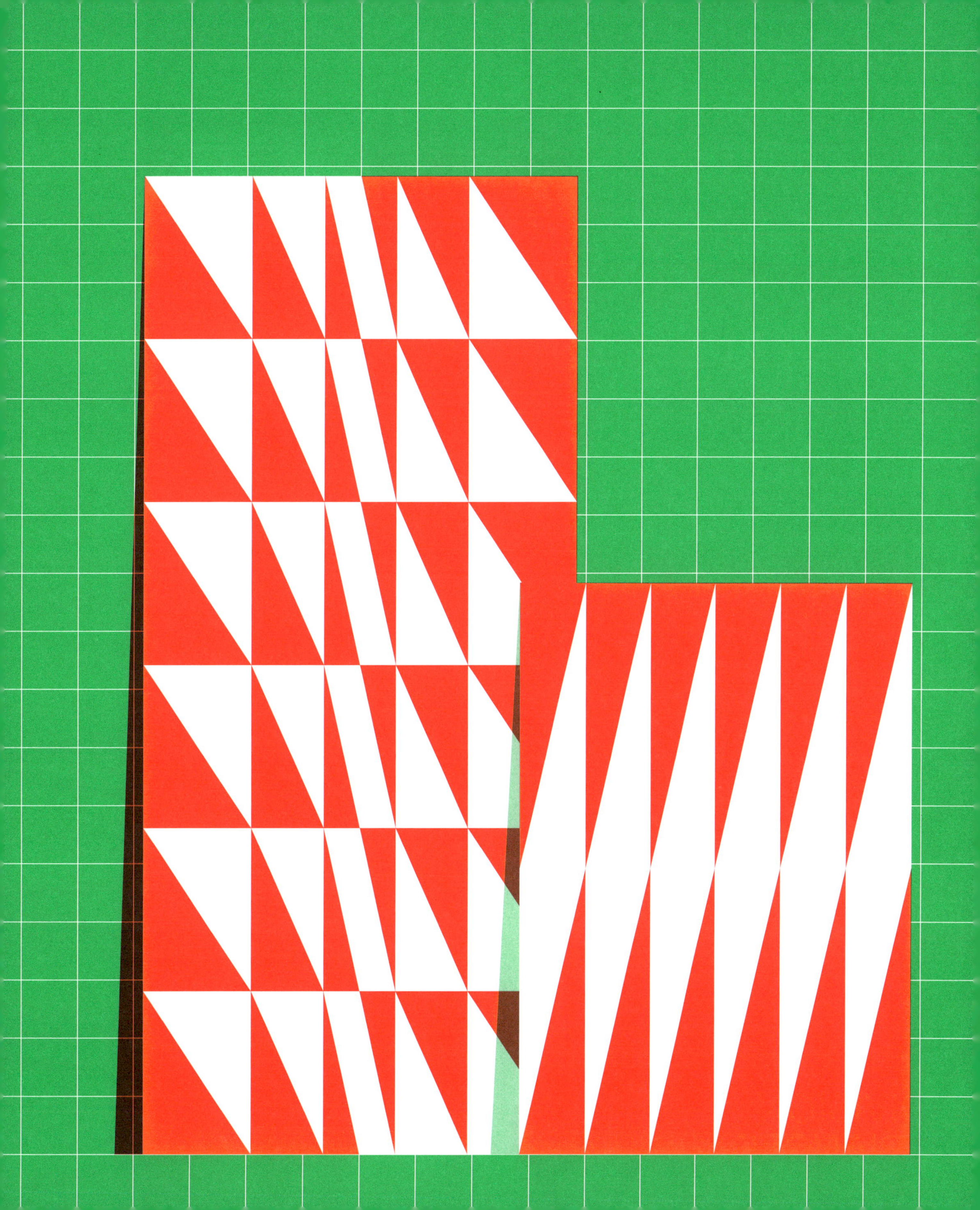

TRANSFORMATION: SHIFT

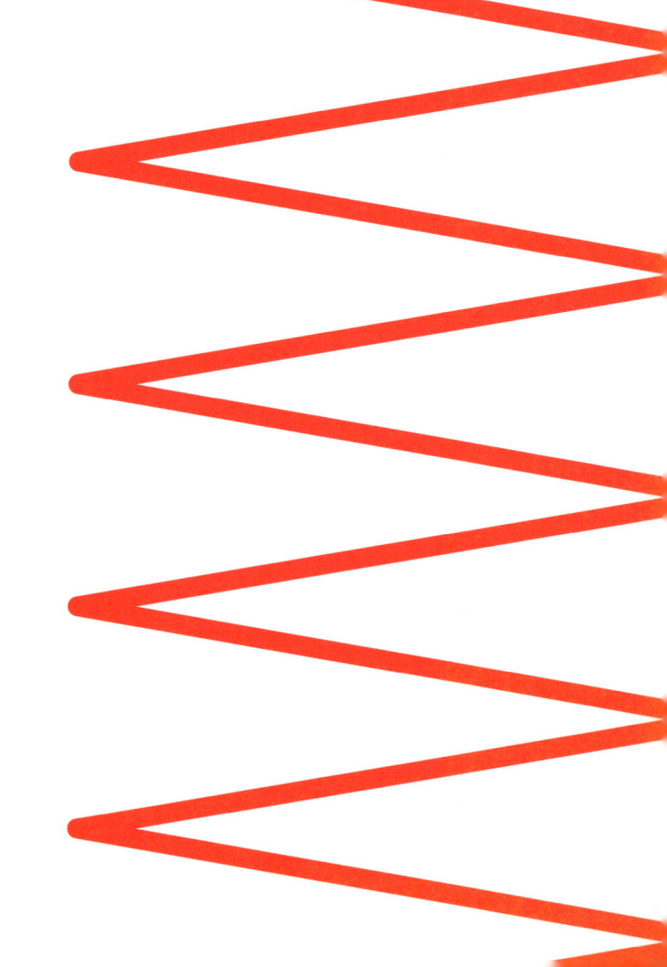

272

DIVISION: TRIANGLE

273

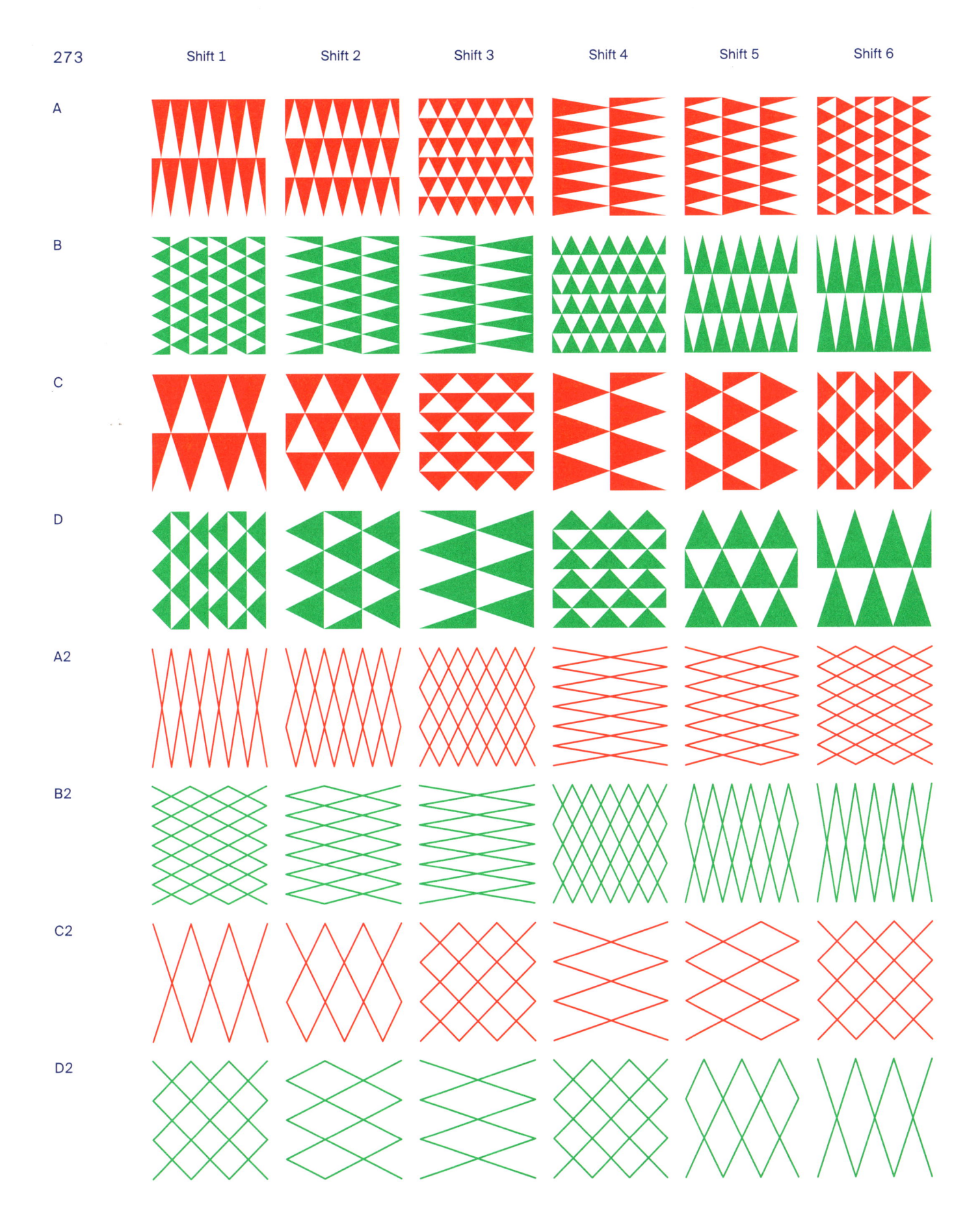

	Shift 1	Shift 2	Shift 3	Shift 4	Shift 5	Shift 6
A						
B						
C						
D						
A2						
B2						
C2						
D2						

	Shift 1	Shift 2	Shift 3	Shift 4	Shift 5	Shift 6	
	A	A	A	A	A	A	A
	B	B	B	B	B	B	B
	C	C	C	C	C	C	C
	D	D	D	D	D	D	D
	FLEXIBLE SYSTEME	FLEXIBLE SYSTEME	FLEXIBLE SYSTEME	FLEXIBLE SYSTEME	FLEXIBLE SYSTEME	FLEXIBLE SYSTEME	E
	VISUELLE IDENTITÄT	VISUELLE IDENTITÄT	VISUELLE IDENTITÄT	VISUELLE IDENTITÄT	VISUELLE IDENTITÄT	VISUELLE IDENTITÄT	F
	TRANSFORMATIVE	TRANSFORMATIVE	TRANSFORMATIVE	TRANSFORMATIVE	TRANSFORMATIVE	TRANSFORMATIVE	G
	TEXT TEXT TEXT TEXT	TEXT TEXT TEXT TEXT	TEXT TEXT TEXT TEXT	TEXT TEXT TEXT TEXT	TEXT TEXT TEXT TEXT	TEXT TEXT TEXT TEXT	H

275

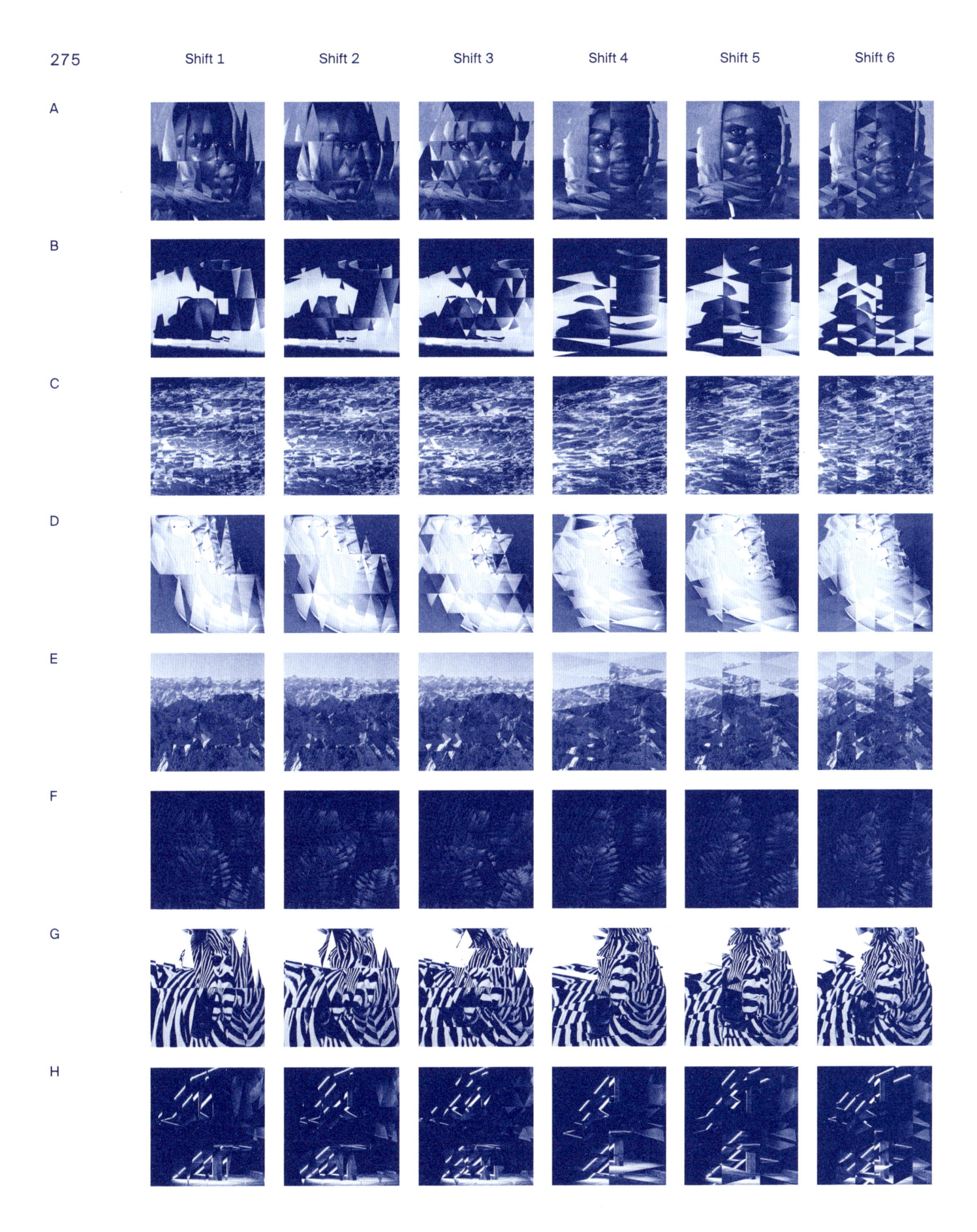

	Shift 1	Shift 2	Shift 3	Shift 4	Shift 5	Shift 6
A						
B						
C						
D						
E						
F						
G						
H						

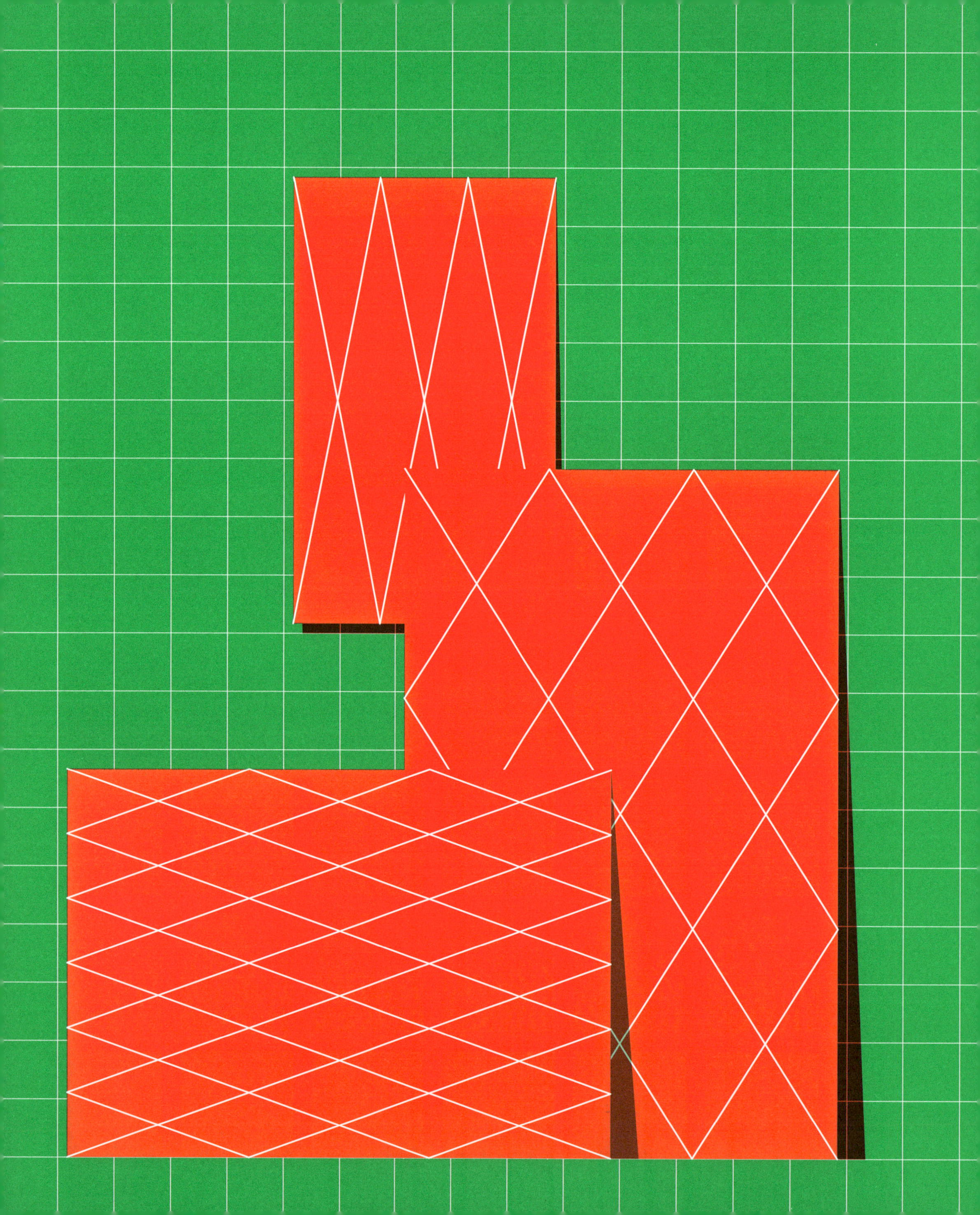

FLEXIBLE
VISUAL
SYSTEMS

TPN
HH BCN

TRANSFORMATION: MIRROR

278

DIVISION: TRIANGLE

279

	Mirror 1	Mirror 2	Mirror 3	Mirror 4	Mirror 5	Mirror 6
A						
B						
C						
D						
A2						
B2						
C2						
D2						

| | Mirror 1 | Mirror 2 | Mirror 3 | Mirror 4 | Mirror 5 | Mirror 6 |

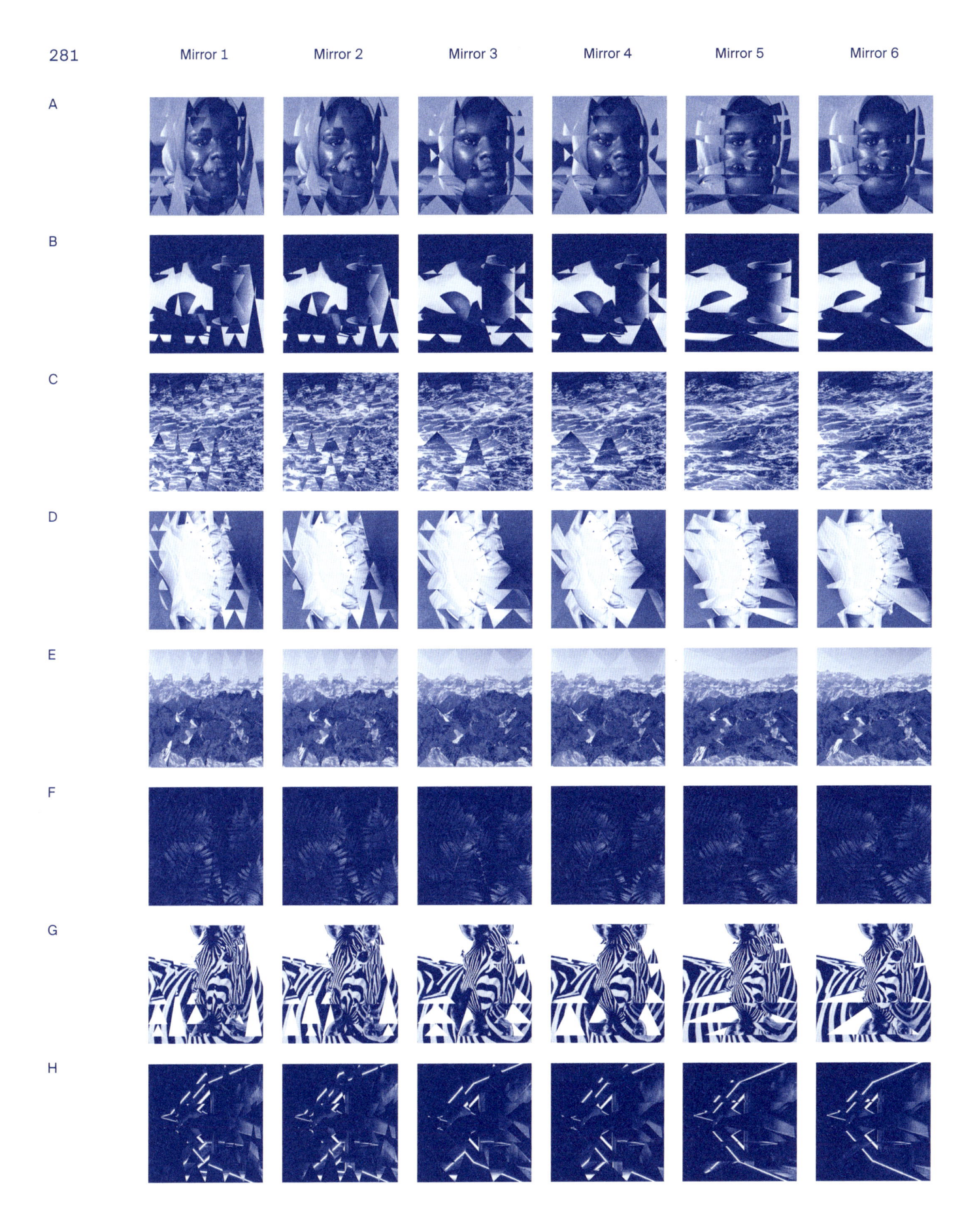

281 | Mirror 1 | Mirror 2 | Mirror 3 | Mirror 4 | Mirror 5 | Mirror 6

FLEXIBLE
VISUAL
SYSTEMS

TPN
HH
BCN

ML

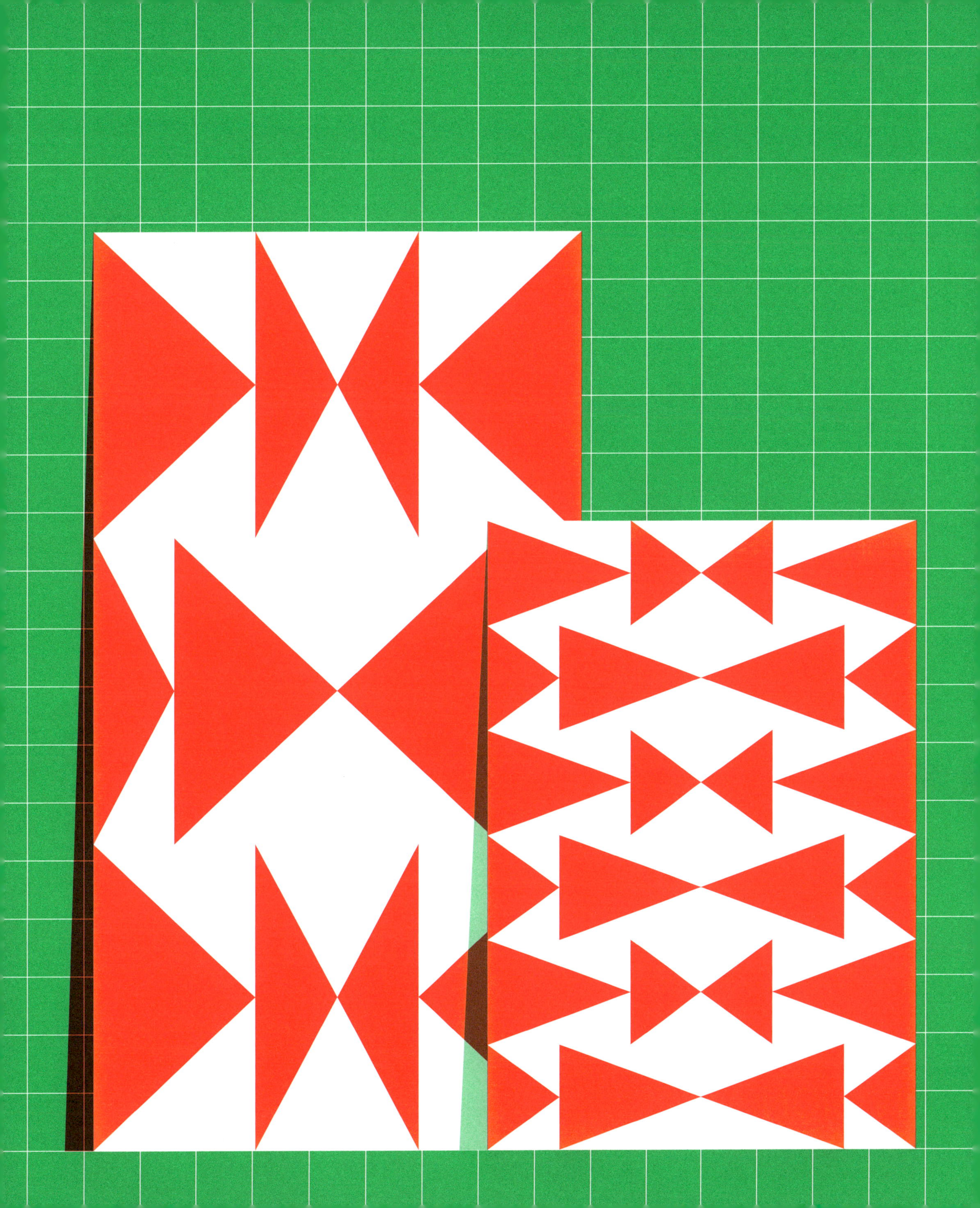

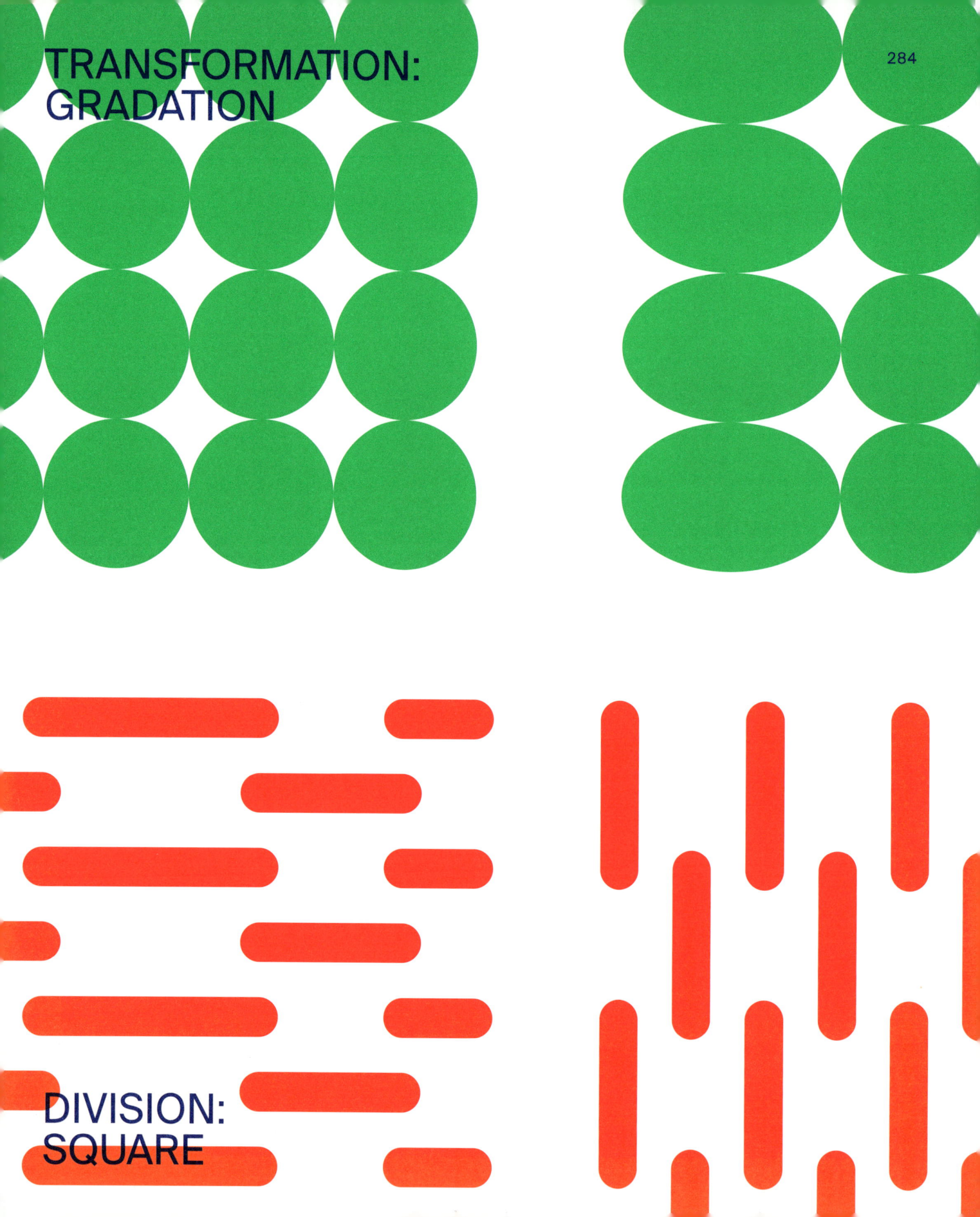

TRANSFORMATION: GRADATION

284

DIVISION: SQUARE

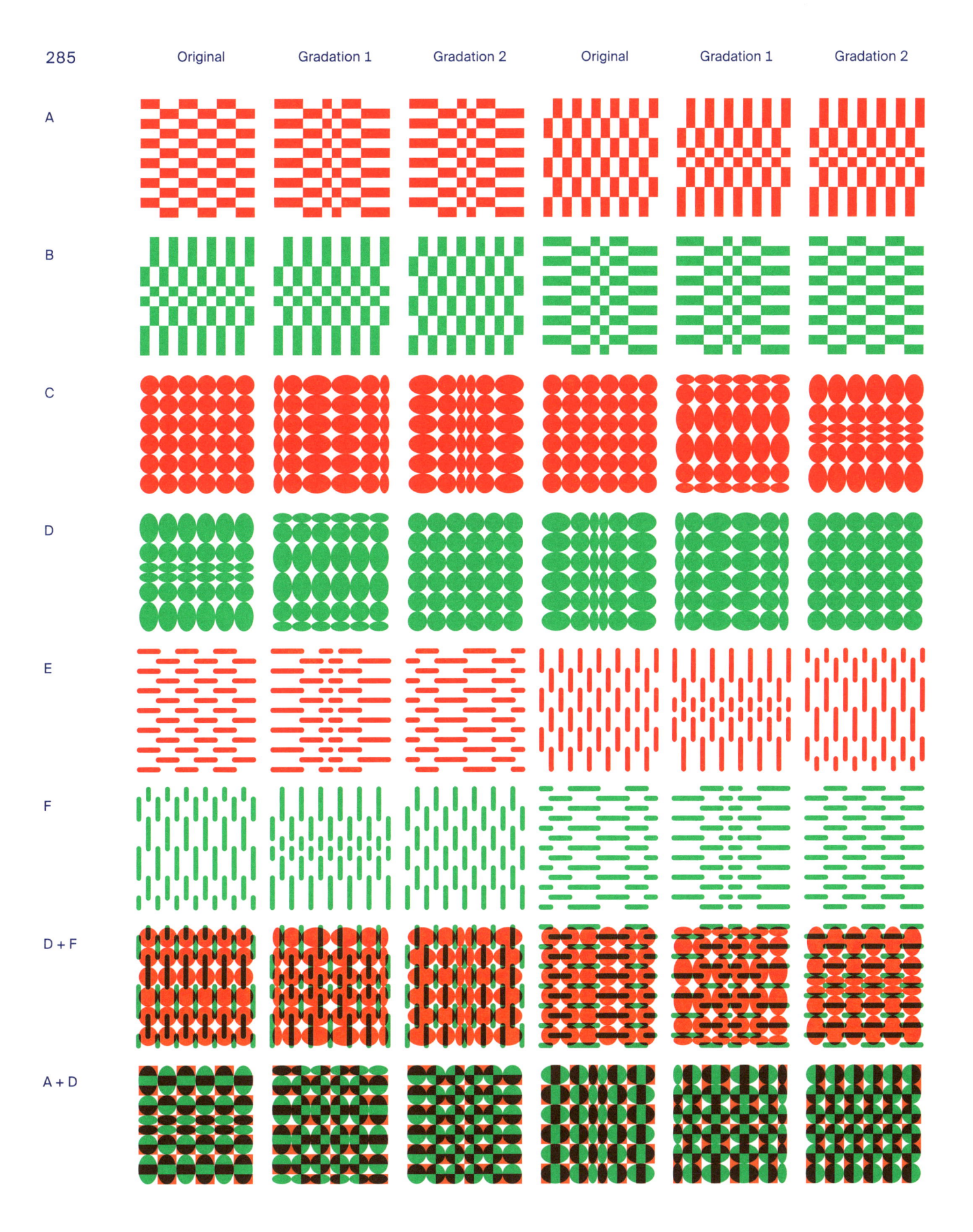

285   Original   Gradation 1   Gradation 2   Original   Gradation 1   Gradation 2

A

B

C

D

E

F

D + F

A + D

Original	Gradation 1	Gradation 2	Gradation 3	Gradation 4	Gradation 5	
A	A	A	A	A	A	A
B	B	B	B	B	B	B
C	C	C	C	C	C	C
D	D	D	D	D	D	D
FLEXIBLE SYSTEME	FLEXIBLE SYSTEME	FLEXIBLE SYSTEME	FLEXIBLE SYSTEME	FLEXIBLE SYSTEME	FLEXIBLE SYSTEME	E
VISUELLE IDENTITAT	VISUELLE IDENTITAT	VISUELLE IDENTITAT	VISUELLE IDENTITAT	VISUELLE IDENTITAT	VISUELLE IDENTITAT	F
TRANSFORMATIVE	TRANSFORMATIVE	TRANSFORMATIVE	TRANSFORMATIVE	TRANSFORMATIVE	TRANSFORMATIVE	G
TEXT TEXT TEXT TEXT	TEXT TEXT TEXT TEXT	TEXT TEXT TEXT TEXT	TEXT TEXT TEXT TEXT	TEXT TEXT TEXT TEXT	TEXT TEXT TEXT TEXT	H

287

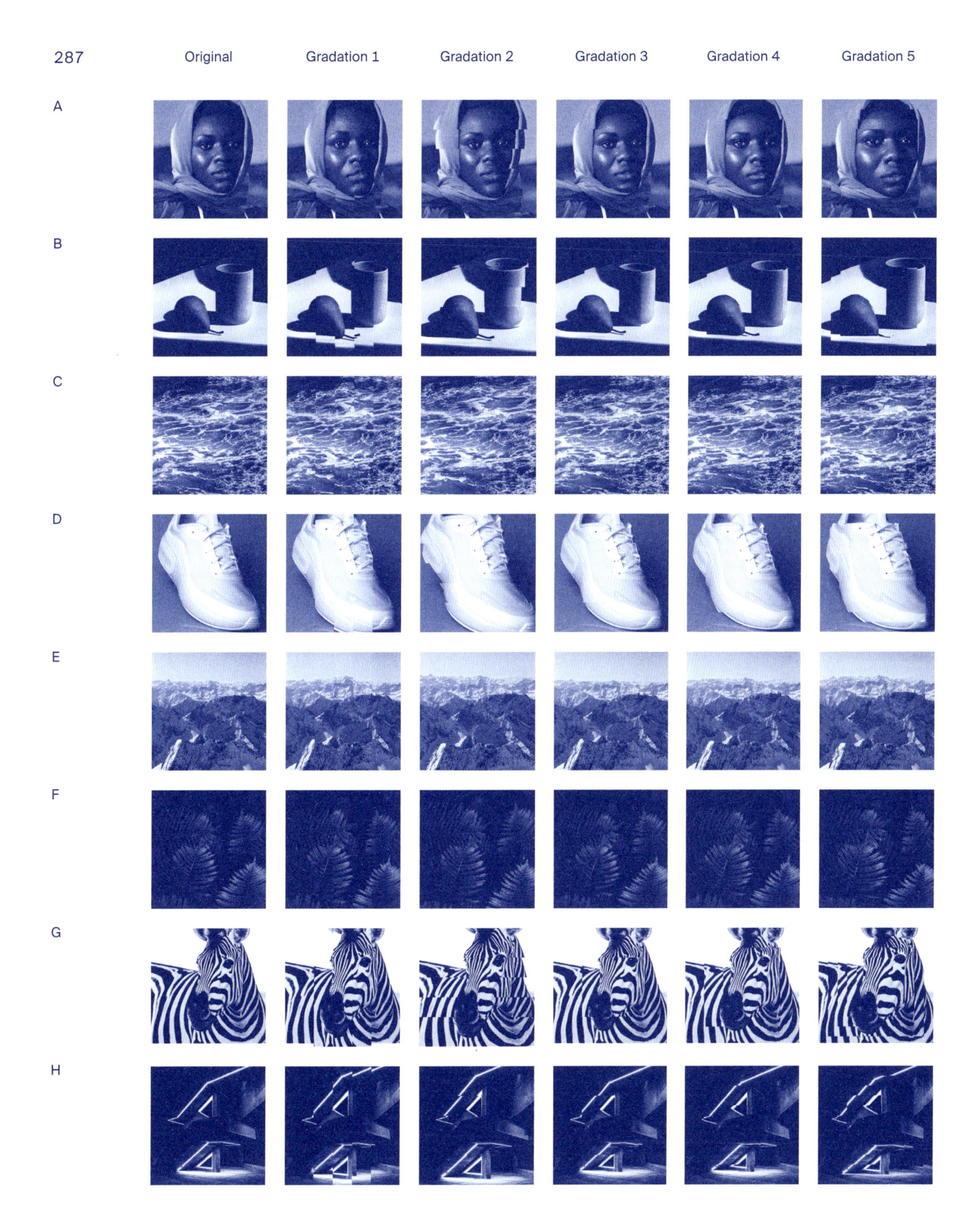

	Original	Gradation 1	Gradation 2	Gradation 3	Gradation 4	Gradation 5
A						
B						
C						
D						
E						
F						
G						
H						

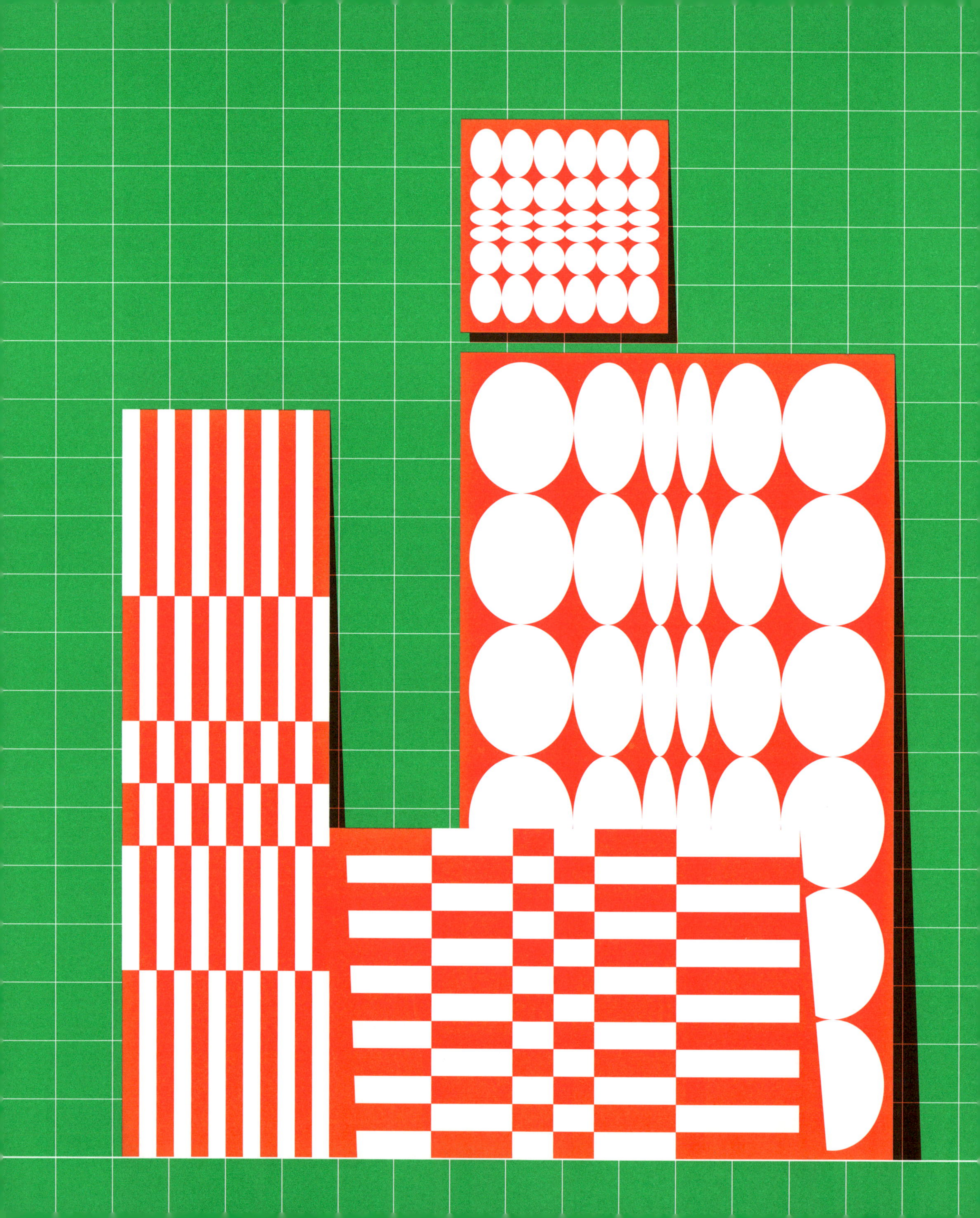

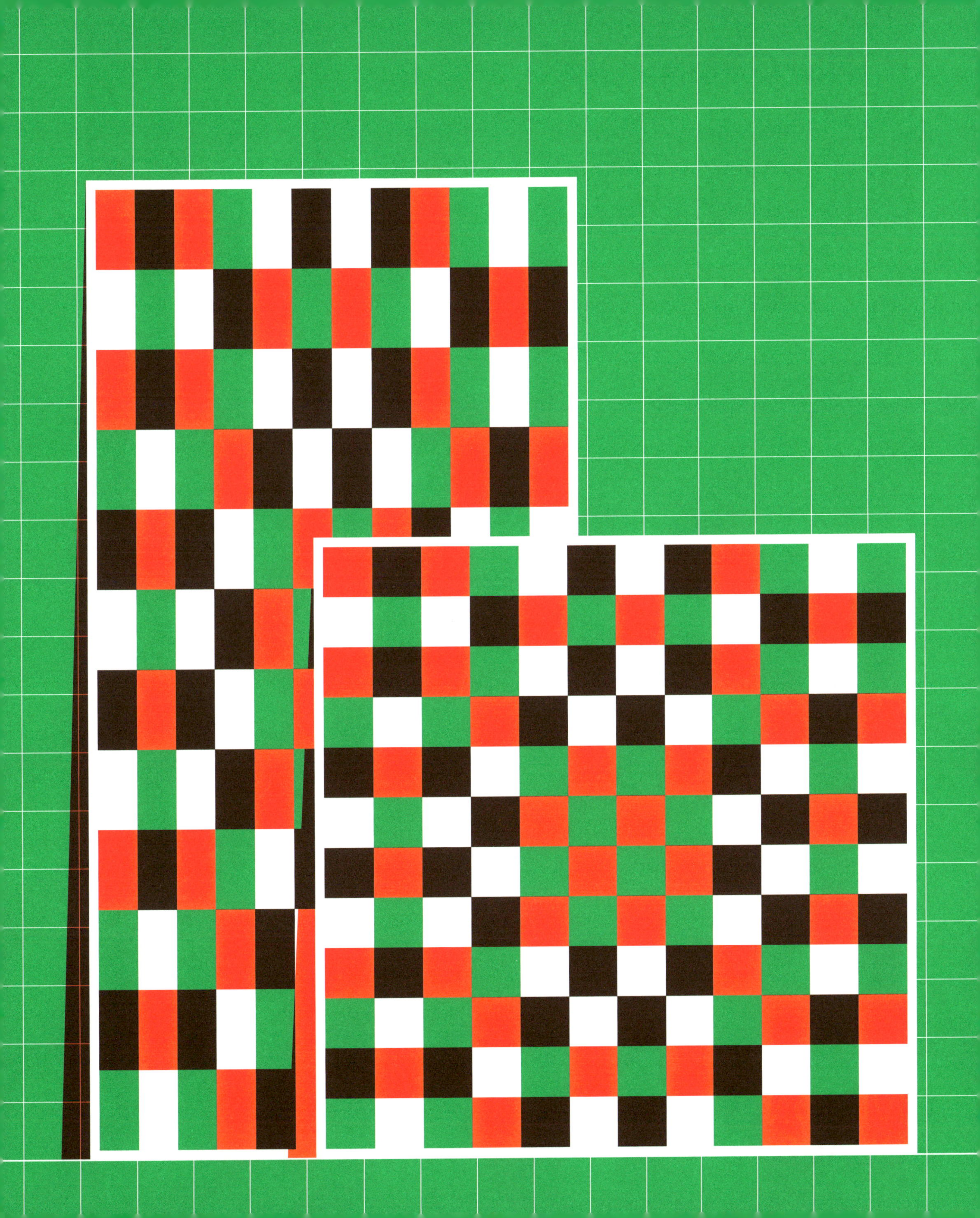

TRANSFORMATION:
SKEW

290

DIVISION:
SQUARE

291 | Skew 1 | Skew 2 | Skew 3 | Skew 4 | Skew 5 | Skew 6

A

B

C

D

E

F

A + B

E + F

Original	Skew 1	Skew 2	Skew 3	Skew 4	Skew 5	
A	A	A	A	A	A	A
B	B	B	B	B	B	B
C	C	C	C	C	C	C
D	D	D	D	D	D	D
FLEX IBLE SYS TEME	FLEX IBLE SYS TEME	FLEX IBLE SYS TEME	FLEX IBLE SYS TEME	FLEX IBLE SYS TEME	FLEX IBLE SYS TEME	E
VISU ELLE IDEN TITAT	VISU ELLE IDEN TITAT	VISU ELLE IDEN TITAT	VISU ELLE IDEN TITAT	VISU ELLE IDEN TITAT	VISU ELLE IDEN TITAT	F
TRAN SFOR MATI VE	TRAN SFOR MATI VE	TRAN SFOR MATI VE	TRAN SFOR MATI VE	TRAN SFOR MATI VE	TRAN SFOR MATI VE	G
TEXT TEXT TEXT TEXT	TEXT TEXT TEXT TEXT	TEXT TEXT TEXT TEXT	TEXT TEXT TEXT TEXT	TEXT TEXT TEXT TEXT	TEXT TEXT TEXT TEXT	H

293

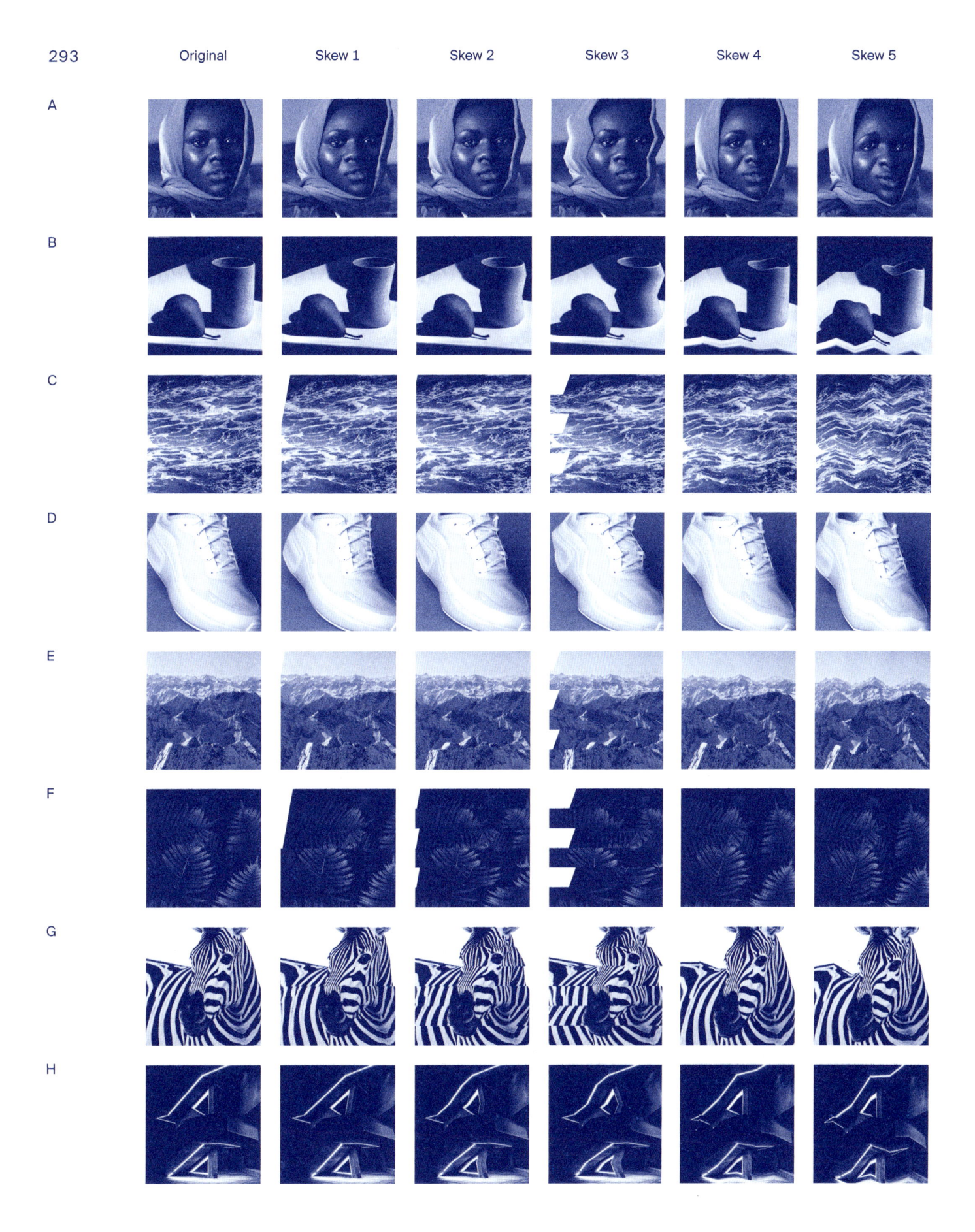

	Original	Skew 1	Skew 2	Skew 3	Skew 4	Skew 5
A						
B						
C						
D						
E						
F						
G						
H						

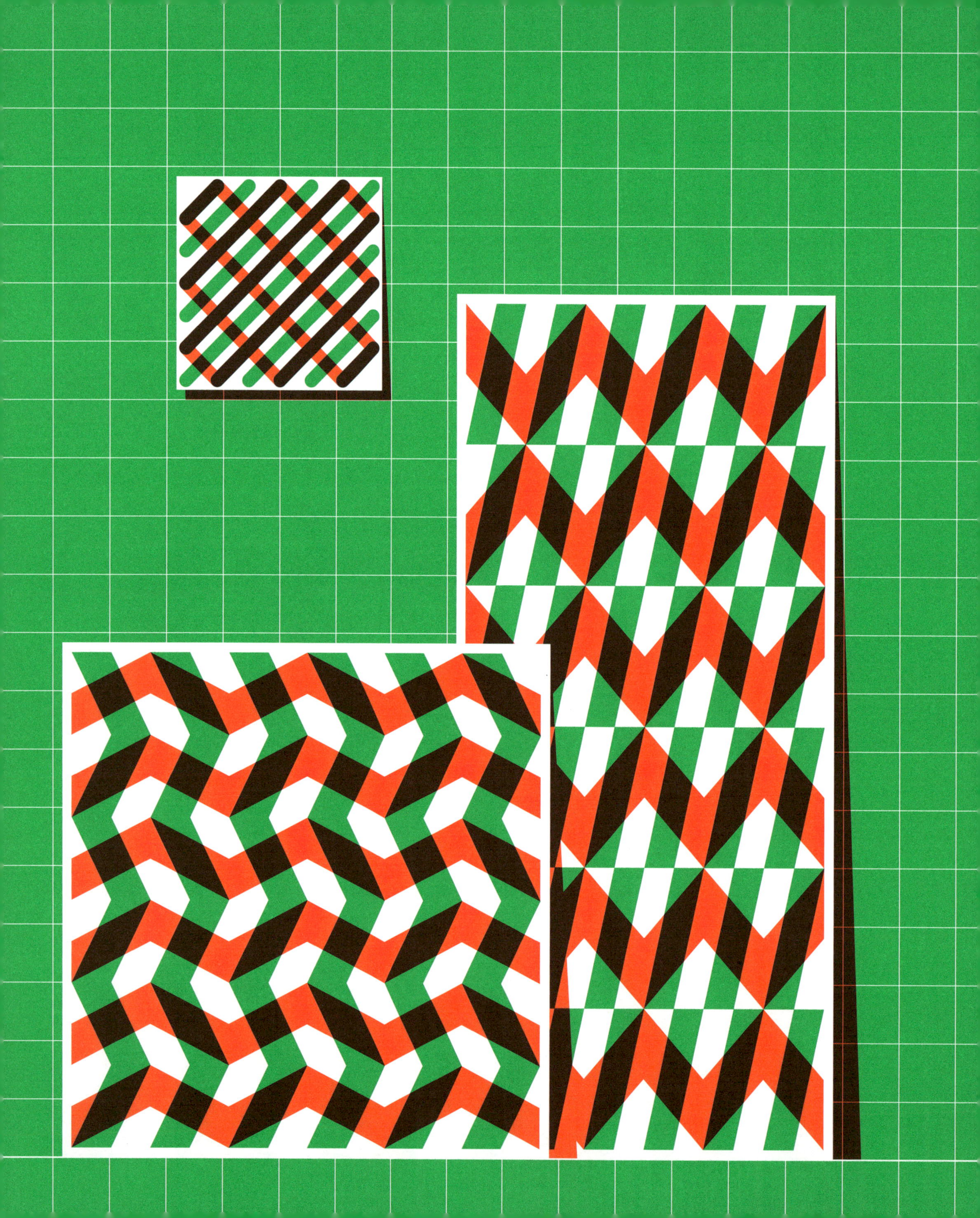

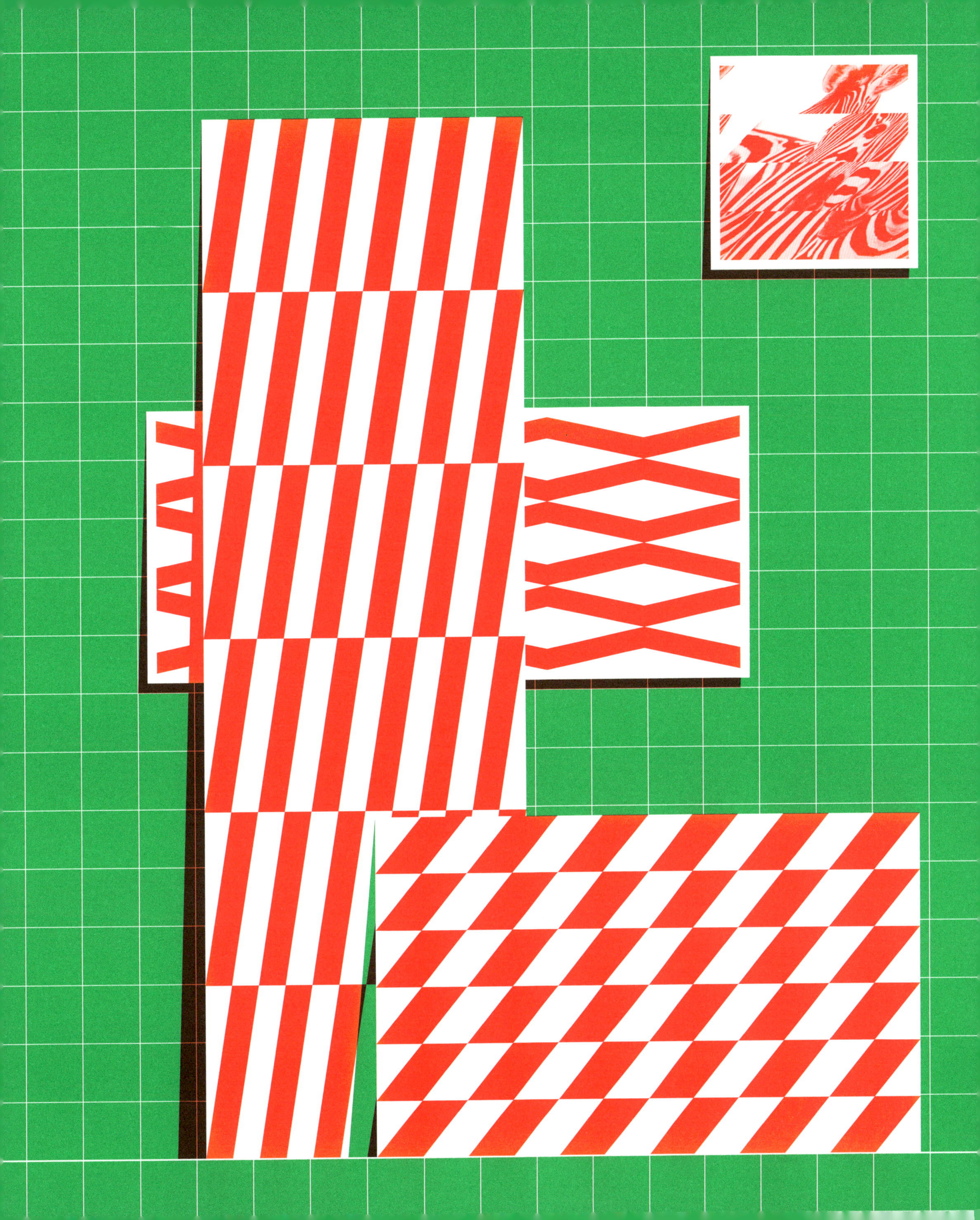

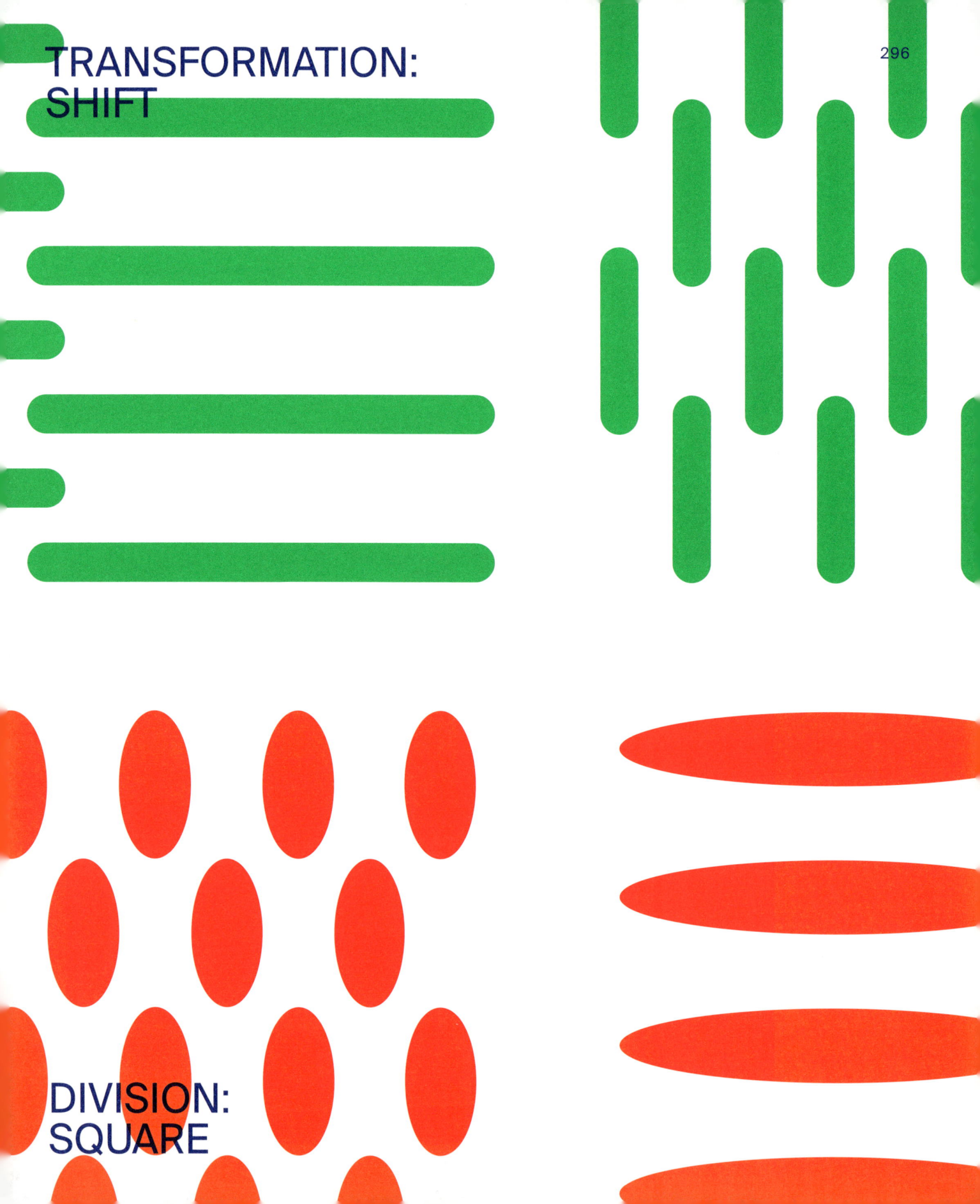

TRANSFORMATION: SHIFT

DIVISION: SQUARE

297 | Shift 1 | Shift 2 | Shift 3 | Shift 4 | Shift 5 | Shift 6

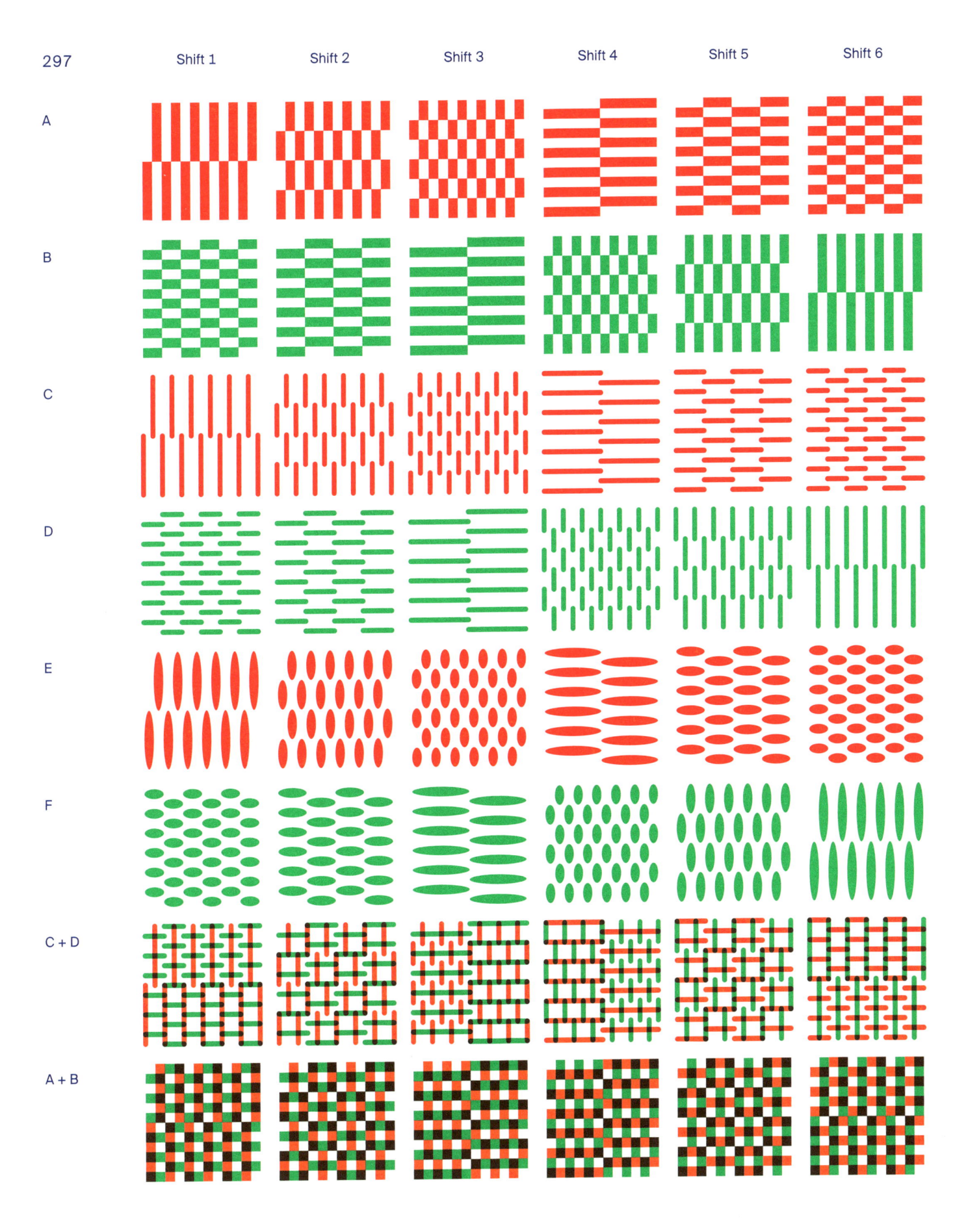

A

B

C

D

E

F

C + D

A + B

| Original | Shift 1 | Shift 2 | Shift 3 | Shift 4 | Shift 5 |

299

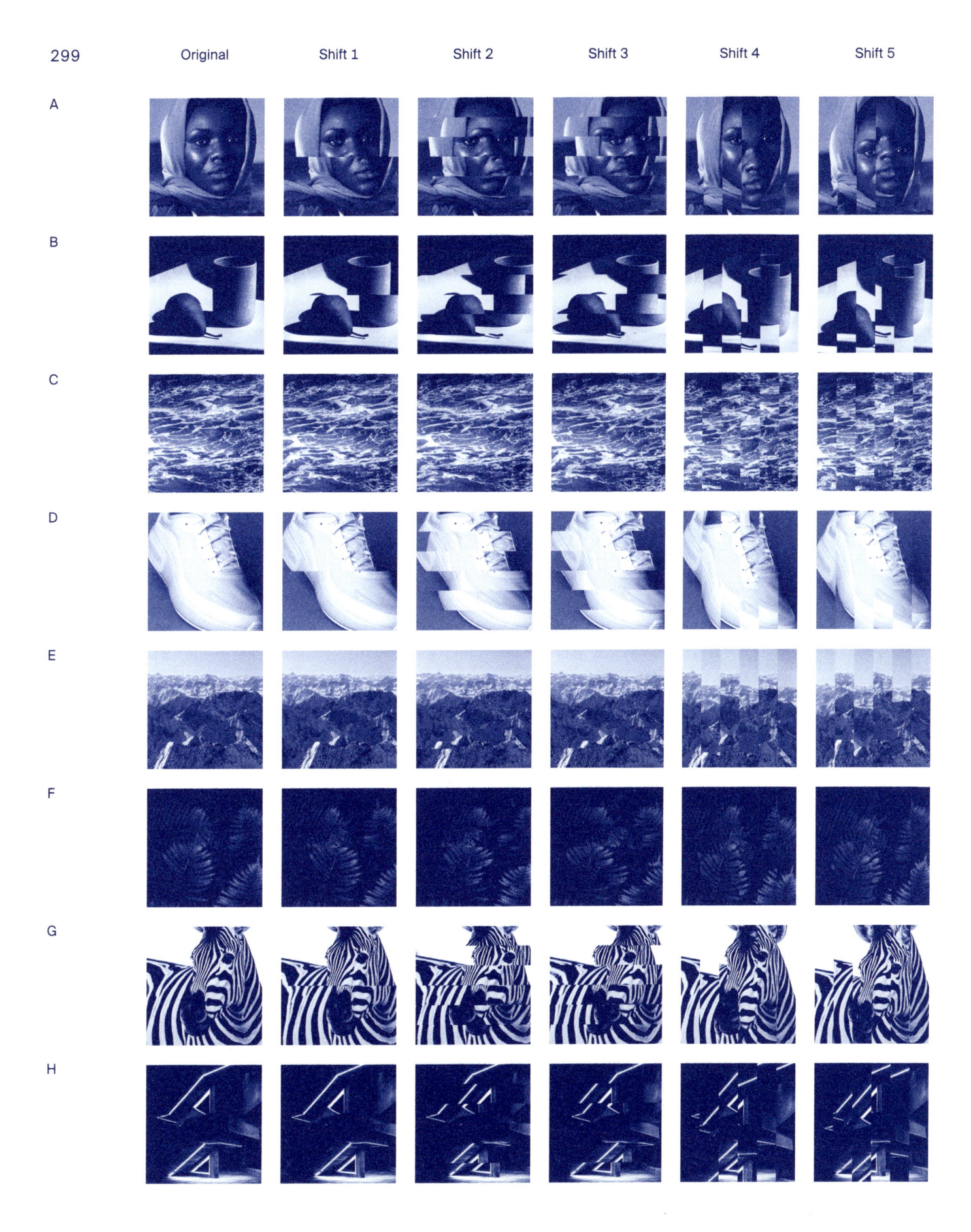

	Original	Shift 1	Shift 2	Shift 3	Shift 4	Shift 5
A						
B						
C						
D						
E						
F						
G						
H						

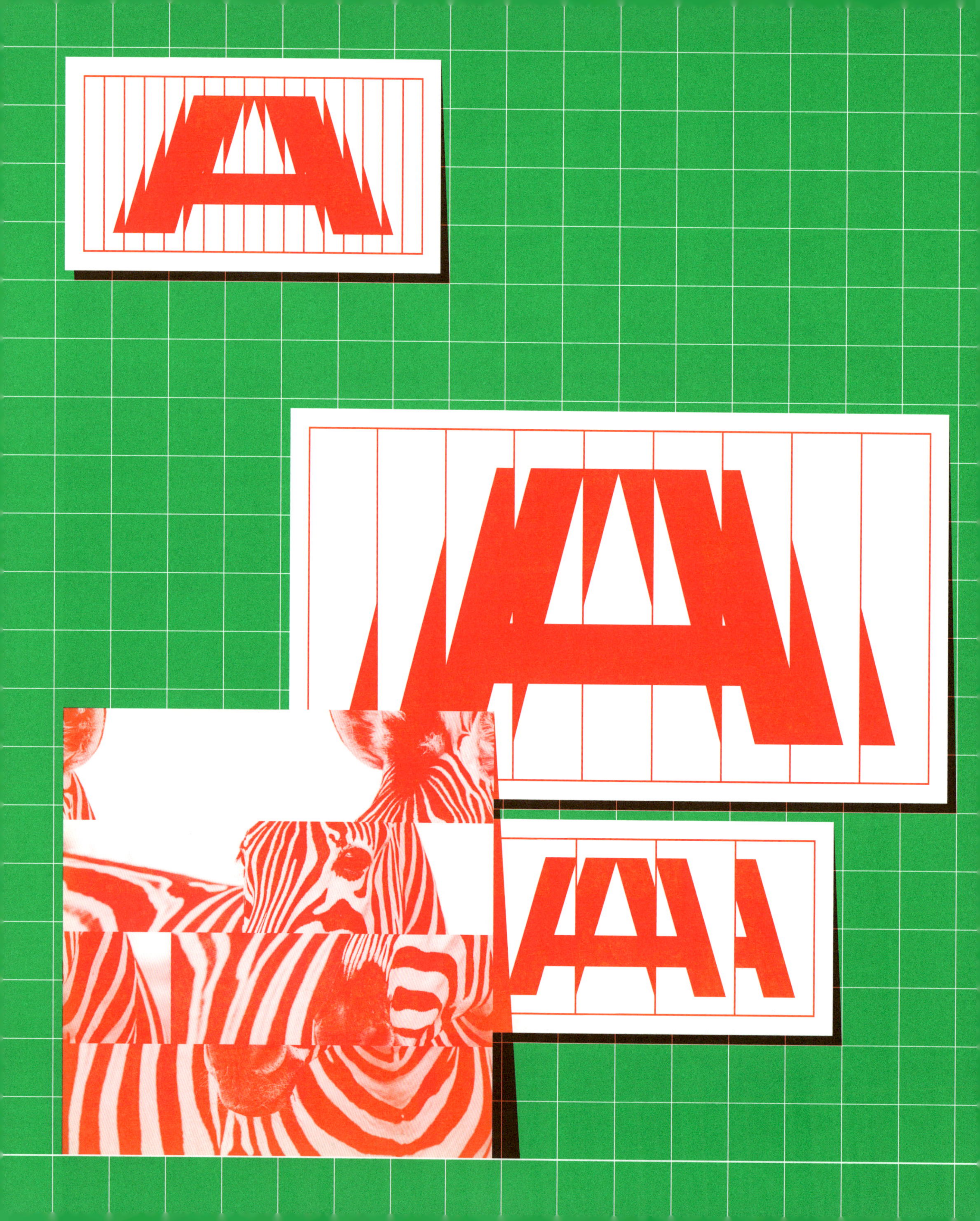

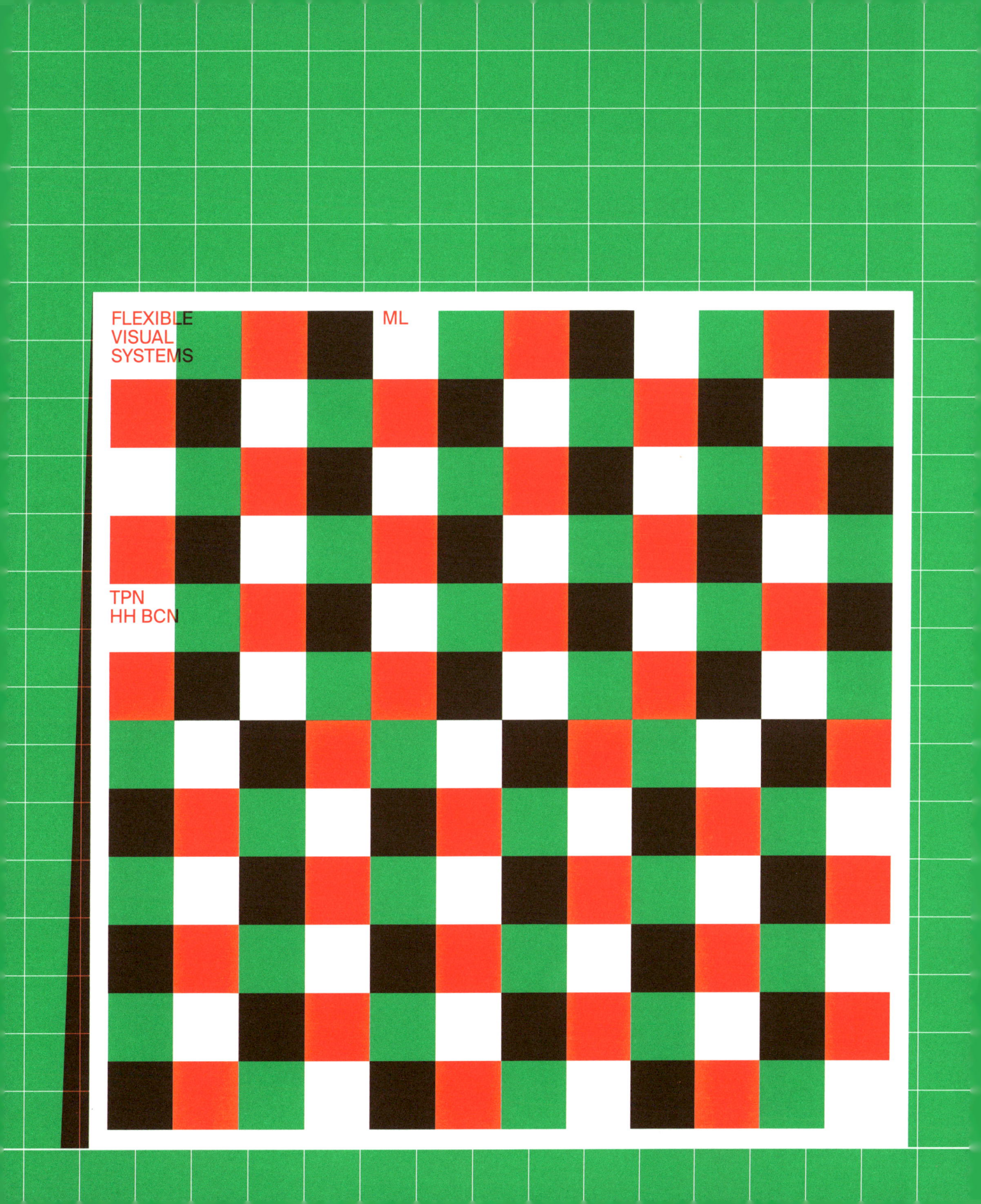

FLEXIBLE
VISUAL
SYSTEMS

ML

TPN
HH BCN

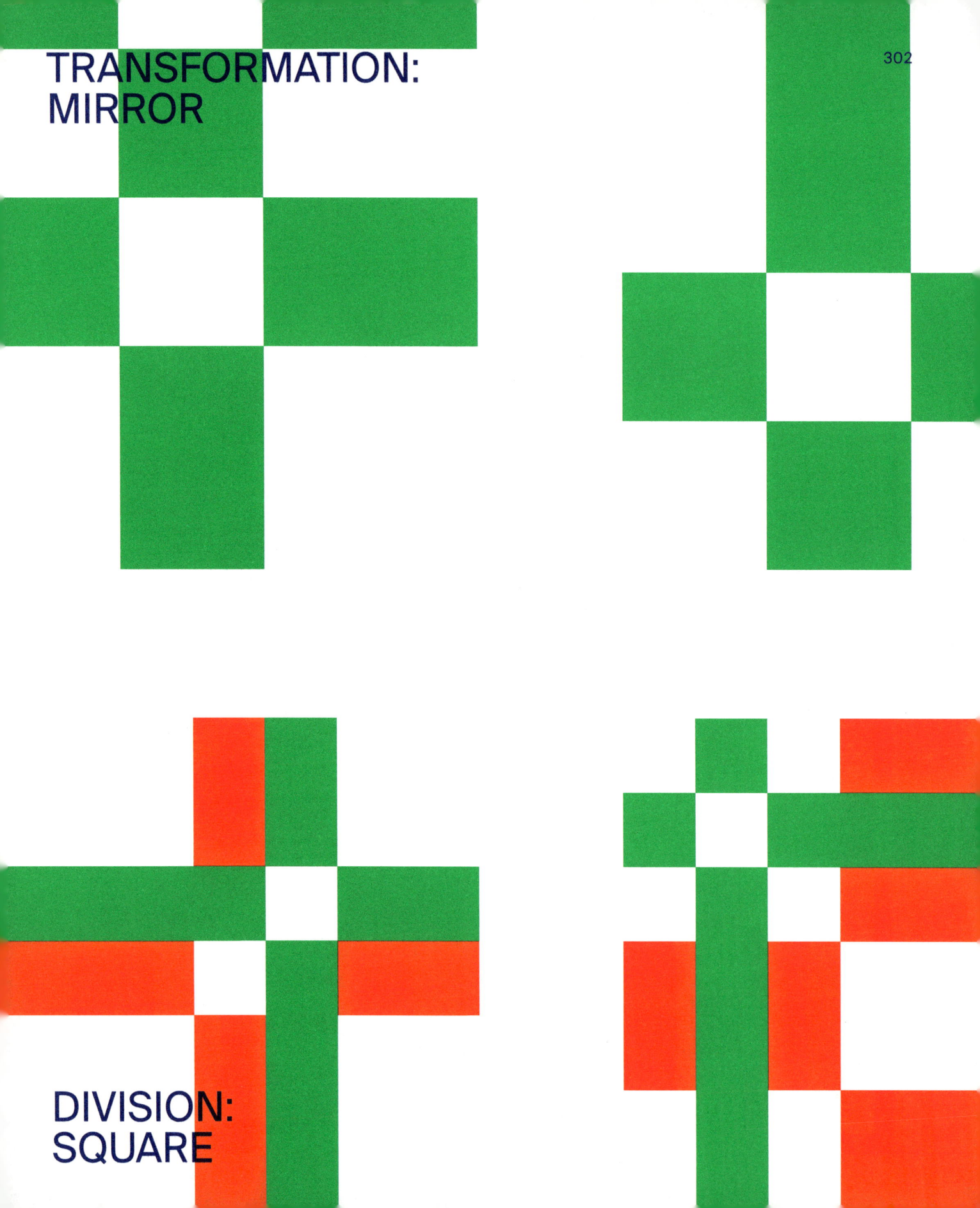

TRANSFORMATION: MIRROR

DIVISION: SQUARE

303

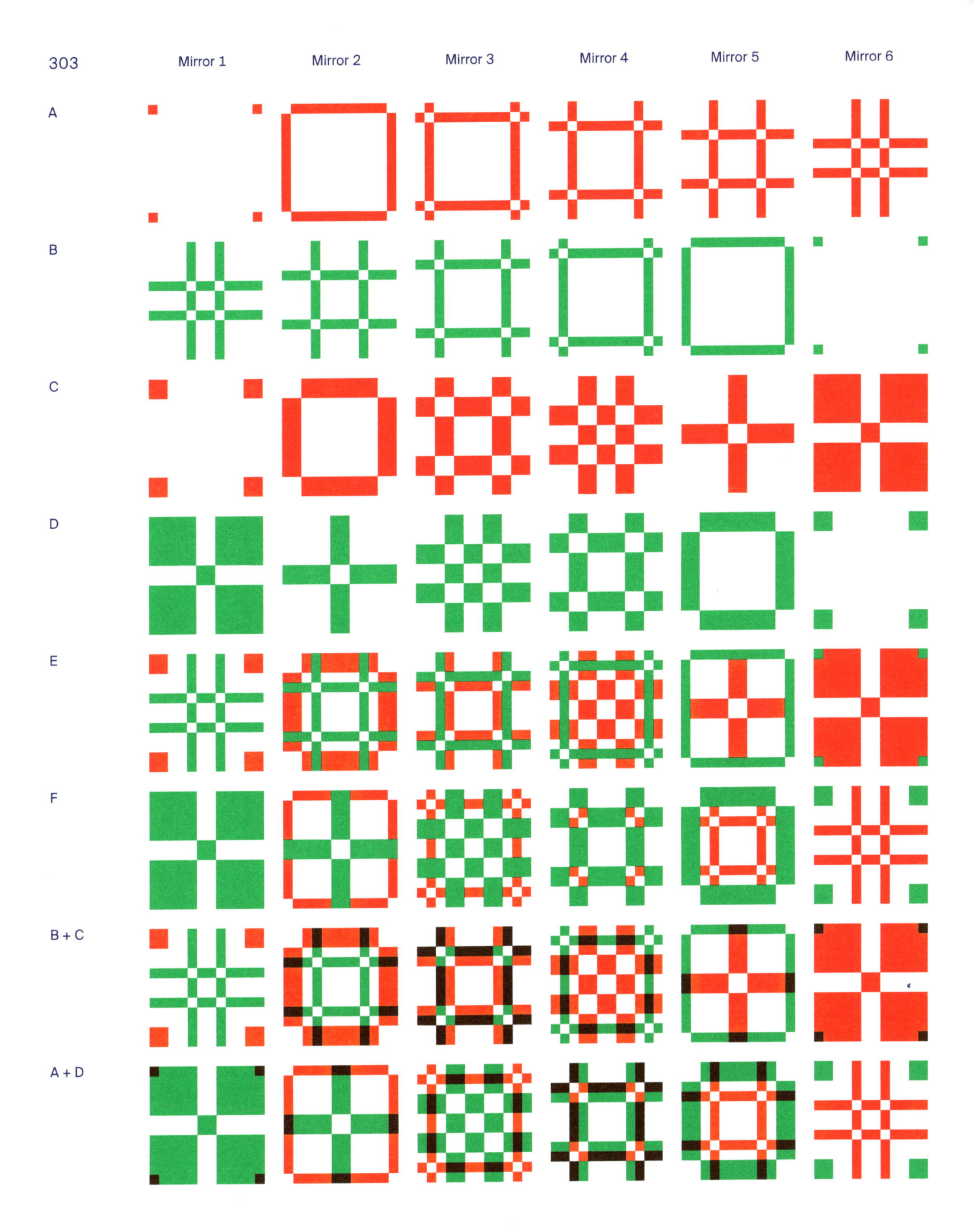

	Mirror 1	Mirror 2	Mirror 3	Mirror 4	Mirror 5	Mirror 6
A						
B						
C						
D						
E						
F						
B + C						
A + D						

Original	Mirror 1	Mirror 2	Mirror 3	Mirror 4	Mirror 5	
A	A					A
B	B	B				B
C	O	C	O			C
D	D	D				D
FLEX IBLE SYS TEME		FLEX IBLE SYS				E
VISU ELLE IDEN TITAT		VISU ELLE			X X	F
TRAN SFOR MATI VE		TRAN SFOR				G
TEXT TEXT TEXT TEXT		TEXT TEXT TEXT TEXT				H

305

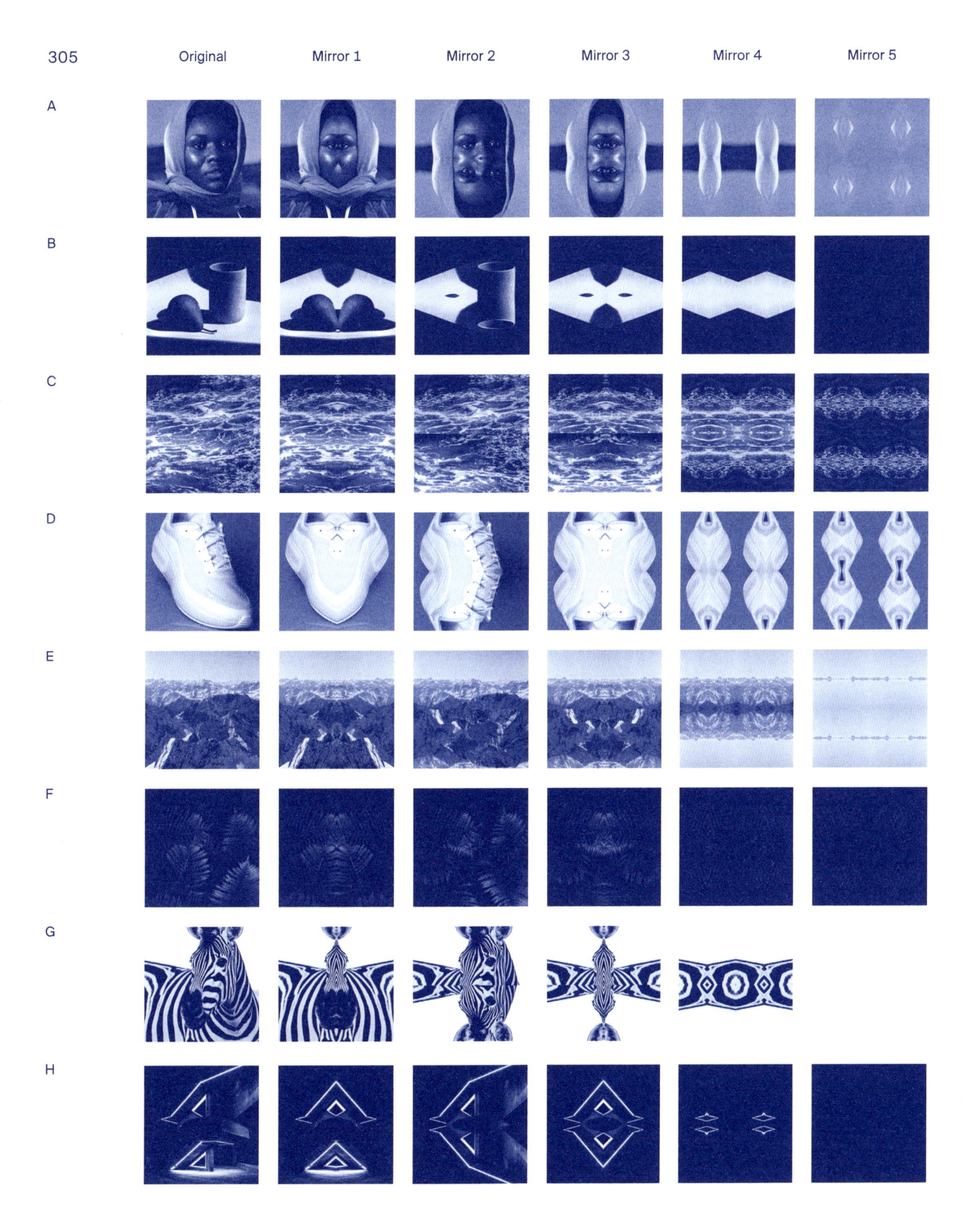

	Original	Mirror 1	Mirror 2	Mirror 3	Mirror 4	Mirror 5
A						
B						
C						
D						
E						
F						
G						
H						

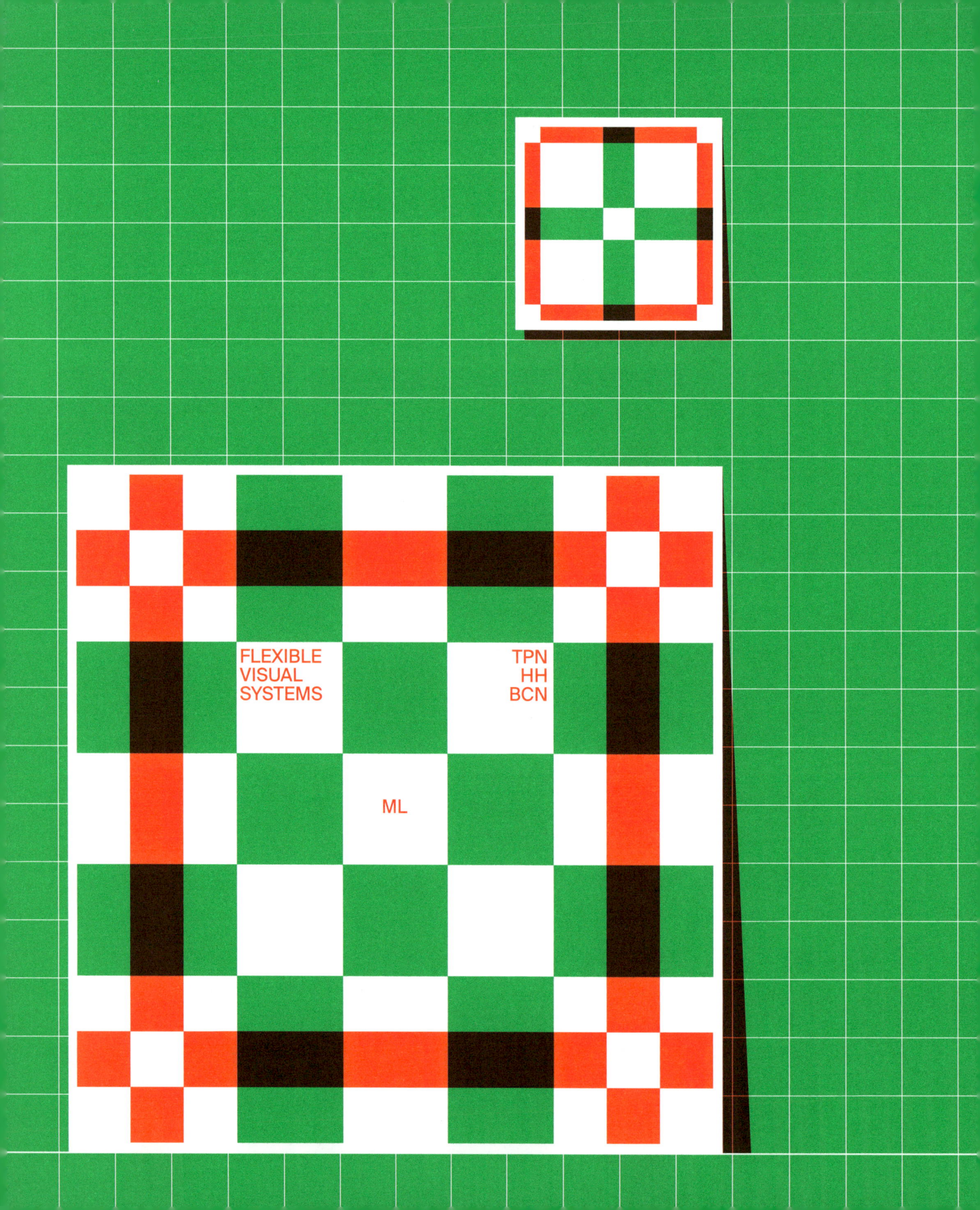

FLEXIBLE
VISUAL
SYSTEMS

TPN
HH
BCN

ML

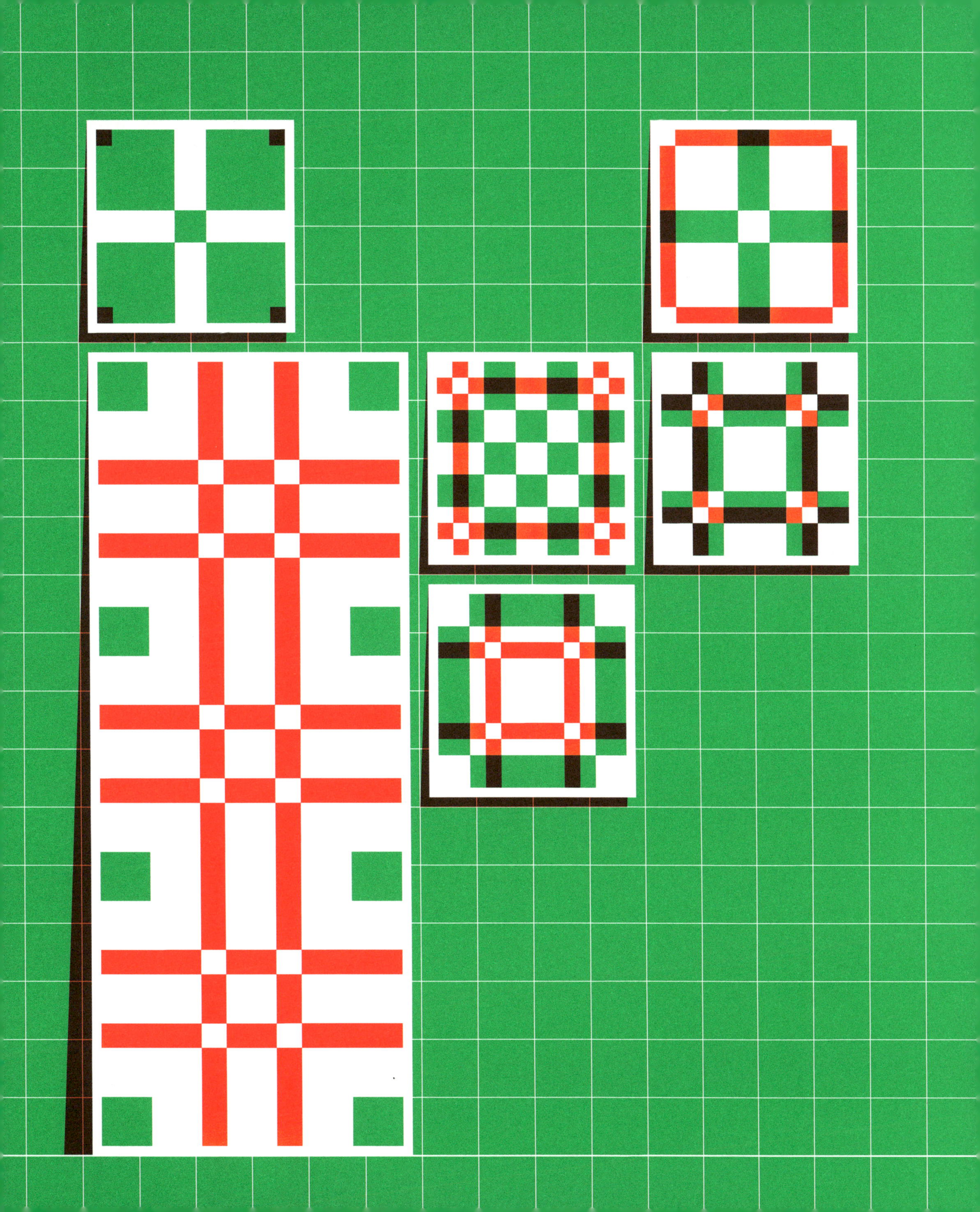

FVS:
3D-TRANSFORMATION-BASED

This book is mostly about two-dimensional visual systems, but three- and four-dimensional systems offer enough possibilities that they would deserve a book on their own. On the next two spreads I give a little insight into some of the possibilities.

TRANSFORMATION: OBJECTS

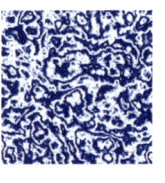

310

Glass Pyramids over Graphic

Glass Pyramids over Typography

Glass Pyramids over Photo

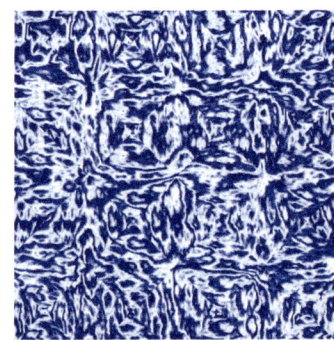

Glass Pyramids over Texture

Graphic projected on Pyramids

Type projected on Pyramids

Photo projected on Pyramids

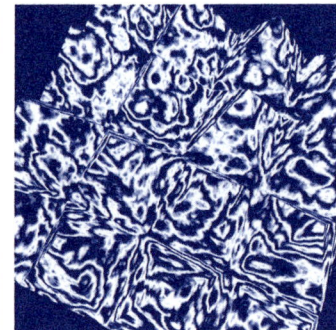

Texture projected on Pyramids

A transformation of graphics, typography, photos, texture or any other image material can be generated through objects too. On this page you see two variations. The transformation through the distortion of a glass object and the projection on an object. There are a couple of other transformation processes imaginable like for example the effect of light on an object or person, as impressively demonstrated by Andréas Winding and Armand Thirard on Romy Schneider in the movie L'Enfer by Henri-Georges Clouzot. A visual system based on a three-dimensional transformation process is especially interesting for motion design, as transitions and variations are easy to produce and feel natural on digital media. Three dimensional design gives us new transformation tools and is a design environment that is worth exploring from the beginning of the design process.

TRANSFORMATION: REPRODUCTION AND RECORDING

Printed Graphic

Printed Typography

Printed Photo

Printed Texture

Scan from printed Graphic

Scan from printed Typography

Scan from printed Photo

Scan from printed Texture

A transformation of graphics, typography, photos, texture, or any other image material through a specific recording or reproduction technique can serve as an identification element too if visible enough. The rasterization, grain, color separation, etc, especially if emphasized are a recognizable filter. Around the 2010's it was trendy to distort images with scanners. Moving an image, while scanning the image, stretched the parts at which the scanner moved at a similar speed as the scanned image. The result was a recognizable distortion of anything scanned. The specific light of a scanner has been used to create visual identities too. In 2004, the design studio Value and Service created posters for Sure Thing Productions by scanning objects related to the production. The unique aesthetic of the scanner was enough to create an easy to recognize visual language. Another example is the revival of Riso printing. The printing technique from the 1980s, with its visible raster dots, bright colors and slight color offset, creates an instant recognition. Used in an environment that does not use Riso printing, the effect can create a distinctive visual language.

FLEXIBLE VISUAL SYSTEMS

ML TPN BCN

WWW.FLEXIBLEVISUALSYST

FLEXIBLE VISUAL SYSTEMS

ML TPN

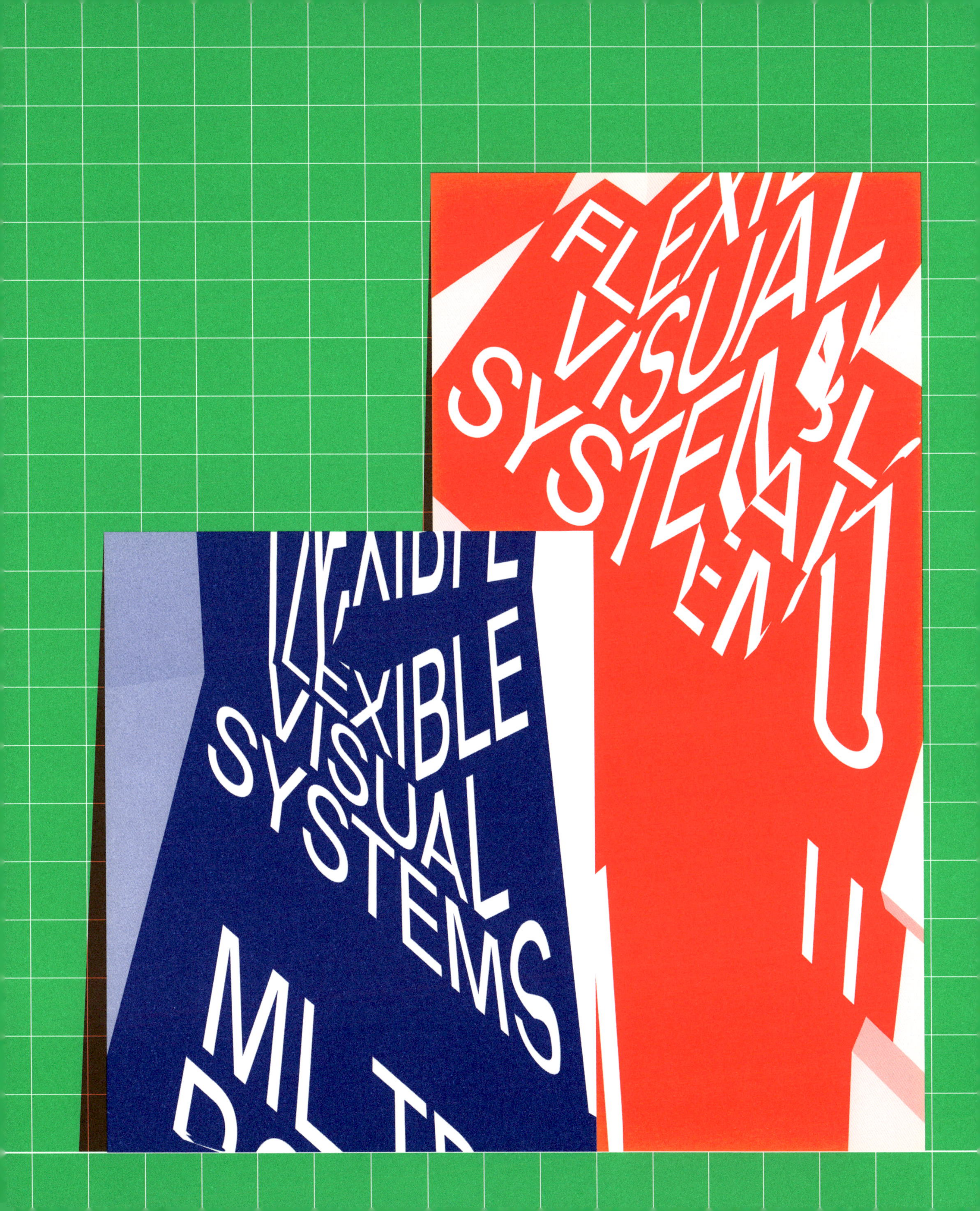
VISUAL

EPILOG

HOW THIS BOOK CAME TO BE

This book took me 20 years to make. To explain why, I need to start at the beginning and introduce myself. Hi, I am Martin, born in 1977 in Hanover, Germany. I am the grandson, nephew, son, brother, friend, and husband of teachers. Studying communication design was my master plan to break free from what everybody around me did.

Before I even knew what communication design was, I did a school internship at the Atelier Müller + Volkmann in 1989 just because I had to, and because it was easiest to do the internship with my neighbors who happened to be communication designers. Being in love with comics, I always thought I would become a comic artist but seeing how versatile and visual graphic design could be, I caught fire.

While still in high school I looked for a university that had a great reputation and, most importantly, would get me to my studies as quickly as possible because I couldn't wait to start a life on my own. It still surprises me how I got into the 10% that got accepted with nothing more than graffiti, comics, and drawings to present, but I did. In 1996 I started studying communication design at the University of Applied Sciences in Darmstadt, Germany, where I received a solid Swiss-German education in color, drawing, typography, photography, design, theory, and even printing techniques, like silk screen printing and movable type setting. I was not aware at that time that the teaching methodologies were Swiss-German, but later on I recognized that I have been studying color with Josef Albers "Interaction of Color" assignments and typography with Armin Hofmann's and Emil Ruder's teaching methods. Sounds exciting, right? Well, it was not. It was hard and dull work. Only in retrospect, I realized how effective the foundation course has been and how much today's design students would benefit from it.[1]

As much as I appreciate what I learned in Darmstadt, I felt that I had reached a dead end after three years. The prospective of graduating in Darmstadt did not excite me. The graduation projects were extremely predictable. If you would show me a project I would have been able to tell you instantly which professor was the tutor. When I heard about the Erasmus scholarship for a student exchange I jumped at it and applied with the Royal Academy of Arts (KABK) in The Hague as my first choice, mainly because it was considered the best European design school and Just van Rossum and Erik van Blokland from Letterror gave a really funny lecture in Darmstadt.

I got the scholarship, moved to The Hague, learned English and Dutch, and immersed myself in my studies. Lupi, who I met in The Hague and is now my dear, charming, beautiful, funny, and spicy wife, had a hard time getting me out of the house. I wanted to absorb as much as I could. So, apart from doing all the courses of the third and fourth year, I also took first year courses in calligraphy with Frank Blokland and joined parts of the "Type and Media" Masters program to carve letters in stone with Françoise Berserik and listen to lectures from Peter Matthias Noordzij. It was a lot, and I was thrilled.

The educational system at the KABK was very different to the one in Darmstadt. There was less dependence on the opinion of one particular teacher. Not because the teachers did not have an opinion, but because the system exposed the students' work to many different teachers with very different opinions, instead of just one. There was no way you could please all the teachers; you could only succeed by finding your own way.[2]

Dutch design in itself was very different too. To be aesthetically appealing seemed to be secondary. First came the wish to surprise with a new take on communication. The experiment, even if ugly, was more appreciated in the Netherlands, than it was in Germany. Still is, in my opinion.

The course that inspired me to follow the path of systemic design was tutored by Petr van Blokland. I do not remember any lectures or assignments, just questions I did not want to hear. I wanted to develop exciting communication, while Petr asked me how my images would work on different media, in different color systems and sizes. I was annoyed by such trivial questions, not realizing that they were not trivial at all, but essential. The image perceived by the audience is not the image you created, but the image that is distributed in different color systems, formats, and sizes.

---

[1] Thank you Sandra Hoffmann Robbiani, Gerhard Schweizer, Ute Osterwalder, Claudia Kerner, and Christian Pfestorf.

[2] Thank you Michel Hoogervorst, Peter Verheul, Frits Dijs, Gijsbert Dijker, Marjan Brandsma, and Petr van Blokland.

The "original" image does not matter. How the image is perceived is what matters.

An idea that kept haunting me was Petr's use of code in his studio to automate design tasks. It enabled him to manage bigger workloads and be independent from common design software.

After graduating in 2001 at the KABK I was offered my first employment by Eike König at the Eikes Grafischer Hort (now just Hort) which at the time was already famous for their innovative record sleeves. While I was hired for my illustration skills, I could not help but further develop my thinking and work with systems. I did not use code as my tool, but pens, scissors, Freehand, and Quark. My systemic approach did not look like code, but it worked like code. It was logical, consistent, and therefore easy to extrapolate to different deliverables: part of an album release, record sleeves, CD cases, booklets, posters, flyers, stickers, etc.

The more systems I designed, the more I became aware that anything could be systematized. The world of visual systems was not as easy to grasp as grid systems. Rather than one tool, it was an approach to design. Everything was possible. Which is fantastic, but also overwhelming. I felt the need to study again. As I was not aware of any person, book, or school teaching visual systems I wanted to start making a book myself, partly because I love books, but also as a research project to learn more about them. It was Lupi who gave me the idea to enroll in a PhD program in Design Research at the university she graduated from, the University of Barcelona.

So I quit Hort, learned Spanish and moved in 2005 with Lupi to Barcelona. Quickly I realized that making a PhD is not like making a book. The methodology and function of a scientific investigation is fundamentally different to personal research. I do not regret the PhD; on the contrary, it gave me the framework and motivation to dive much deeper into the subject than I would ever have, but I came very close to quitting on more than one occasion. Having to work and raise two kids at the same time, it took me 10 years to finish my dissertation.[3] I would not have made it without the constant support of Lupi and my dissertation supervisor Jesús del Hoyo Arjona.

But then something I have tried to avoid my whole life happened. I was about to become a teacher, like everyone else in my family. Lupi pushed me in her role as a director of a Master Degree in Graphic Design, because apparently students enjoyed my classes and I was able to teach them something others did (or could) not. At the beginning of the 2000s, visual identities started to become more flexible, but the academic world still had not really caught up yet. There were no courses, only a couple of articles and books, but all using a thousand different terms to talk about the same paradigm change from static to flexible systems in communication design.

Teaching during and after the PhD at more than ten different design schools in Spain, Germany and the Netherlands helped me to put my theory into practice and develop a curriculum for flexible systems in communication design.[4] Depending on the group of students and the university I am teaching at, I still adapt the structure, content, and approach, but the theoretic model I base my courses on stays the same. It provides structure to the apparent infinite possibilities to design flexible systems, but it does not limit creativity. My students learn to think and work in systems and, what I am most proud of, apply systems to their own individual trajectories based on their own interests.

This book obviously can't be a one to one translation of my courses, as I am not present as a teacher and tutor, but in the last five years I worked on a way to teach you through this book how to design flexible visual systems. The structure of this book, as well its articles and examples guide you through the possible approaches. Each of the examples are starting points for your own exploration. You will get the most out of this book if you do not read through this book at once, but stop every now and then, take an idea and explore it visually. Think with your hands and enjoy the process. I am looking forward to seeing your experiments[5] and how they will change future editions of this book.

---

3   One memory I won't forget is working at Mario Eskenazi's house in Cadaques. The beauty of the house, the village, the good food, the sun, the sea, and ability to learn new things were some of the most perfect moments in my life. Thank you Mario.

4   There were references from the 1970ies, like Herbert Kapitzki, Karl Gerstner, and Armin Hofmann, but nothing contemporary I found applicable.

5   Tag me (@martinlorenz) so I can see and share them.

ACKNOWLEDGEMENTS

First of all, I would like to thank Lupi for being at my side since 1999, believing in me and my abilities when I was not believing in them and supporting me wherever and whenever she could. In the case of this particular book, I want to thank her for her feedback and, as in most of our TwoPoints.Net projects, the color scheme and the production of this book.

To my sons Adrian and David, thank you for loving me unconditionally and keeping me from being a complete workaholic.

With Bryan Boyer I've had a decade of inspiring collaborations, expanding my horizon with each and pushing them to the next level. In this particular case, I want to thank him for making my book readable.

To Elio Salichs, for being supportive beyond expectations and part of TPN family since 2015.

To Tim Rodenbröker, who pushed me and keeps on pushing me to use my full potential. He also played an important role in the last steps of this book.

Without my family, friends, colleagues, and 621 Kickstarter supporters this book would not have become what it is.

I want to thank as well my current and former students at the Royal Academy of Art (KABK), The Hague, ELISAVA; Pompeu Fabra University, Barcelona, European Institute of Design (IED), Madrid/Barcelona, University of Media, Communication and Economy (HMKW), Frankfurt/Berlin, Hamburg University of Applied Sciences (HAW), Hamburg, Art School Wandsbek (KW), Hamburg, IDEP; Abat Oliba CEU University, Barcelona, Muthesius Academy of Fine Arts and Design, Kiel, Konstanz University of Applied Sciences (HTWG), Constance, Blanquerna; Ramon Llull University, Barcelona, Abat Oliba CEU University, Barcelona, University of the Arts (HFK), Bremen, Willem de Kooning Academy (WDKA), Rotterdam, University and Art and Design (HfG), Offenbach, School of Design, Münster, Film Academy Baden-Württemberg (FABW), Ludwigsburg, Typographic Society (TGM), Munich who helped me to shape my curriculum for flexible visual systems.

Last, but not least, I want to thank the Slanted team: Lars, Julia, and Clara, for their support which made this book finally become real and reach you, my dear reader.

BIBLIOGRAPHY

Albers, J. 1995, *Kombinationsschrift, 1930, Prospektblatt der Metallglas Aktiengesellschaft Offenburg-Baden, 298 x 212 mm*. Published in Fleischmann, Gerd. 1995. Bauhaus – Drucksachen, Typografie, Reklame, Oktagon, Stuttgart.

Bayer, H. 1967, *Herbert Bayer – Das Werk des Künstlers in Europa und USA,* Otto Maier Verlag, Ravensburg.

Bertin, J. 2011, *Semiology of Graphics; Diagrams, Networks, Maps,* Esri Press, Redlands.

Bill, J. 2008, *max bill – funktion und funktionalismus. Schriften: 1945-1988,* Benteli, Zurich.

Bohnacker, H., Groß, B., Laub, J., Lazzeroni, C 2009, *Generative Gestaltung, Entwerfen, Programmieren, Visualisieren,* Verlag Hermann Schmidt, Mainz.

Bosshard, H. R. 2000, *Der typografische Raster,* Verlag Niggli AG, Zurich.

Bringhurst, R 1992, *The Elements of Typographic Style,* H&M Publishers, Vancouver.

Broos, K. 2003, *Wim Crouwel Alphabets*, Bis Publishers, Amsterdam.

Brüning, U., Büchner, J., Haldenwanger, M. 1991, *Die neue plastische Systemschrift, Typographie kann unter Umständen Kunst sein: Kurt Schwitters – Typographie und Werbegestaltung,* Landesmuseum, Sprengel Museum and Museum für Gestaltung, Hanover.

Burke, C. 1998, *Paul Renner – The art of typography,* Princeton Architectural Press, New York.

Burnhill, P. 2003, *Type spaces, in house norms in the typography of Aldus Manutius,* Hyphen Press, London.

Cabezas Gelabert, L., Ortega de Uhler, L. F. 2001, *Anàlisi gráfica i representació geomètrica,* Universitat de Barcelona, Departament de Disseny i Imatge, Barcelona.

Cranfield, B. 2003, *Examining the visual culture of corporate identity,* Systems Design Ltd. Idn Pro, Hong Kong.

Critchlow, K. 1969, *Order in Space – A Design Source Book,* Thames & Hudson, London.

Doczi, G. 1981 (2005), *The Power of Limits – Proportional Harmonies in Nature, Art & Architecture,* Shambhala, Boston.

Dondis, D. A. 1973, *A Primer of Visual Literacy,* mit press, Boston.

Erlhoff, M and Marshall, T 2008, *Design Dictionary, Perspectives on Design Terminology,* Birkhäuser Verlag, Basel.

Felsing, U., Design 2 context, ZHdK. 2010. *Dynamic Identities in Cultural and Public Contexts*. Lars Müller Publishers, Baden.

Fineder, M., Kraus, E., Pawlik, A .2004, *Postcript – Zur Form von Schrift heute, A/CH/D,* Hatje Cantz, Ostfildern.

Fleischmann, G. 1995, *Bauhaus – Drucksachen, Typografie, Reklame,* Oktagon, Stuttgart.

Friedl, F., Ott, N., Stein, B. 1998, *Typography – when who how,* Könemann Verlagsgesellschaft mbH, Cologne.

Froshaug, A. 1999, *'Typography is a Grid',* Heller, S, Bierut, M (ed.), *Looking Closer 3. Classic writings on graphic design,* Allworth Press, New York.

Frutiger, A. 2001, *Der Mensch und seine Zeichen. Schriften, Symbole, Signete, Signale,* Fourier Verlag GmbH, Wiesbaden.

Gerstner, K. 1986, *Die Formen der Farben – Über die Wechselwirkung der visuellen Elemente,* athenäum, Bodenheim.

Gerstner, K. 1986, *Die Formen der Farben: Über die Wechselwirkung der visuellen Elemente,* Athenäum, Frankfurt.

Gerstner, K. 2000, *Kompendium für Alphabeten – Systematik der Schrift,* Verlag Niggli AG, Zurich.

Gerstner, K. 2007, *Karl Gerstner: Programme entwerfen. Statt Lösungen für Aufgaben Programme für Lösungen,* Lars Müller Publishers, Zurich.

Gobé, M. 2010, *Emotional Branding: The New Paradigm for Connecting Brands to People,* Allworth Press, New York.

Hofmann, A. 2004, *Methodik der Form- und Bildgestaltung; Aufbau, Synthese, Anwendung,* Verlag Niggli AG, Sulgen, Zurich.

del Hoyo Arjona, J. 2001, El módulo tipográfico. Aproximaciones a su conocimiento contemplado desde la comprensión, el estudio, el análisis y la catalogación sistemática de la obra de Juan Trochut Blanchard, Universitat de Barcelona, Departament de Disseny i Imatge, Barcelona.

Kandinsky, W. 1979, *Point and Line to Plane,* Dover Publications Inc., New York.

Kapitzki, H. W. 1997, *Gestaltung: Methode und Konsequenz.* Edition Axel Menges, Stuttgart / London

Kapitzki, HW 1997, *Methode und Konsequenz – Ein biografischer Bericht,* Edition Axel Menges, Stuttgart, London.

Khazaeli, C. D. 2005, *Systemisches Design, Intelligente Oberflächen für Information und Interaktion*, Rowohlt, Hamburg.

Kindle, E. 2007, The 'Plaque Découpée Universelle': a geometric sanserif in 1870s Paris, Typography papers 7, Hyphen Press, London.

Klanten, R., Mischler, M., Brumnjak, B. 2006, *Serialize. Family Faces and Variety in Graphic Design,* Gestalten, Berlin.

Klanten, R., Mischler, M., Brumnjak, B. 2006, *Serialize – Family Faces and Variety in Graphic Design,* Gestalten Verlag, Berlin.

Kress, G., van Leeuwen, T. 2010, *Reading Images – The Grammar of Visual Design,* Routledge, London.

Leborg, C. 2006, *Visual Grammar*, Princeton Architectural Press, New York.

Leda, 1984, La Rotulacion al pincel, Leda, Barcelona.

Lindinger, H. 1991, *Ulm... Die Moral der Gegenstände,* Ernst und Söhn Verlag, Berlin.

Lohse, R. P. 1966, 'Standard, series, module: new problems and tasks of painting', Kepes, G (ed.) *Module, Proportion, Symmetry, Rhythm,* George Braziller, New York.

Middendorp, J. 2004, *Dutch Type,* 010 Publishers, Rotterdam.

Müller-Brockmann, J. 1996, *Grid Systems / Raster Systeme,* Verlag Niggli Ag, Fürstentum Liechtenstein.

Müller, L. 1994 / 2001, *Josef Müller-Brockmann, Ein Pionier der Schweizer Grafik,* Lars Müller Publishers, Zurich.

Munari, B. 2006, *Diseño y comunicación visual. Contribución a una metodología didáctica,* Editorial Gustavo Gili, Barcelona.

Nikkels, W. 1998, *Der Raum des Buches,* Tropen Verlag, Cologne

Noordzij, G. 1985, *The stroke. Theory of writing,* Hyphen Press, London.

Norm, 2002, *The Things*, Die Gestalten Verlag, Berlin.

Opel, A. 2010, *Adolf Loos – Gesammelte Schriften,* Lesethek Verlag, Vienna.

Richard, H. 2006, *Swiss Graphic Design: The Origins and Growth of an International Style,* Laurince King, London.

Roberts, L., Thrift, J. 2005, *The designer and the grid*, Rotovision, Hove.

Rothenstein, J., Gooding, M. 2003, *ABZ. More Alphabets And Other Signs,* Redstone Press, London.

Schmidt, C. 1997, *Klassische Alphabete,* Art Stock / Fourier Verlag GmbH, Wiesbaden.

Smeijers, F. 1996, Counterpunch, Hyphen Press, London.

Simón, B. 2001, *Sistemes d'ordenació de la imatge gràfica l'arquitectura gràfica en la metodologia del projecte gràfic,* Universitat de Barcelona, Departament de Disseny i Imatge, Barcelona.

Tschichold, J. 1987, *Die neue Typografie– Ein Handbuch für zeitgemäss schaffende,* Berlag Brickmann & Bose, Berlin.

Unger, G. 1975, T*ekst over tekst – een documentaire over typografie,* Drukkerij en uitgeversbedrijf, Lecturis bv, Eindhoven.

Van Leeuwen T., Jewitt, C. 2001 *Handbook of Visual Analysis*, Sage Publications, New York.

Van Nes, I. 2012, *Dynamic Identities, How to create a living brand,* BIS Publishers, Amsterdam.

Wong, W. 1972, *Principles of Two-Dimensional Design,* John Wiley & Sons, Inc, Hoboken.

IMPRINT

Slanted Publishers UG (haftungsbeschränkt)
Nördliche Uferstraße 4–6
76189 Karlsruhe
Germany
T +49 (0) 721 85148268
info@slanted.de
slanted.de
@slanted_publishers

© Slanted Publishers, Karlsruhe, 2021
Nördliche Uferstraße 4–6, 76189 Karlsruhe, Germany
© Dr. Martin Lorenz, TwoPoints.Net
All rights reserved.

ISBN: 978-3-948440-30-5
5th edition 2023

Idea, Content, and Design: Martin Lorenz, TwoPoints.Net
Publishing Direction: Lars Harmsen, Julia Kahl
Production Management: Julia Kahl
Editing: Bryan Boyer, Dash Marshall
Proofreading: Julia Kahl, Clara Weinreich, Lupi Asensio
Print Management: Lupi Asensio, TwoPoints.Net
Printer: Printmedia Solutions, Germany

Unsplash Photography
Bird by Zdenek Machacek
Flower by Mio Ito
Person by Nana Kwame
Shoe by Izzy Gibson
Plants by Omid Armin
Stairs by Ryunosuke Kikuno
Sea by James Eades
Zebra by Frida Bredesen
Still Life by Jocelyn Morales
Mountains by Alexander Kaufmann

Disclaimer
The publisher assumes no responsibility for the accuracy of all information. Publisher and editor assume that material that was made available for publishing, is free of third party rights. Reproduction and storage require the permission of the publisher. Photos and texts are welcome, but there is no liability. Signed contributions do not necessarily represent the opinion of the publisher or the editor.

The German National Library lists this publication in the German National Bibliography; detailed bibliographic data is available on the Internet at dnb.de

About

Slanted Publishers is an internationally active independent publishing and media house, founded in 2014 by Lars Harmsen and Julia Kahl. They publish the award-winning print magazine *Slanted,* which twice a year focuses on international design and culture. The Slanted blog www.slanted.de and social media have been publishing daily news and events from the international design scene and presenting inspiring portfolios from around the world for 18 years. In addition to the Slanted blog and magazine, Slanted Publishers initiates and creates projects such as the Y*earbook of Type,* tear-off calendars *Typodarium* and *Photodarium*, independent type foundry *VolcanoType* and others. Slanted's publishing program reflects their own diverse interests, focusing on contemporary design and culture, working closely with editors and authors to produce outstanding publications with meaningful content and high quality. These publications can be found in the Slanted Shop alongside other extraordinary products by young design talents and established producers from all over the world. Slanted was born from great passion and has made a name for itself across the globe. Its design is vibrant and inspiring—its philosophy open-minded, tolerant, and curious.

About the author

Martin Lorenz (1977, Hanover, Germany) graduated in 2001 from the Graphic Design department at the Royal Academy of Art (KABK) of The Hague, Netherlands, after having previously studied communication design at the University of Applied Sciences in Darmstadt, Germany. In January 2016, he successfully defended his PhD dissertation about flexible visual systems in communication design at the University of Barcelona, Spain. He is cofounder of the graphic design studio, TwoPoints.Net and co-author of *On the Road to Variable*, *I Love Helvetica*, *I Love Times*, *I Love Franklin Gothic*, *I Love Gill Sans*, *I Love Bodoni*, *I Love DIN*, *I Love Avant Garde,* and *I Love Futura*, published by Viction:ary, Hong Kong, *Left, Right, Up, Down*, *latino—grafico*, *Pretty Ugly,* and *Type Navigator*, published by Gestalten, Berlin, *Neuland* and *The One Weekend Book Series*, published by Actar, Barcelona. He currently teaches at the Bachelor and Masters Degree of Graphic Design of Elisava, Barcelona and the Graphic Design Department of the Royal Academy of Arts (KABK), The Hague.

flexiblevisualsystems.info
@flexiblevisualsystems
martinlorenz.com
@martinlorenz
twopoints.net
@twopointsnet